Reg Carter

The Transparent Accountability Paradigm

An Outcome-Based Management Approach for Government and Nonprofit Organizations

D1390904

Reginald K. Carter, Ph.D.
Adjunct Professor
Master of Science in Administration
Central Michigan University
Mount Pleasant, Michigan

Transparent and Accountable Manager Press

Additional copies may be ordered from:

Transparent and Accountable Manager Press
1777 Colorado Drive
East Lansing, MI 48823
(517) 337-2266
http://www.reginaldkcarter.com

The author can be contacted by e-mail at:
reginaldkcarter@aol.com

The material provided by Frederick Richmond on
return on investment that appears in Chapter 5 is
copyrighted, and is used with permission. The North
Carolina 20/20 Update Report included as Appendix
A is copyrighted, and is used with the permission of
the North Carolina Progress Board.

Cover photo credits: Cover combines two images
licensed for use by Getty Images: Cleaning Giant
Glasses by Jonathan Evans and U.S. Capitol by Tom
Grill. Additional cover image design was provided by
Jerry Gates, i2integration.

ISBN: 978-0-615-45463-4

Table of Contents

Dedicated to Sandy and MacNichol

Acknowledgments

The author gratefully acknowledges the helpful comments and suggestions offered by many colleagues who reviewed various drafts. They include Gus Breymann, Western Michigan University; Rick Cole, College of Communication Arts and Sciences, Michigan State University; Stuart Doneson, Michigan State University; Tom Hoisington, CEO, Public Affairs Associates; Armaud Lauffer, School of Social Work, University of Michigan; Mike Moore, School of Labor and Industrial Relations, Michigan State University; Susan Parlato; Fred Richmond, CEO, Center for Applied Management Practices; Doug Roberts, Director, Institute for Public Policy and Social Research, Michigan State University; Spencer Johnson, President, Michigan Health and Hospital Association; Bill Bolton, President, Master Machine; Paul Willging, Bloomberg School of Public Health, Johns Hopkins University; Frank Wronski, CEO, Medilodge Group; Mike Duda, Superintendent, Haslett Public Schools; and Larry Yachcik, CEO, Porter Hills.

Thanks also to Fred Richmond's continuous support and commitment to Results Oriented Management (ROMA) and the creation of the Carter-Richmond Methodology for performance monitoring of Community Action Agencies and HUD programs. I was also honored when he agreed to write the Foreword for this book.

Thanks also are due to Gary Grobman and Linda Grobman, White Hat Communications, for editing the manuscript and designing the cover. Both greatly improved the final product. I am grateful for the additional editing and review provided by Kari Sederburg. Finally, I want to thank my wife, Sandy Carter, for her substantive and editorial contributions through various revisions. I am truly blessed with a partner who is so bright, generous, and encouraging.

R.K.C. March 2011

Foreword
by Frederick Richmond

Peter Drucker is the premiere writer on effective management practices for both private and nonprofit organizations. For decades, I have combined Drucker's writings *(The Drucker Foundation Self-Assessment Tool)* with Reg Carter's earlier book *(The Accountable Agency)* in my own consulting practice with government and nonprofit agencies. Reg Carter's second book follows in the tradition of Peter Drucker and presents a challenging new way of thinking about a more transparent and accountable government. Both elements are important for a new social contract between citizens and their government: The Transparent Accountability Paradigm. It is a call to action and redefines what is expected of government. It captures a new vision of a preferred future and provides a way to focus the current frustration and anger of the taxpayers who are clearly unhappy with the political leadership as reflected in the low Congressional approval ratings and the emergence of the Tea Party movement to rein in federal spending. It describes a practical solution for citizens who are convinced that the country is going in the wrong direction.

The paradigm has ten elements that clarify the expectations for government to demonstrate outcomes for the clients and communities that receive their services. Currently, government is largely invisible to the public and needs to be more visibly accountable to its citizens. This book shows how some local, state, and federal government programs have attempted to demonstrate their outcomes through public disclosure of relevant benchmarks, how two program managers measured their program's impact by following their clients after they completed the program, how nursing homes in Michigan voluntarily released transparent outcome information (family satisfaction survey results) for each home to help future consumers make more informed choices, and how you can be involved with establishing the new paradigm in your community, agency, or nonprofit organization.

The Transparent Accountability Paradigm is particularly relevant today because there is increased scrutiny of all currently funded programs. The economic and financial crisis of 2008 has enlarged the federal deficit by several trillion dollars. The state and local government tax bases are severely affected by the housing decline that directly reduces the revenues available to fund programs. No program is necessarily exempt from such a massive reduction in jobs and wealth. Education, public safety (police and fire), Medicaid, and all publicly funded programs may experience extensive funding reductions or elimination.

An outcome-based management approach focuses on client/community changes resulting from programs (employment as a result of training programs, graduation rates and educational achievement levels as a result of attending school, and new jobs as a result of economic development initiatives). Reg Carter argues convincingly that outcomes need to be defined, shared publicly, and be the basis of future funding decisions. This is the main message of the book. It is not a new message, but it is a more urgent message because there is a need to reduce funding—and there is no outcome basis for making the decision about the programs to be funded.

During my formative years in school and throughout my work life, I have been fortunate to have had several teachers who opened pathways with original and innovative thought and had the skills to bring their ideas into the workplace. One such teacher is my friend and colleague, Reg Carter, who I first encountered in the fall of 1980. His seminal book, *The Accountable Agency*, published in 1983, identified seven key questions that all program managers should be able to answer of their programs:

1. How many clients are you serving?
2. Who are they?
3. What services do you give them?
4. What does it cost?
5. What does it cost per service delivered?
6. What happens to the clients as a result of the service?
7. What does it cost per outcome?

At the time, I did not know the profound influence these seven questions would have on my career and life work and ultimately on the work of the numerous public and private agencies that have adopted and integrated these simple questions into the ongoing management of their organizations. As remarked by a colleague, these questions are "so simple, so complex, and yet so simple." Fast forward to 2011 and these same seven questions are the basis for accountability that is on the forefront of any discussion about funding, quality program management, evidence based research, and generation of outcomes to measure impact.

As the founder and CEO of the Center for Applied Management Practices, Inc., I have worked with Reg Carter to implement these fundamental management and accountability questions in state and federal government, as well as in the nonprofit sector. In 1993, we introduced these questions and management methodologies to the national Community Action Network, a group of more than 1,000 public and private nonprofit agencies across the United States, Puerto Rico, and the District of Columbia engaged in the delivery of community based self-sufficiency and community revitalization programs. The principles of sound management and accountability that were so clearly presented in the 1983 publication originally targeted to state government had applicability beyond its original audience and could be adopted by the nonprofit sector, as well as local and municipal governments engaged in the delivery of human services.

One of the key factors influencing the transference of these management and accountability practices beyond state government was the Government Performance and Results Act of 1993, which required federally-supported programs to demonstrate measurable outcomes and other sound management practices. It was this driving force that prompted the initial interest of the Community Action Network to become more familiar with, and later adopt, the fundamental precepts in *The Accountable Agency*.

By 1998, a management curriculum known today as Results-Oriented Management and Accountability, or ROMA, was developed by the Center for Applied Management Practices, Inc. (CAMP) to support the ongoing management of these human service agencies and other community-based organizations with similar missions. Today, ROMA, with its focus on outcome based management, has become a standard curriculum used in county human services, the broad spectrum of nonprofit agencies, and other units of local and municipal government. As a foundation for accountability and sound management practices, the ROMA curriculum integrated key elements of *The Accountable Agency*, specifically the seven key management questions. In FY2000, a National ROMA Peer-to-Peer Training Program was initiated by the U. S. Department of Health and Human Services, Office of Community Services, which formalized a national certification program for developing ROMA trainers.

In 2005, in a collaborative effort with the Center for Applied Management Practices, Inc., the original seven key questions from *The Accountable Agency* were augmented with two additional questions that I developed, and together, these questions were published as the Carter-Richmond Methodology, a financial accountability and return-on-investment methodology. In 2005, this methodology was published in the Federal Register and adopted by the U.S. Department of Housing and Urban Development (HUD) for required use in its annual Notice of Funding Availability (NOFA) for its annual Discretionary Grants program, which releases close to $3 billion annually to thousands of community-based organizations and units of state and local government. The term *Carter-Richmond Methodology* appears on every grant application/eLogic Model® in the Discretionary Grants program.

This outcome-based approach to management has a long history. Reg Carter provides an historical perspective and draws several valuable lessons for implementing this style of decision-making. He is optimistic and skeptical at the same time. This is a teaching moment with hope that the current crisis may catch the attention of both leaders and the citizens.

This book is a must read for managers at all levels of government and nonprofit organizations. Such managers are very familiar with the legislative resistance to making difficult appropriations decisions based on performance criteria as opposed to continued funding based on the "intrinsic goodness" of programs. More importantly, it is a must read for any informed citizen who is ready to commit to the next steps in defining our preferred future, measuring progress toward it, and holding legislators and government leaders accountable to reach the preferred future.

Frederick Richmond, CEO
Center for Applied Management Practices

Chapter 1
Introduction

The public believes the country is going in the wrong direction. Public opinion polls reflect significantly low ratings for the Congress, which, along with President Obama, are considered by many to be responsible for the current level of dissatisfaction with the direction of our country. Many Americans are frustrated by our collective inability to define a preferred future for the country. We no longer trust our political leadership to tell the truth about current conditions or the capacity to fulfill the promise for a better future.

How would we know if we were going in the right direction? There is no consensus on the right direction. There is a need to define and measure our preferred future and mobilize the resources to get there. We need national progress benchmarks and the leaders who can make progress toward our preferred future.

The Transparent Accountability Paradigm: An Outcome-Based Management Approach for Government and Nonprofit Organizations provides the beginning stages of this initiative by providing a summary of how some states, local governments, and individual programs have created outcome-based benchmarks. They are models for a national set of accountability standards. There is a common set of benchmarks used by various states to define the expectations for its citizens. All share a common vision similar to the North Carolina Progress Board (2006):

- healthy children and families,
- safe and vibrant communities,
- quality education for all,
- high performance environment,
- a prosperous economy,
- a modern infrastructure, and
- an accountable government.

This book proposes a new social contract between citizens and their government. The new model is called *The Transparent Accountability Paradigm*, and it includes the following ten components:

1. Taxpayers want a government that works. They want a positive relationship between taxes and tangible program success.
2. Government programs should demonstrate a positive impact on citizens and communities they serve.
3. Government should share results with all stakeholders, including the public.
4. Results should be measurable, simple, realistic, manageable, and easily understood.
5. Results should be the primary basis for important resource decisions.
6. Program managers should maximize results.
7. Program managers should create results measures and obtain the necessary consensus/acceptance from various stakeholders.
8. Government should only fund programs that improve results and remove those that cannot.
9. Voters should elect leaders who demonstrate this level of accountability.
10. Voters should become better educated on the performance of government and communicate directly with their leaders about their "ask" of government.

This new paradigm is necessary because we have lost trust in our leadership and need to clarify a new consensus agenda and process. When any institution loses the trust of its stakeholders, there are serious consequences for future commitments. We have seen the loss of trust in:

- priests and the leadership of the Catholic Church for allowing child sexual abuse,
- airlines for allowing inadequate protection from terrorists,
- accounting companies for allowing corporations to dramatically overestimate the value of their corporate clients like Enron, and
- banks, brokerage firms, security rating agencies, and other financial institutions for not disclosing the risk to investors.

The latter resulted in the collapse of the financial system in 2008 with devastating consequences to individuals who placed their savings and trust in these institutions.

All institutions rely upon trust for re-investment commitments from stakeholders. Schools and universities rely upon the perceived ability to provide educational value in order to experience high enrollment, tuition increases, and alumni support. Fire and police rely upon the perceived value to provide safety to receive on-going funding from taxpayers. Government and nonprofit organizations likewise rely upon the perceived ability to improve the quality of life for citizens and communities served to receive donor funding.

In most cases, the loss of trust is usually confined to a limited number of stakeholders within a given church, industry, corporation, or geographic region—such as the Gulf of Mexico coast in the cases of Hurricane Katrina and the British Petroleum oil spill. This limited impact allows the vast majority of citizens to define it as an isolated example with little or limited impact on their lives. The financial disaster of 2008 is unique because it significantly affected the savings/jobs of so many citizens. Only the Great Depression of the 1930s did such damage to an entire generation. The 2008 dramatic loss of personal wealth due to the collapse of the international financial system is similar and provides a sobering lesson in understanding the fragile nature of trust. A dramatically more effective transparent accountability system across federal government would have prevented this event or provided early warning signs of the threats.

President Obama, on his second day in office, declared that he would have a transparent government:

> *My administration is committed to creating an unprecedented level of openness. We will work together to ensure the public trust and establish a system of transparency, public participation, and collaboration. Openness will strengthen our democracy and promote efficiency and effectiveness in government* (White House, 2009).

As President, Mr. Obama has taken several steps to implementing transparency through the use of the Internet as a communication vehicle to share information. Among them are:

- publishing the list of visitors to the White House,
- vastly expanding the availability of 118,000 federal agency data sets,

- directing federal agencies to be more responsive to Freedom of Information Act requests,
- requesting C-SPAN coverage of the health care reform debate,
- promising the availability on the Internet of pending federal legislation before it is voted on by legislators,
- directing federal agencies to disclose more information that would be helpful to consumers at the point of purchase, such as average expected miles-per-gallon for automobiles that are prominently displayed on the window of the car in the dealer's showroom, and
- providing a summary of the transparency initiatives in a report entitled *Open Government: A Progress Report to the American People* (2009).

There are a number of citizen advocacy groups that focus on transparency in government, such as the Sunlight Foundation, OMB Watch, the Center for Public Integrity, and the National Security Archive. They provide valuable balance in understanding and assessing federal agency budgets and proposed legislation, and expose the role of special interest groups. They attempt to interpret government to a public that is largely uninformed and cynical of the political process.

In addition, there are some university research projects that focus on transparency and appear to have influenced the Obama administration's emphasis on providing helpful consumer information at the point of purchase. The Transparency Project at Harvard University (Fung, 2007) is one example. The researchers reviewed the results of eight laws from 1933-1997 that attempted to increase transparency across several areas, including corporate financial disclosure, restaurant hygiene, nutritional labeling, toxic release disclosure, workplace hazards, patient safety, and timely notice of plant closures. They identified several important characteristics of the most effective strategies. The most effective was a simple ABC grading of Los Angeles restaurants that displayed their rankings in the window so that consumers at their decision points would be aware of the assessment of risk by the Department of Public Health. This project influenced the number of customers who patronized these restaurants. The researchers referred to this type of approach as targeted transparency.

The ingeniousness of targeted transparency lies in the mobilization of individual choice, market forces, and participatory democracy through relatively light-handed government action (Fung 2007, p.5).

In these examples, government and legislation is necessary to require disclosure by organizations that otherwise would keep such information secret. Government is necessary because it can mandate disclosure, maintain permanency, periodically update and publish reports, and enforce compliance. This approach works to varying degrees to help consumers to select better quality products and services and subsequently alter corporate strategies to improve. This sequence assumes that the consumer is making informed decisions and the disclosed information accurately reflects the risks for the consumer. Clearly, this does not always happen, as previous financial disclosure requirements did not accurately reflect the risks to investors in 2008.

This same approach to targeted transparency has been available for many years through The Consumers Union's monthly publication of *Consumer Reports*. Its assessment of a wide array of home and auto products is often used by consumers at the point of purchase. *Consumer Reports* is supported by sales of the publication. In turn, such disclosure may motivate manufacturers to improve their product design and performance.

A recent example (April 13, 2010) is the *Consumer Reports'* assessment of the Lexus GX 460 SUV, which led to a recommendation not to purchase the car because of the risk of a roll-over. This was uncharacteristically negative, as *Consumer Reports* generally ranks various options to purchase, but it seldom recommends not purchasing a product. Toyota chose to immediately stop production of this vehicle until the problem was corrected. This example demonstrates the importance of trusted information for potential Lexus customers. This same type of oversight needs to be more widely available across such other complex decisions such as insurance and financial products.

This book is about the need to move from a country where 80% of Americans believe the country is moving in the wrong direction to 80% believing the country is moving in the right direction. To do this, we need to agree on the direction, measure it, and hold government and ourselves accountable for achieving this direction.

We need a set of progress benchmarks that keep us focused on what is important. Such standards are especially important with an increasing noise level of irrelevant distractions provided by multiple media options. We can no longer allow political party differences to define and dominate the dialogue about our preferred future. We need to clarify our expectations for progress, prevent politicians from defining a Democratic or Republican agenda, and demand an American agenda.

This book continues the process of creating outcomes, transparency, and accountability across institutions. Such an initiative demands a significantly better informed public with a strong and clear advocacy voice to keep us focused on the most important common benchmarks of our preferred future. With such a focus, we can restore our sense of investment and trust in these institutions. However, it requires a greater interest in defining a common direction than fighting about political and ideological differences.

Four key benchmarks are initially defined:

1. improving educational achievement,
2. increasing the movement out of poverty,
3. increasing median household earnings, and
4. lowering health system cost and increasing health outcomes.

A complete list is provided in Appendix A. These benchmarks will be presented as easy-to-read charts that can be updated regularly. For them to be effective, however, a critical mass of stakeholders needs to pay attention to these benchmarks and become actively involved in keeping our collective resources focused on these outcomes.

My favorite cartoon is from the *New Yorker* magazine. It shows a pack of wolves howling at the moon. One wolf says to another wolf, *"My question is: Are we making an impact?"* Most of the other wolves are busy howling. But only one is asking for feedback about the impact of the howling. We need more wolves asking the important impact question rather than simply howling.

Most government programs focus on inputs (number of employees, funding levels) and outputs (number of services provided, clients served) rather than on outcomes (employment from training programs) that affect the lives of clients and communities.

This is true at the local, state, and federal agency levels. There are pockets of cities, states, and federal initiatives that recognize the importance of the impact question and are committed to answering the question for employees, managers, legislators, funding sources, and the public. I am obsessed with this outcome question and have spent most of my career trying to convince others about why the question is relevant. I am simply wired this way. It is part of my DNA. It is a big part of who I am and enjoy being. I do not know any other reason why I keep coming back to the same question. I do know that it is important in a very fundamental way. I hope to convince the reader why it is important not only to government programs but also to schools, churches, faith-based agencies, foundations, and nonprofit organizations like the United Way.

Program outcome information (e.g., increasing academic achievement for students, securing jobs for employment and training programs, and decreasing re-abuse rates for child protective service intervention agencies) is more available but rarely used as the main criteria for resource decisions made by politicians and managers across government and nonprofit organizations. Some examples of using outcome information include:

- All federal agencies are required to collect performance results as part of the Government Performance and Results Act of 1993. This information can be accessed via the Internet, in many cases.
- Amazon welcomes consumer's assessment of products purchased. These are made available for future potential customers so that they can benefit from prior user's experience.
- Colleges and universities are ranked across a variety of measures to help families select their choice for higher education.
- College and university classes are ranked by students who have taken the class and results shared online for the next cohort of students selecting their classes.
- Grade school achievement levels are widely available by school.

I am optimistic that outcome information may ultimately become the norm rather than the exception to good management practices. There are many resources available to pursue outcomes used by government, public policy institutes, and nonprofit organizations. Some of the best include publications by the General Accountability Office, the Governmental Accounting Standards Board, the National Conference of State Legislatures, and the Urban Institute.

Outcomes are one way to educate the public on government performance and create trust in government by taxpayers who are hungry to be told the "truth." Government needs to become more accountable as well as transparent and learn the lessons from the other sectors and organizations—among them the Catholic Church, Enron and Arthur Anderson Consultants, airline security, and the 2008 failures of the banking and brokerage firms— that have recently suffered the consequences of not being either.

In 2002, a small number of Catholic diocesan priests were accused of sexually abusing children. The Vatican had been aware of the problem since the early 1920s. The U.S. scandal revealed 5,000 victims and $2 billion in litigation costs. Catholic bishops were aware of this abuse and reassigned the priests to other parishes placing additional children at risk. Although only five percent of all priests may have been involved in the abuse, the consequences are large. This failure to be accountable and transparent was avoidable. It was a calculated risk.

Also in 2002, Enron filed for bankruptcy, and the auditing firm, Arthur Anderson, was convicted of obstruction of justice in the subsequent federal investigation. Both firms misled investors and shareholders regarding the financial viability of Enron. Both firms suffered irreparable consequences for high risk initiatives in addition to failures in accountability and transparency. In 2002, after the 9-11 terrorist attack on the United States, the airline industry paid a huge price as a result of inadequate security at the airports that allowed the hijackers to secure control over the aircraft used to destroy the World Trade Center in New York and the Pentagon building in Washington, D.C.

There is a need for government to be accountable and transparent to taxpayers in a way that is easily understood and appreciated. Americans have become educated and accustomed to the realistic success levels of baseball players where one hit out of three is considered to be outstanding. It's about telling the truth. Americans have never been educated about realistic success levels for government programs. This book provides some insight into this world of defining government performance expectations.

This book illustrates how some government programs are changing as a result of a continuing focus on results. Outcome reporting is now required for some public and nonprofit agencies like the United Way and select foundations. One of the next major challenges is for all managers—regardless of whether they are based in government, schools, churches, faith-based agencies, or nonprofit organizations—is to learn how to use outcome information to explain excellence and to improve performance levels as a result of this understanding. It is not just about government agencies documenting their impact. It is about all major institutions sharing their results with stakeholders and the general public, who currently are uninformed and skeptical that there are any results. Distrust of government and politicians is based, in part, on their lack of honesty in communicating the impact of programs on the lives of clients and communities.

There have been remarkable initiatives in government accountability and transparency over the past 30 years. The following leaders are some of the pioneers who have been most responsible for encouraging the impact approach to managing government programs:

- Harry Hatry, the Urban Institute
- Fred Richmond, Center for Applied Management Practices
- Vice-President Al Gore (Government Performance and Results Act, 1993)
- Jay Fountain, Governmental Accounting Standards Board
- Judy Zelio, National Conference of State Legislatures
- Davis Osborne, Ted Gaebler, and Peter Hutchinson (*Reinventing Government* and *The Price of Government*)
- General Accountability Office
- Oregon and North Carolina (benchmarking)
- city managers in Sunnyvale, California; Palo Alto, California; and Portland, Oregon
- program managers like Vergil Pinckney (Maxey Bays Training school), Clark Luster (Pressley Ridge), and Barbara Dorf (HUD), and the
- Alfred Sloan Foundation.

Their contributions to government performance remain largely invisible to the general public and many of their initiatives are only at the early stages of development and acceptance. The reader will be introduced in this book to some of their findings and recommendations. They have succeeded in spite of powerful forces of tradition and practice that prevent the disclosure of government performance. Accountability and transparency are necessary, in my opinion, for providing a basis for trust in government and other institutions like schools and churches.

This book is organized into 11 chapters.

The first chapter provides an overview.

Chapter 2 focuses on baseball as the transparency model for performance reporting.

The third chapter describes *The Transparent Accountability Paradigm* and provides examples at the federal, state, and local level. It includes the 13 questions legislators should ask (but seldom do) on the effectiveness of any government-funded program and how to best present performance information to citizens. The chapter also presents Oregon's benchmarks as a model of how to create a statewide set of progress measures. Oregon has the greatest experience in setting and maintaining benchmarks and attempting to link programs to these standards. The final section lists the major reasons why individuals are in favor of, or against, increased levels of transparency along with an example of a transparency initiative by WikiLeaks in 2010 to release thousands of classified documents on the Iraq and Afghanistan wars.

The fourth chapter discusses the "ethic of intrinsic goodness" as the biggest barrier to answering Carter's basic seven questions of stewardship that focus on client outcomes after the service has been delivered. It concludes with a discussion of the seven management strategies necessary to define and implement an outcome focused accountability system.

Chapter 5 introduces the concept of return on investment.

Chapter 6 portrays two managers' approach to stewardship through being accountable and transparent.

Chapter 7 provides some lessons learned about the risks of being transparent and telling the truth about a program's impact. The example of transparency is the publication of the *Consumer Guide to Michigan Nursing Homes*, which included the average family satisfaction score and the Department of Public Health's inspection citations for each of 420 facilities. The challenges faced by the nursing home providers as they considered the release of such transparent performance information included the fear of low outcomes, fear of high outcomes, misinterpreting outcomes, fear of litigation, and not knowing what causes high performing nursing homes.

Chapter 8 focuses on "connecting the dots," which explains how specific outcomes are used to explain program excellence. The example used is the six key factors associated with quality care in nursing homes. This concise summary is particularly useful in explaining the program to representatives from the media, legislature, or funding sources. More importantly, such an exercise challenges program advocates and program managers to validate and provide documentation for the causal factors most likely responsible for quality outcomes.

Chapter 9 defines the concept of the public good with benchmarks and recommends widely sharing this information with the public. The benchmarks clarify the "ask" of government to improve the benchmarks. This, in turn, will pressure politicians, government officials, and nonprofit agencies to become better stewards of resources entrusted to them. If the truth about performance is openly shared, stakeholders may increase their trust in these institutions. The chapter provides an example of how to measure trust as an important component of the most successful relationships between auto companies and their suppliers. The reasons for distrust of government are reviewed, and a strategy is developed for using performance measures as an approach to regain the trust. The chapter concludes with a set of historical charts as examples of potential benchmarks.

Chapter 10 provides readers answers to eight key questions, such as why legislators are reluctant to require government to be accountable.

Chapter 11 summarizes the argument for a more accountable and transparent government and provides a set of strategies for organizations and individuals to participate in creating this preferred future.

Appendix A includes North Carolina's benchmarks of progress report. Appendix B, intended to be particularly helpful for students of organizational behavior, public administration, and the management of nonprofit organizations, provides discussion questions and activities for each chapter.

Chapter 2
Government Should Be More Like Baseball

Baseball is transparent. Government is not. Government should be more like baseball. It would be more fun for everyone. In baseball, all the players know how their performance compares to other players. All managers know how well their team's performance compares to all other teams. Most baseball fans are familiar with the best player and team performance standards. Excellent batters hit the ball successfully 3 out of ten times. Only rarely does an individual hit the ball successfully 4 out of ten times (Ted Williams, Boston Red Sox outfielder, was the last to achieve this feat in 1941 when he finished the season with a .406 batting average). No one has ever consistently hit the ball successfully 5 out of ten times over the course of an entire season. In short, everyone involved (players, managers, owners, fans, and media) know the same outcomes and appreciate the rareness of any player who can attain a high level of achievement.

Baseball player performance information is widely available on newspapers' sports pages, and this is routinely part of the American socialization process. Every professional baseball player has his own baseball "card" with his picture and uniform and number on one side and his performance history on the back of the card. These cards are widely distributed and collected by fans. For baseball, all important historical performance information is collected at the individual level and made public so that all stakeholders share the same results. Baseball has made a huge investment in having outcomes by individuals and teams. It has a rich history of the average performance levels so that everyone understands what are reasonable expectations based on historical information. Baseball is the ultimate form of transparency—everyone knows the same truth.

Baseball is fun to watch, in part, because everyone knows what reasonable performance is. These expectations are unlikely to change because of improved training techniques, rules, stadium enhancements, or ball or bat design. Baseball has largely remained unchanged for over 100 years. Baseball performance levels are unlikely to significantly change over the next 100 years.

The performance levels are not negotiable. A knowledgeable fan not only has favorite players and team, but also appreciates how their performance compares to all other players or teams.

Government has almost none of baseball's characteristics and could benefit greatly from adopting many of its performance measurement strategies. Over the past 25 years, there have been several initiatives to require outcome measurement of government so that everyone could have a realistic expectation of success. In 1989, Oregon established a Progress Board to measure the state's progress across various indicators of success for education, health, a clean environment, public safety, and economic growth and diversity. Oregon provides a scorecard for the taxpayer. Government needs a scorecard to compare current performance with historical performance across a set number of important outcome measures, such as:

- high school and college graduation rates,
- academic achievement levels,
- unemployment rates,
- average family income levels,
- poverty levels,
- clean water and air quality,
- crime rate,
- rate of avoidable health care provider errors, and
- deaths due to auto accidents.

Individual programs also need their own scorecards so that everyone can share in the same measure of success. Most have a scorecard, but it generally reflects the amount of money spent, clients served, or services delivered—rather than the results of their efforts to change the lives of their clients or communities. It would be the equivalent of knowing the number of baseball games played and the times at bat, but not the players' batting averages or number of home runs.

Most government programs have no way to know their own success rates. This robs their managers and staff of ever knowing how to improve their services or to appreciate their own success level. It is like bowling with a curtain in front of the pins so that one cannot know the impact of his or her technique of throwing the bowling ball. There is no way to improve one's score without knowing the impact of the previous effort. In this bowling example, one may hear some noise from the pins falling but no score is signaled above the pins. The bowler would never know if he or she had a "strike." If there was no noise, the bowler would probably assume a "gutter ball." However, there are many rules about how to throw the bowling ball, such as not crossing over the foul line with your foot after you have released the ball. These rules are enforced and, if violated, disallow the score. Government work is a lot like bowling with a curtain in front of the pins example. The bowlers are being paid to bowl, but not given meaningful feedback about the success of their efforts. Instead, they are measured and rewarded based on their compliance with the rules and regulations for throwing the ball and the number of years they show up to play the game. Government employees without outcome focus and feedback create alternative meaning for their work day, including:

- high value on compliance with rules and regulations,
- high interest in gossip about administrative decisions of agency managers,
- low respect for legislative and agency leadership who often have short tenure,
- skepticism and cynicism about initiatives to improve performance, and
- planning the work day around personal agendas with more meaning such as breaks, lunch, errands, and exploring Internet diversions.

It is counter-productive to hire someone to do a job and not provide meaningful feedback on their success and then expect them to be committed and invested in a success they cannot know. In this context, the concept of government employees as civil servants makes sense. This is what we have done with government programs and many faith-based agencies. We have denied them a chance to know if they are successful, because we have failed to define the impact of their efforts on the lives of clients and communities served.

We have also not asked for a return on our tax investment. Effective government is a resource we cannot continue to squander. It is a luxury we can no longer afford. We need a federal government league. Each state would be a team. The collective effort would be the national measure of government outcomes. The results would be reported regularly in the media, and children would be introduced to these measures in their schools so that they could be knowledgeable consumers of government services since they will be contributing 37% of their earnings to pay for government.

A similar effort could be launched by nonprofit organizations like the United Way. This type of transparency would unleash a healthy competition among states to become the best across a variety of measures of outcomes. It would also be a constant reminder of what is important as opposed to what is often irrelevant, but is the temporary distraction of the media or politicians. The Oregon benchmarks would be an ideal starting point and will be discussed in the next chapter.

In this scenario, every taxpayer would receive in April each year the latest benchmark scores reflecting how each state has performed historically and is performing now, along with a national average. As taxpayers complete their tax returns, they will know if we are better off under specific political leadership within the state and nationally. They will be capable of "connecting the dots" between their tax investment and the outcomes. They will be informed consumers and demand that politicians and government officials become more effective, especially if they are asking for additional taxes. I expect that most politicians will be opposed to this level of transparency.

I suspect that many politicians will claim their state's uniqueness that would then excuse any comparatively low performance levels. State leaders generally give the greatest credence to the performance of adjoining states of similar size. For example, Oregon compares itself to national averages or to the performance of the adjacent state of Washington. Michigan leaders often consider as valid the comparisons of Michigan with other states in the Great Lakes region (Ohio, Wisconsin, Indiana, Minnesota, and Illinois). It is as if the Midwest state economies and governments are comparable but not the east, west, or southern states.

In baseball, there is always the complaint that the New York Yankees have a huge advantage in purchasing the most talented baseball players because of that team's large consumer and media base. allowing them to offer attractive player salary packages. This objection does not change the way baseball compares the performance levels of players or teams. They all compete and there is only one baseball champion.

Ultimately, historical benchmarks will be the test of how well each state performs, given its unique challenges. Most state leaders and citizens generally want the same outcomes regarding their communities:

- safe and healthy,
- beautiful,
- a vibrant economy with job opportunities,
- accessible and cost-effective health services, and
- an education system that prepares students for a rewarding economic and civic life.

Benchmark comparisons between states are the focus of this book. The appropriate comparisons at the national level are among other industrialized countries. With globalization of trade, the United States should rank in the top five countries across all important benchmarks to continue its status as a world leader and assure opportunities for its citizens. This is particularly challenging in the area of education and health care outcomes and expenditure rankings.

Chapter 3
The Transparent
Accountability Paradigm

A paradigm is an example, model, or pattern that illustrates a particular perspective. The new hybrid automobile engine, which combines electrical battery energy and gasoline to operate the car, is a new paradigm, because it provides an alternative way to generate energy for a car. The long standing social contract between citizens and government has perpetuated a paradigm of citizens paying taxes to fund government's provision of services for the public good (national defense, fire safety, police, schools, clean environment, regulation of financial markets), which otherwise would not be available. Citizens have trusted government to effectively operate these services to provide the greatest return on the resources committed to them. The trust in politicians and government has never been high, in part, because there has not been any systematic way for citizens to know the positive impact of government on the lives of clients and communities. Governments have not been good stewards of the resources committed to them, because they have not measured their success and have not informed the taxpayers of the results.

Paradigm is used within natural sciences to refer to a pattern or model of thinking. Thomas Kuhn (Kuhn, 1962) describes the transition from one paradigm to the next as a shift that rarely occurs but it has huge consequences. The process usually occurs over a period of years and the following steps facilitate the acceptance of any new science paradigm:

- professional organizations that give legitimacy to the paradigm,
- dynamic leaders who introduce the paradigm,
- journals and editors who write about the system of thought,
- government agencies who give credence to the paradigm,
- educators who propagate the paradigm's ideas by teaching it to students,
- media coverage,
- other interest groups embrace the beliefs central to the paradigm, and
- sources of funding to further research on the paradigm.

The Transparent Accountability Paradigm

This is a trickle down approach to the introduction of a new paradigm. Similar conditions currently are facilitating the acceptance of *The Transparent Accountability Paradigm* and will be described and documented throughout the book. A quicker acceptance process is more likely to result from sharing ideas through rapid technology mechanisms like YouTube, Facebook and Twitter and reaching a "tipping point" of acceptance. Malcolm Gladwell (2000) provides many examples of rapid changes such as the dramatic reduction in crime in New York City in the early 1990s due to a number of causal factors.

This traditional paradigm of citizens funding government programs with no meaningful results for the taxpayers' investment is now being challenged, and a revised contract is being tested in specific locations at the federal, state, and local levels. I call this new paradigm *The Transparent Accountability Paradigm*. It is being created out of the frustration of taxpayers and a small number of courageous legislators, foundations, and government program managers. The heart of the new paradigm is honest governance that will help generate taxpayers' trust of politicians and government. It will not guarantee support for new taxes, but it will generate a more informed debate about how taxes are currently used and should be used in the future. Taxpayers deeply resent taxation without true accountability, and this is at the heart of the low approval rating of politicians and government that are inevitably linked together in the minds of the citizens. This level of resentment existed before the eight-year Iraq war, the inadequate regulation of banks to avoid the sub-prime mortgage collapse with lowering home values, and the Federal Emergency Management Agency's flawed provision of assistance for Hurricane Katrina victims. This resentment has only deepened as a result of government's inability to meet the public's expectation.

The Transparent Accountability Paradigm is largely invisible to the general public, which remains skeptical of government performance and largely perceives taxes as a necessary financial burden with limited positive consequences. The press continuously covers examples of the misuse of government resources. This feeds the public's sense of low government performance expectations and reinforces the resentment for new taxes. There is no way to know how current resources are being used, let alone if there is a compelling need for additional resources.

The Angry Taxpayer

The taxpayer has been angry for some time. California Proposition 13 (1978) limited the growth of government in the largest state. Other states, such as Massachusetts, passed similar legislation to curb the expansion of state services. Five months after passage of Proposition 13, the *Washington Post* conducted a survey that indicated that American taxpayers were not nearly as angry with their tax bills as they were with how little they got from their government in return. Taxpayers are largely uninformed about how their tax dollars are spent, let alone how much impact these dollars have on the lives of clients or communities. "Tax money," said the *Post* story announcing poll results, "is seen as largely wasted by local state and federal governments that have padded payrolls and employees who are overpaid, lazy, discourteous and inefficient" (Greiner, Hatry, Koss, Millar & Woodward, 1981, p. xv).

In January 1992, *Money Magazine* contracted with Gallup Organization pollsters to survey 300 randomly selected readers about the perceived value of taxes. Only 25% of respondents perceived their federal taxes as being spent "well." The perceptions of state taxes fared somewhat better at 36% and local real estate taxes (largely for schools) peaked at only 58% (Dingle, 1992, p 2).

Taxpayers have more positive perceptions of the use of their taxes at the local level and the most negative perceptions at the federal level. That reinforces the need to have a state-specific report of the effectiveness of programs at the state and local level. For example, each state has several offices of the Social Security Administration and post offices. Outcome information at this level needs to be shared with citizens in each separate location.

In 1994, Mario Cuomo was defeated after serving 12 years as Governor of New York. In his typical reflective style, Mr. Cuomo echoed a familiar theme to the national wave of voter anger at Democratic politicians:

> *It is difficult to know exactly what the negative votes are saying because they are probably saying more than one thing. It is clear that they are saying that much of America is unhappy. This is not a joyous vote. This is condemnatory, frightened, and angry. Now the question*

> *is why. I think a lot of people are saying government doesn't appear to be using my money well, therefore I resent their taking it* (Sack, 1994, p. A17).

Mario Coumo's son was elected Governor of New York in 2010 and faces some of the same difficulties as his father. The mid-term national elections that same year transferred control of the House of Representatives to Republicans, in part, because of the emergence and influence of a new populist political movement called the Tea Party. It focused on the need to reduce the increasing federal deficit.

Democrats and Republicans are at risk when taxpayers are un-focused in their anger. Both parties need to understand the root cause or causes of this anger and what they can do to lower the simmering rage and replace it with a minimal level of support for government's use of tax dollars. At this point, neither the Democratic rhetoric of expanded government nor the Republi-can rhetoric of less taxes and smaller government appears to have resonated with the majority of voters. A number of strate-gies have been tried to limit government spending and to bring more accountability to government. Each has had only limited success. They are more a reaction to unfocused taxpayer anger than any effective long term solution. Some of the more popu-lar ineffective strategies include: caps on spending, term limits for politicians, privatization of public services, less government, sun-setting of legislation (requiring re-authorizing of programs after a set number of years), performance-based budgeting, and zero-based budgeting (Osborne and Gaebler, 1992). None of these initiatives has resonated with the public, in part, because of the limited transparency in communicating how tax dollars are used to improve the lives and communities where they live.

Neither Democrats nor Republicans have been honest about the results of their program initiatives. They filter their messages to enhance their political agenda. Any taxpayer who is motivated to be informed must sort through the rhetoric to arrive at the total picture and make an assessment of the "truth." Some would con-tend that this is the responsibility of citizens. There is no neutral entity that focuses on the truth. The media presents both po-litical interpretations and provides controversy. However, in the end, the citizen is often confused and distrustful of both political parties' "spinning" of the truth. Adding to the difficulty of obtain-ing objective information is the recent creation of Internet blogs that provide a wide range of perspectives and limited assurances about the validity of the sources of the information. It is similar to the skepticism of tabloids. Blogs are often consistently providing a vehicle for readers to reinforce their biases. This is one of the main reasons for their popularity. This is a miniaturized version of a talk show like the Rush Limbaugh program. Conservatives support Limbaugh's perspective because they want an interpretation that reinforces their current beliefs.

In *The Price of Government* (Osborne and Hutchinson, 2004), the authors conclude that "...the American people are immensely frustrated. They pay the price of government and they want a government that is worth what they pay" (p. vii). The cost of government has remained within 35-37% of personal income for the past three decades (1972-2000). This breaks down into three categories: 20-22% for federal taxes, 7.3-8.3% for state taxes, and 6-6.6% for local taxes. Their assessment of the current budgeting process at all levels is that the process and rhetoric may include performance information but the decisions continue to remain largely based upon political considerations, influenced by stakeholders of currently funded programs.

> *What citizens care most about is the relationship between the taxes they pay and the quality of services they receive. If it takes an extra employee to produce the results they want they are willing to pay, that's fine with them. No one, for example, argues that public education would improve if we had fewer teachers. What people want is more effective teachers* (p. 134).

Osborne and Hutchinson are clear about the need for public leaders to tell the truth to voters.

> *Citizens do not want their leaders to flinch from open discussions of fiscal reality when voters are in the room. They can deal with bad news. They simply want leaders who will lead with them. And more often than not, they can tell when talk is on the level and when it is smoke and mirrors* (p. 309-310).

The Transparent Accountability Paradigm

I created *The Transparent Accountability Paradigm* to articulate a new type of accountability that focuses on government outcomes and the responsibilities of stewardship. It is a revised social contract between taxpayers, their elected representatives, and government. The ten key characteristics include:

1. Taxpayers want a government that works. They want a positive relationship between taxes and tangible program success.
2. Government programs should demonstrate a positive impact on citizens and communities they serve.
3. Government should share results with all stakeholders, including the public.
4. Results should be measurable, simple, realistic, manageable, and easily understood.
5. Results should be the primary basis for important resource decisions.
6. Program managers should maximize results.
7. Program managers should create results measures and obtain the necessary consensus/acceptance from various stakeholders.
8. Government should only fund programs that improve results and remove those that cannot.
9. Voters should elect leaders who demonstrate this level of accountability.
10. Voters should become better educated on the performance of government and communicate directly with their leaders about their "ask" of government.

New paradigms most frequently develop on the "edges" of the mainstream. Examples of organizations that are promoting elements of *The Transparent Accountability Paradigm* include the Urban Institute, the Governmental Accounting Standards Board, the National Conference of State Legislatures, and selected cities and states. These examples will be the focus of the next section.

The Urban Institute

Harry Hatry is the Director of State-Local Government Research for the Urban Institute, a research and public policy firm in Washington, D.C. It was established in 1968 and has demonstrated an extensive commitment to outcome measurement throughout its history.

Harry Hatry has worked for the Urban Institute in his current capacity for most of the 50 years since the organization was founded. His leadership and intellectual curiosity has nourished the interest and legislation for government accountability and transparency. I have known Harry Hatry since 1974, and worked with him in producing the publication *Developing Client Outcome Monitoring Systems: A Guide for State and Local Social Service Agencies* (Millar & Millar, 1981) and on an advisory panel for the Commission on the Accreditation of Rehabilitation Facilities. Mr. Hatry has published many books on government performance and has been actively involved with the Governmental Accounting Standards Board, National Conference of State Legislatures, and Oregon's Progress Board Assessment. His influence is found throughout the Government Performance and Results Act and countless other initiatives. In 2005, he was named the first Urban Institute Distinguished Fellow. His books have been translated into Japanese, Russian, and Polish. His imprint is both broad and deep. His influence is ubiquitous. I cannot overestimate his personal impact on *The Transparent Accountability Paradigm.*

Government Performance and Results Act (1993)

On March 3, 1993, President Clinton announced the National Performance Review, a six-month assessment of federal government programs. The subsequent report by Vice-President Gore was entitled *The Gore Report on Reinventing Government* (Gore, 1993). Vice-President Gore fully recognized Washington's preoccupation with program scandal rather than program outcomes:

> *The greatest risk is not that the program will perform poorly, but that a scandal will erupt. Scandals are front-page news, while routine failure is ignored. Hence, control system after control system is piled up to minimize the risk of scandal. The budget system, the personnel rules, the procurement process, the inspector generals—all are designed to prevent the tiniest missteps. We assume that we cannot trust employees to make decisions so we spell out in precise detail how they must do everything, then audit them to assure that they have obeyed every rule. The slightest deviation prompts new regulations and even more audits* (p. 3-4).

As Vice-President, Gore provided excellent insight into the motivation of elected officials and described the link between government and the media, which is more pre-occupied with scandal than effectiveness. Reporters and editors contend that scandal sells and effectiveness is not newsworthy. Both, I believe, should be newsworthy. Vice-President Gore articulated a six-step process for reinventing government: decentralizing the decision-making process, holding all federal employees accountable for results, giving federal workers the tools they need to do their jobs, enhancing the quality of work life, forming a labor-management partnership, and exerting leadership.

The second step of holding all federal employees accountable for results is the most important for our purposes. Gore recognized the current inappropriate focus on process rather than on the outcomes of programs:

> *Management in government does not judge most programs by whether they work or not. Instead, government typically measures program activity—how much it spends on them, or how many people it assigns to them. Because government focuses on these inputs instead of real results, it tends to throw good money after bad. It pours dollars into old education programs even as student performance sinks* (p. 72).

In July 1993, Congress passed the Government Performance and Results Act (GPRA) which required ten federal agencies to complete three-year pilots beginning in fiscal 1994 to develop measures of progress. It also required that all federal programs develop five-year strategic plans linked to measurable outcomes in FY 1998. The Senate Committee on Government Affairs held hearings in 1993 on the proposed legislation. The committee's overview summarized the need for this initiative.

> *Public confidence in the institutions of American government is suffering from a perception that those institutions are not working well. Recent public opinion polls indicate that this is particularly true with respect to the Federal government, as both Congress and the Executive Branch are held in low esteem by the American people.*

> *Much has been made of the seeming inconsistency between the public's desire for a wide range of government services and the same public's disdain for government and objections to paying higher taxes. The committee believes that part of the explanation for this*

apparent inconsistency can be seen in the results of a recent opinion poll which shows that Americans, on average, believe that as much as 48 cents out of every tax dollar is wasted. In other words, the public believes that it is not getting the level of government services for which it is paying (Committee on Governmental Affairs, 1993, p. 5-6).

The Committee heard testimony of successful results oriented programs from Florida's Department of Health and Rehabilitation Services; the city of Sunnydale, California; Australia; and Britain. Encouraging testimony was also supplied by the General Accountability Office's (then named the General Accounting Office) Comptroller General, the National Academy of Public Administration, and the American Society for Public Administration.

Since 1993, all federal agencies have completed annual reports specifying performance expectations including program outcomes that are assumed to be a result of the federally funded program interventions. For example, the Community Services Block Grant (CSBG) program within the Department of Health and Human Services' Office of Community Services funds to support approximately 1,000 local anti-poverty agencies that provide programs such as Head Start, home energy assistance programs, and low-income housing. The following outcome expectations are a collective effort by many anti-poverty programs. The six national performance indicators (with multiple outcome measures within each) for CSBG include:

1. low-income people become more self-sufficient (employed),
2. the conditions in which low-income people live are improved,
3. low-income people own a stake in their community,
4. partnerships among supporters and providers of services to low-income people are achieved,
5. agencies increase their capacity to achieve results, and
6. low-income people, especially vulnerable populations, achieve their potential by strengthening family and other supportive environments.

The General Accountability Office (GAO) has monitored the implementation of GPRA since 1993. The GAO found that federal agencies were collecting more performance data, but there has been no change in the use of such information for purposes of improving the management of these programs. This was disappointing to the GAO 13 years after passage of this legislation:

> *The benefit of collecting performance information is only fully realized when this information is actually used by managers to make decisions oriented toward improving results. While our surveys found that managers reported having more performance measures in 2003 than in 1997, the data showed the use of performance information for program management activities did not increase significantly from 1997 levels. In our survey, we asked managers about their use of performance information for specific purposes, such as setting program priorities, allocating resources or adopting new program approaches....The extent of use in 2003 was not sufficiently different from 1997 levels for any category of use except for adopting new program approaches or changing work processes, where use actually decreased* (General Accountability Office, 2005, p. 5).

The use of performance information by federal managers is high. Approximately 60-70% of federal managers surveyed by GAO report the use of performance data across a wide range of decisions. This level of use has not changed as a result of GPRA. GAO attempted to obtain examples of the use of performance information. There were few examples. This has led to additional research into how best to use outcome information. There is a recognition that managers at all levels could benefit from additional training in interpreting and appropriately utilizing this kind of information to improve their programs. This will be the topic of Chapter 8 (Connecting the Dots).

If compliance with GPRA has resulted in better federal programs, it has neither been obvious to the GAO or to the general public.

OMB Watch is a nonprofit organization created in 1983 to monitor the federal budget process. Its assessment of GPRA is that it has little impact.

> *In reality, GPRA has done very little to improve the public perception of government performance, since public awareness of GPRA is almost non-existent, there is al-*

most no media coverage and very few policy types are engaged. In most agencies GPRA appears to have become a compliance activity and nothing more. Although agencies are required by GPRA to seek and consider stakeholder comments as they prepare their strategic plans, few citizens or non-profit organizations have even heard of GPRA, let alone provide input. Congress also has shown limited interest in GPRA, even though it is designed to ultimately lead to 'performance budgeting, with performance assessments being used as a basis for authorization and appropriation funding levels' (OMB Watch, 2004 p. 1).

National Conference of State Legislatures

The National Conference of State Legislatures (NCSL) is a bipartisan organization that serves state legislators and staff of the states, its commonwealths, and territories. One of its initiatives is *Legislating for Results* (NCSL, 2003), a joint project with Harry Hatry of the Urban Institute. *Legislating for Results* provides legislators and their staff members with a process that focuses on performance and outcomes. Several states (Florida, Louisiana, New Mexico, and Texas) are used as examples of legislating and implementing a performance-based budgeting system. This initiative is a step-by-step process for any legislator interested in obtaining performance information on state-funded programs.

The following 13 questions give the legislator a sense of the basic questions to ask of agency managers during the appropriations and program review hearings. They are particularly helpful for new legislators who often have limited understanding of the various programs. Seldom have I heard such questions routinely asked in such hearings in Michigan over the past 30 years, at least in the social and health program areas.

The 13 questions are:

1. What is the program's primary purpose? What citizens are affected?
2. What key results are expected from this use of taxpayers' funds?
3. What key performance indicators are used to track progress in attaining these results?
4. What were the results in the most recent year?

5. How do these results compare to the targets? Have any results been unexpectedly good or unexpectedly poor?
6. How do the results compare to other benchmarks (e.g., other states)?
7. For which citizen groups have the results been less than desired? (Examples: groups by location, gender, income, race/ethnicity, disability, etc.)
8. If any targets were missed, why were those targets missed?
9. What is being done to improve deficiencies?
10. What actions does your new/proposed budget include that would improve results?
11. How would the results change if funding is increased by 5%? Decreased by 5%?
12. Which group of citizens might benefit? Which might lose? To what extent?
13. What other programs and agencies are partners in producing desired results?

These are appropriate questions if results refer to actual outcomes such as jobs for employment training programs or learning for educational programs. Most frequently, results refer to services delivered. Most state legislators do not know the expected outcome as a result of any given service. The agency's program manager knows that the legislators do not know what an appropriate outcome would look like. Moreover, they do not take the time to find out. So the game continues with funding at or above last year's appropriation. Seldom are program managers ever able to systematically justify how their program caused an impact positively or negatively on the clients or communities served. Anecdotal testimony is substituted for outcomes across the population served.

NCSL also provides legislators with very practical examples of what different states have used results to bring accountability to state government. Judy Zelio, a staff member of NCSL, constructed steps to walk any interested legislator through the process.

Generally speaking, performance measures include:

1. *input indicators—funding amounts or state personnel,*
2. *output indicators—number of things such as miles paved or clients served (e.g., children vaccinated,*

prison beds occupied, emergency room visits, hunting licenses issued), and

3.   *results indicators—history or changes in rates of things like accidents, diseases, crime, adoption, graduation, recidivism, job placement.*

Many agency and program managers commonly keep records of inputs and outputs. A typical example would be the cost per person to provide job training and the number of people who received it. Far less common is performance information about results. Policymakers interested in program results beyond input and output indicators may want to know, for example, how many people in a job training program actually got jobs, and how long they kept them. They may ask whether domestic violence has increased or decreased rather than how many clients receive shelter and counseling. They may ask about the percentage of state college graduates employed in the state instead of how many graduate. They may want to know the proportion of welfare recipients who became self sufficient after receiving state assistance. Until such information is available, it is difficult to know whether a program is accomplishing its purpose and whether funding changes need to be made (Zelio, 2005).

NCSL and the Urban Institute provide valuable leadership and practical steps to implement results oriented budgeting. This is especially needed in states with term limited legislators. However, even with legislators with many more years in elected office, there were remarkably few interested enough to actually pass results oriented legislation or appropriations. There are reasons for this legislator reluctance to enter this arena of controversy and possible loss of re-election support. If the stakeholders who support the program perceive result oriented questions as challenging the "intrinsic goodness" of the program, then they may withhold their support for re-electing the legislator. This fear often prevents legislators from pursuing this level of accountability. In the end, it is far easier to not ask the results oriented questions than to risk the political consequences.

This approach is an uphill battle because of the status quo forces against such a direction. With a critical mass of legislative and executive branch leadership, some states have institutionalized this direction. NCSL recommends the following seven steps:

1. Focus on outcomes that are of importance to constituents, such as highway accident rates, number of child abuse cases, infant mortality, incidents of communicable disease, unemployment rates, air and water pollution levels, and prisoner escape rates.
2. For advocacy groups or groups that are interested in specific, current issues, focus on outcome data relevant to those issues.
3. Where possible, provide breakouts of the outcomes by particular cities or counties or by demographic groups (e.g., gender, age group, racial/ethnic group, income group, or particular disabled group).
4. Show constituents how outcomes for their location or group compare to others.
5. Obtain information in advance that helps explain why low outcomes of interest to the audience occurred.
6. Be objective in reporting the outcome information and in providing explanations about why poor outcomes and good outcomes occurred.
7. Identify what legislators plan to do about low outcomes.

An outcome approach is important because sharing such effectiveness information is being honest and straightforward. It is about telling the truth and establishing trust with the taxpayers. Most state legislators are not interested in program outcomes. They are primarily focused on their own political outcome and representing their political party's caucus and the party's re-election. During the annual appropriations process, state legislators are assigned to appropriations committees that hold public hearings to review proposed budgets for various programs. Agency staff members provide an overview of the program and then the legislators call on various stakeholders to provide testimony regarding their support or opposition to this proposed budget.

For example, the Medicaid Director would provide an overview of the Medicaid program and proposed budget and the appropriations committee would ask various stakeholders their assessment of the proposed budget. Stakeholders in the Medicaid example would include representatives of physicians; hospitals; nursing homes; health plans; home health agencies; Home and Community Based Care organizations; and professional advocacy groups like AARP, Office of Services to the Elderly, and State Ombudsman programs. The same program's stakeholders are often the biggest contributors to the political campaigns of the legislators sitting on the appropriations committee. I know this from my experience as President/CEO of the Health Care Association of Michigan (HCAM) for ten years (1996-2006). Our members were nursing home owners. I testified at the annual appropriations hearings in support of continued Medicaid funding for nursing homes. HCAM also contributed to the political campaigns of the appropriations committee members, especially the chair and vice-chair.

There is a common bond of interest between the legislator and the stakeholders to maintain or expand a specific program's budget. The legislator is seldom motivated to reduce funding. He or she is motivated to increase funding whether the program is performing or not. The irony, of course, is that regardless of the outcome information, it is highly likely that any given program will continue to receive funds. Thus, the fear of outcome information damaging a program is largely unfounded. It is, nevertheless, perceived as a possible threat and a disincentive to require accountability. It is a rare politician who will raise the important questions of program outcomes and hold program managers responsible for their performance level. Term limitations for politicians have only increased the prevailing practice of approving or increasing funding without requiring outcome information. For those rare legislators committed to accountability and transparency in government, the NCSL has provided valuable examples and a process to implement such an approach.

One of the fundamental barriers to implementing performance monitoring systems is that legislators, their staff members, and the staff members of the agencies rarely have any formal training in evaluation, research, and analysis. The MPA (Masters of Public Administration) is seldom a formal educational prerequisite for government or political leadership positions. If the public demands more accountability and transparency, there will be a subsequent need for better training and experience of program managers and legislative staff.

Governmental Accounting Standards Board

The Governmental Accounting Standards Board (GASB) is an organization that sets standards for government financial reporting. For many years, the GASB has encouraged the inclusion of services efforts and accomplishments as performance measures. Although not yet required, this initiative encourages all governmental entities to explore ways to report their performance along with their financial information.

Jay Fountain, formerly GASB's Director of Research, has dedicated a large portion of his career to expanding the traditional role of accounting to include program results as part of this important accounting function. He has successfully partnered with Harry Hatry of the Urban Institute and the Alfred Sloan Foundation over the past 30 years to conduct impressive research and practical suggestions on how to most effectively collect and report program outcomes to a broad group of interested citizens. GASB's Government Service Efforts and Accomplishments Performance Reports recognizes the need for information about whether the government agency was "successful in maintaining or improving the well-being of citizens and other stakeholders—its primary purpose" (GASB, 2002). The report provides valuable examples of how city and state governments have attempted to summarize their programs' impact on their citizens and communities. GASB recognizes that each specific government function has unique performance measures and has developed program specific performance reports for the following services: elementary and secondary education, water and wastewater treatment, mass transit, sanitation collection and disposal, fire department programs, public health programs, police department programs, and road maintenance. The report can be downloaded on the GASB's Web site (www.gasb.org), and it includes numerous references to other Internet sites illustrating the use of performance measurements.

Although these GASB efforts are experimental and voluntary at this point in time (GASB, 2007), GASB will hopefully prevail in mandating some form of public reporting on service outcomes as part of the current accounting standards. A larger challenge (even if GASB does prevail) is the difficulty of securing the attention of the taxpayer to read and react to any document summarizing either financial or outcome information.

The following brief excerpt from an op-ed article in the *New York Times* by Cynthia B. Green (Green, 2003), a GASB Board member, articulates the role of GASB and why performance measurement is important for New York as well as all states. It is entitled *The Way to a Better Budget:*

> *Useful reforms have been suggested, from better financial management systems to more stringent lobbying*

laws. None of these proposals, however, deals with the crux of the problem: the State of New York does not regularly measure and report on the performance of its programs, a system known as managing for results. In other words, no one in charge knows where our money is making a difference and where it isn't. Every spending cut is basically a shot in the dark. Until the state evaluates the efficiency and effectiveness of its services, and does so seriously and regularly, it will never have adequate information to make these important decisions, let alone debate the issues.... Reporting the performance of individual programs allows elected officials, advocates and citizens to consider what their government is (and is not) accomplishing and to suggest how to improve performance. And while this information is always helpful, it is critical in the face of sizeable budget deficits. With performance data at their fingertips, state and local officials can develop ways to achieve better results at lower costs. ... (A17).

In 2000-2001, GASB held citizen discussion groups to identify how the taxpayer best understands public service performance information to best present this type of information. The results of these focus groups were reported in a GASB publication entitled *Report on the GASB Citizen Discussion Groups on Performance Reporting* (GASB, 2002). This was the first look at how citizens view local and state government performance reporting. There were four primary research questions:

1. What performance information should be reported?
2. How should performance information be communicated?
3. How important are data verification and external review or evaluation?
4. How can citizens use performance information?

GASB held 19 focus groups comprised of 133 participants representing nine cities, two counties, and four states. The nine cities were Austin, Texas; Boston, Massachusetts; New York, N.Y.; Orlando, Florida; Phoenix, Arizona; Portland, Oregon; Tuscan, Arizona; Winston-Salem, North Carolina; and Worcester, Massachusetts. The two counties were Multnomah County, Oregon; and Prince William County, Virginia. The four states were Massachusetts, New York, Oregon, and Texas.

Neither the 133 focus group participants nor the cities, counties, and states were randomly selected. The entities were already involved with government performance monitoring in some way. There were 110 citizens who were not government staff and ten other participants with independent roles such as audit staff or members of an oversight board. In general, the focus groups were comprised of individuals with varying backgrounds and different interests in government including neighborhood or homeowner associations, interest groups such as senior citizens, civic organizations like the League of Women Voters, public policy institutions, media, nonprofit community service agencies like the United Way, consultants to government, appointed citizen committees advising government on improving performance, and citizen boards or commissions. These focus group results do not represent an unbiased random sample of citizens. These are citizens with a strong interest in government and performance monitoring of government. Nonetheless, the results are indicative of the challenges facing any effort to communicate government performance to a group of informed citizens who are already engaged in local or state government at some level of volunteering their time to improving government. The following 12 significant findings all have important insights into practical ways to communicate government performance:

1. Participants want to see performance information reported that citizens say is important, determined by involving citizens in selecting performance measures.
2. Participants want a range of different types of performance information reported (outcomes, citizen and consumer perceptions, and program costs).
3. Measures of outcomes were considered important by participants in all discussion groups.
4. Measures based on surveys of citizens and consumer perceptions and satisfaction were discussed and supported in 16 of the 19 discussion groups.
5. Participants were interested in disaggregation of some performance information.
6. Participants want performance information reported in several comparative contexts.
7. Participants want explanatory information reported along with performance data.
8. Participants urged the use of multiple communication modes with citizens about performance (print, Internet, press, public forums).

9. Participants want performance information to be provided in more than one "layer" or level of detail with different communication channels used for different layers. For example, there should be a printed, condensed version widely distributed with more details available on the Internet.
10. Participants encouraged educating citizens about performance information and its use.
11. Participants want to know performance information has been independently verified.
12. Participants identified and discussed five main uses of performance measurement: increase government accountability; increase citizen engagement; enable citizens to analyze, interpret and evaluate public performance; support citizen decision making; and increase citizens' confidence in government.

GASB (2005) has summarized the results of the focus groups in a citizen-friendly guide to understanding service efforts and accomplishments at the local and state level of government. GASB has provided strong leadership and primary research in our understanding of how to communicate government effectiveness so that citizens can appreciate their tax investments. Unfortunately, GASB's contribution is largely unknown by politicians, the media, and the public. Nonetheless, when accountability and transparency become a specific "ask" of government, the GASB pioneering work will be extremely valuable.

Oregon Benchmarks Progress

There are a number of cities and states (Connecticut, Florida, Maine, Minnesota, North Carolina, Oregon, and Vermont) that benchmark important measures of progress. Their efforts are summarized in various publications such as *Reinventing Government* (Osborne and Gaebler, 1992) and *The Price of Government* (Osborne and Hutchinson, 2004). GASB, NCSL, and the Urban Institute have also published materials on government benchmarking. Oregon is my favorite state example. In 1989, the Oregon legislature created The Progress Board to implement its strategic plan and to set benchmarks to track its progress in attaining three major goals: quality jobs; safe, caring, and engaged communities; and healthy sustainable surroundings. This initiative was called Oregon Shines, and progress was shared each year with the major stakeholders including the general public. The Progress Board, before it was defunded as of June 30, 2009, was comprised of 11 voting members, which, at the time it was disbanded, included the Governor (chair), a member of the U.S. House of Representatives, a member of the state House and Senate, a county commissioner, a newspaper editor, a retired academic, and business leaders. There were also two ex-official members: the Director of the Department of Administrative Services and a student. The Board also had an executive director and several analysts who prepared various reports, benchmarking measurements, and interpretation of progress movement.

There are 91 benchmark and performance measures across seven broad categories—economy, education, civic engagement, social support, public safety, community development, and environment. Examples include:

- national rank of cost of doing business,
- per capita personal income as a percent of U.S. per capita income,
- unemployment rate as a percent of U.S. unemployment rate,
- percent of children entering school ready to learn,
- percent of eighth graders who achieve established skill levels (reading and math),
- percent of adults with a Bachelor's degree,
- state general obligation bond rating (Standards and Poor),
- *Governing* magazine ranking of public management quality,
- infant mortality rate per 1,000 live births,
- percent of families below poverty,
- percent of seniors living outside of nursing facilities,
- crimes per 1,000 citizens,
- percent of roads and bridges in fair or better conditions, and
- percent of owner-occupied houses.

Whenever possible, these benchmarks are compared to the adjacent state of Washington and nationally. Many of these benchmarks have been tracked since 1992 and are displayed as historical trends. The whole report is available online at: http://www.oregon.gov/DAS/OPB

Individual state departments select the benchmarks most relevant to their programs and report on their progress in reaching targets of performance.

Each of the benchmarks is assessed annually in terms of progress. Broad assessment categories include these possible responses:

- *yes,*
- *yes, but,*
- *no, but,* and
- *no.*

With 81 total comparisons with the state of Washington, Oregon does better or is similar 60% of the time. Against 70 comparisons to the U.S. average, Oregon does better or is similar 65% of the time (2003-2005).

A number of other states and countries have been interested in monitoring the Oregon benchmarking experiment. North Carolina has largely modeled its approach from the Oregon design. There have been a number of assessments of the Oregon benchmarking process (Leichter and Tyrens, 2002; Torruellas, 2004; Misaeas, 2007). They recognize the benefits of benchmarks as a way to focus state priorities and progress efforts. However, there remain important difficulties in obtaining a strong commitment from state agency management and legislative leadership to integrate benchmarks into agency and appropriations decision-making.

The amazing thing is that Oregon has collected longitudinal benchmark measures, openly share the data, and analyzed it so that everyone is able to see the extent of the state's progress across a wide range of important measures of performance. Benchmarks prioritize what is important. The *Oregon Shines Vision Highlights 2009 Benchmark Report* is available at: http://www.oregon.gov/DAS/OPB/docs/2009Report/2009_Benchmark_Highlights.pdf.

The report "is intended to inspire productive exploration of why Oregon's results are the way they are and how to make them better."

Included as Appendix A of this book is the North Carolina Progress Board report, *North Carolina 20/20 Update Report.* It is modeled after the Oregon initiative and provides a simple comparison with United States measures along with some analysis on each benchmark.

The biggest challenge facing any state, in my opinion, is that the individual state agencies' benchmarks currently are not, but need to be, aligned with the statewide benchmarks. In Oregon, like other states, many programs are unrelated or only marginally related to such benchmarks. Many programs and agencies have historically emerged spontaneously without any systematic linking back to a broader set of prioritized expectations reflected in the statewide benchmarks. Programs are funded because federal and state funds become available to meet the needs of specific interest groups independent of any relationship to a broad set of benchmarks. Ultimately, states need to figure out a way to demonstrate the contribution of each funded program to improving the public good as reflected in statewide benchmarks.

This is a huge analytic challenge which will require a significant intellectual investment to sort out the most important factors causing the initial benchmark levels to increase or decrease. Oregon and North Carolina are best positioned to answer the question originally posed in Chapter One with the cartoon of wolves howling at the moon: Are we having an impact?

The anti-poverty benchmark is a good example of the need to link programs with a specific benchmark. All states have an array of anti-poverty programs designed to reduce poverty. Factors related to poverty are widely known and documented: minority status, single parenthood, low education, and limited employment skills. Some of the more common state or federal programs in this area include: day care, dental clinic services, early start, employment and training skills development, energy assistance programs, families in partnership, fatherhood, food/clothing pantry, foster care, foster grandparents, GED preparation, Head Start, health services like Medicaid, home repair, homeless shelters, homeownership, literacy programs, parenting skill development, recycling, taxi services, weatherization for homes and the Women, Infants and Children special supplemental nutrition program (WIC).

National poverty levels have persistently ranged within a relatively narrow band between 12-15% of families since the beginning of the Great Society programs of the 1960s. We do not know which of the anti-poverty programs or combination of programs are causing any reduction in the poverty level. There is currently no way to track movement out of poverty and isolate which programs, if any, are responsible for economic mobility out of poverty especially because of the long timeline that usually spans generations. Successfully emerging from poverty during the period from 1900-1960 was assumed to result from success in school, athletics, crime, business, or entertainment, and often requires geographic relocation as with the mass movement from the south to the north with auto factories, steel mills, or shoe manufacturers.

Currently, most anti-poverty programs assume that economic mobility out of poverty is the result of schools; pre-school programs; family support systems; employment training programs; and providing various basic necessities like housing, energy, safety, and health services. These programs are embedded in state agencies and often are supplemented by faith-based efforts. The public policy challenge is to sort out the most important causal factors and the most effective intervention programs. In that context, stakeholders are in a better position to consider funding for those programs that can demonstrate the highest return on the taxpayers' investment. The anti-poverty benchmarking example only illustrates the underlying difficulties of linking specific programs and agencies with statewide benchmark measures of the public good. We generally do not collect the necessary information to answer such a fundamental question of accountability. The same question remains unanswered for crime rates, graduation rates, teenage pregnancy rates, health outcomes, and the other benchmarks. We do not know what works and why!

There is much controversy and remarkably little consensus on the most basic cause-effect relationships between government programs and outcomes. A good example is the testing controversy about the No Child Left Behind program and the appropriateness of these federal learning standards as accurately reflecting student progress. For decades, the National Assessment of Educational Progress (NAEP) scores have remained unchanged regardless of the increasing funding for elementary and secondary education. Essentially, we have not sorted out which of the array of factors (classroom size, teacher credentialing, busing of students, pay and benefit levels of teachers) is most responsible for the greatest improvement in student learning. We are still unclear about how to measure learning let alone the programs that are most effective at enhancing student learning.

The Transparent Accountability Paradigm

The assumption that legislators make each time they appropriate funds for a program is that the intervention will improve the public good and they generally require little or no evidence that this is the case. This most basic assumption is being challenged by *The Transparent Accountability Paradigm*. The taxpayer needs to know the relationship between the investment in state or federal programs and the subsequent return to the public good as a result of that investment. Faith-based foundations are asking the same question about their investments as reflected in a recent summary by the Heritage Foundation (Fagan, 2007). Most taxpayers probably fear that there is no relationship between publicly funded programs and any measurable outcomes. This fear, I believe, leads to cynicism, anger, and frustration with government officials and politicians who are not "watching the store" and not being good stewards of the taxpayers' trust. I believe that if government measured and shared their program results, there would be less cynicism, anger, and frustration by taxpayers. The Oregon Progress Board and benchmarking reporting is a good example of government accountability and transparency. However, until the investment in each publicly funded program is linked to the benchmarks, there is no way for the legislature or the public to know if their investments are causing the progress reflected in the benchmark measures.

Conclusion

The Transparent Accountability Paradigm reflects a government that honestly accounts to taxpayers for the resources provided to them to improve the lives of clients and communities. There is a difference between accountability and transparency. Accountability refers to the reporting of performance information such as inputs, outputs, and outcomes to various layers of oversight (governors, legislators, agency directors, auditors, and accountants). Transparency refers to the open sharing of performance information with a much broader audience of stakeholders including the media, public, and taxpayers. The Oregon Progress Board is a good example of both accountability and transparency. Everyone shares the same information. The Oregon benchmarks define "the public good." Oregon has yet to demonstrate the relationship between the state funded programs to the public good. However, they are farther along, in my opinion, than any other state.

The initiatives in this chapter illustrate some of the ways federal, state, and local governments are attempting to be both more accountable and more transparent. GPRA, NCSL, and GASB have created valuable basic research and advocacy for this approach to governing. However, these initiatives have been unable to attract a public or political constituency necessary to significantly change the current budget decision-making process that includes neither accountability nor transparency. Even assessments within the Executive Office of Management and Budget like the Program Assessment Rating Tool (PART) have not made significant progress and are unlikely to be continued into the Obama administration.

Fortunately, transparency is being demanded across a broad spectrum of institutions including the Catholic Church, publicly held corporations and their accounting firms, universities' relationships with student lending institutions, elementary and high schools, in addition to the news media. Transparency is voluntarily and routinely telling the truth without "spin" or defensiveness. Transparency instills trust. I think a trustworthy person or institution has the following seven characteristics:

1. a history of telling the truth regardless of the consequences to the institution,
2. unequivocal clarity and brevity so that there is no "spinning" about his or her position on a given issue,
3. no ulterior motive such as personal or political gain,
4. quick ownership of mistakes, practical solutions to prevent similar future mistakes, sincere acts of forgiveness for past mistakes, and pledges to self-correct,
5. aggressive disclosure of mistakes emerging naturally from a continuous self-monitoring of outcomes and other measures of performance,
6. an easily recognized core set of values which are continuously communicated and are the basis for key decisions, and
7. explicit recognition that there are limits to performance expectations—similar to professional baseball players accepting historical batting averages as reasonable expectations for their performance.

There are few individuals or organizations that share these traits of trustworthiness. I will give a couple of examples of individuals I trust. I trust my doctor because over the years, his diagnoses have been accurate and his recommended course of treatment has corrected my ailments. I trust a mechanic who would tell me that my brakes do not need to be repaired even though there is no way for me to independently know the current condition of my brakes. I trust my veterinarian because of the accuracy of his past diagnoses and because he phrases his recommendations in terms of "this is what I would do if this Scottie was my dog." He treats my problem as if it were his problem and preferred solution.

Politicians and government officials need to become transparent in order to be trusted. Many constituents do not believe they have been told the truth. There is no way they can know the truth because of the knowledge base and complexities of the issues. It isn't any different than the inability to know if individuals are being told the truth by their physicians, lawyers, mechanics, priests, teachers or any other consultants. Trust is the short cut to truth. We use the short cut all the time. My Michigan state representative for the East Lansing district sends his constituents a weekly e-mail report on his daily routine. It includes who he is meeting with and their agendas. It provides an excellent way for his supporters to understand the life of a legislator. It is frank, clear, and educational. It is a daily political journal. However, when it comes to the Democratic caucus meetings, he cannot share these debates with his constituents. He is sworn to secrecy so that the opposing party cannot know their strategy. And neither can his supporters!

This is an excellent example of the absence of transparency—secrecy. At this critical point in key decision-making (caucus meetings) like tax increases, there is no willingness to share openly the real dimensions of the debate. Even after the votes have been made public, there is no open discussion of the dimensions of the debate within the caucus meetings. There is only one reason for such secrecy—politicians do not want to share the truth because they have been telling different versions of it in different settings. At best, the taxpayer may ultimately find out years later when it is too late to affect the decisions. This certainly was true for the decisions surrounding the Vietnam War and Watergate, and is likely to be the case with the wars in Iraq and Afghanistan.

The following example illustrates how transparency is an important dimension of how government responds to the release of classified information about the wars in Iraq and Afghanistan. WikiLeaks is an activist organization that publicly shares information that is generally not available for purposes of creating a better informed public. It defines itself as "a multi-jurisdictional public service designed to protect whistleblowers, journalists and activists who have sensitive material to communicate to the public" (Lendman, 2010). It sees itself as following a similar path of public disclosure as Daniel Ellsberg who released the Pentagon Papers, a meticulously kept record of the U.S. military and strategic planning to deceive the public throughout the Vietnam War. Criminal charges against Ellsberg were dropped and the U.S. Supreme Court ruled in his favor concluding that "only a free and unrestrained press can effectively expose deception in government." WikiLeaks believes that the exposure of government activities leads to reduced corruption, better government, and stronger democracies.

In 2010, WikiLeaks released a 39-minute video of U.S. soldiers in an Apache helicopter killing civilians in Baghdad, including two Reuters' journalists. It also released a set of classified cables to four European newspapers—*Der Spiegel* in Germany, *El Pais* in Spain, *LeMonde* in France, and *The Guardian* in England. The Guardian shared the documents with the *New York Times.* These documents included 1,325 of 251,287 cables, daily traffic between the U.S. State Department and 270 diplomatic outposts around the world over a six-year period (January 2004 to December 2009). The documents revealed extensive detail about the Iraq and Afghanistan wars that were largely hidden from the public such as a secret commando unit like Task Force 373—a classified group of U.S. Army and Navy operatives focused on capturing/killing 70 top insurgent commanders. The *New York Times* justified the decision to print some of the cables to tell "the unvarnished story of how government makes the biggest decisions, the decisions that cost the country most heavily in lives and money" *(New York Times, 2010).*

Julian Assange, founder of WikiLeaks, an Australian activist and computer specialist, is the spokesperson for WikiLeaks. He travels extensively and appears to have no permanent address. He is currently under investigation for alleged non-consensual sex with two women in Sweden. Private Bradley Manning, a 22-year-old U.S. Army military intelligence analyst, is considered responsible for releasing the video and classified documents to WikiLeaks. He was based east of Baghdad, Iraq, and he is now being held in solitary confinement at Quantico, Virginia. He is expected to be prosecuted for releasing classified information. Several companies, including Amazon, PayPal, and a Swiss bank that enabled WikiLeaks to operate and receive funds, have ended their commercial cooperation with WikiLeaks for various reasons. Finally, U.S. Attorney General Eric Holder is attempting to bring criminal charges against Mr. Assange for violating the Espionage Act of 1917, a statute that has never been successfully used to prosecute a third-party recipient of leaked material. The Espionage Act prohibits the unauthorized disclosure of national security information.

The arguments against transparency in this case include:

- U.S. national security has been put at risk.
- Lives of people who work for the American people have been put at risk.
- Terrorist groups are aided by giving them information about military strategies and diplomatic partners in Iraq, Afghanistan, Pakistan, and other allied countries.
- Relationships with foreign diplomats are damaged by making it more difficult to gather future intelligence information and secure the trust of informants who may fear future public disclosure of confidential exchanges.

The arguments in favor of transparency in this case include:

- The first amendment to the Constitution of the United States protects freedom of the press, and this protects WikiLeaks from being prosecuted for publishing information, even classified information.
- The release provides valuable unfiltered information that educates the public about its government. It is similar to investigative journalists exposing inside information from trustworthy sources that remain anonymous.
- The government could use the classified information to expose and eliminate fraud, inappropriate military practices, misuse of military resources, and embarrass uncooperative foreign countries in order to improve counterterrorism effectiveness.

Transparency is risky. So is secrecy, as the Catholic Church, Anderson Consulting, and Enron now know. The following lists provide a rationale for and against transparency. Try to envision a meeting of executives from Enron, Anderson Consulting, Catholic bishops, or *New York Times* editorial staff debating the issues of transparency before and after they were exposed for not being transparent.

Rationale Against Transparency

- It is only a problem for five percent of our customers.
- We have more important priorities than to deal with this issue.
- We are already dealing with the problem successfully without disclosure.
- We have a strong core of member/customer support for our product. We can endure any exposure of this problem.
- Full disclosure could put the organization at such great risk that it is not worth the risk on my watch.
- We have successfully kept the secret without much damage for decades. We can probably continue indefinitely.
- It is going to be very difficult for anyone to actually trace the problem back to us. We can find someone else to blame.
- We can always hire a public relations expert or legal counsel to explain or delay any significant negative impact on the organization. We have done this before and we can do it again. Ultimately we can "settle" any specific case and basically continue our current practices.
- We cannot afford to disclose the truth now because we would be admitting culpability and will incur lawsuits for damages. It would be irresponsible for us to voluntarily place the organization at high risk. That would be reckless management.

Rationale for Transparency

- It is the morally right thing to do.
- The member/customer deserves to know the truth.
- Full disclosure is a sign of responsible stewardship worthy of trust.
- Full disclosure is a sign of responsible management because it reflects a commitment to honesty.
- It is proactive to recognize a problem and solve it rather than be forced to respond once a problem has erupted into a scandal or a disaster.
- Once trust has been lost, it will be expensive, difficult or not possible to regain.
- Tremendous internal resources are being consumed in keeping "the secret" a secret.

- It is only a matter of time before "the secret" will be exposed especially during a period of new information technology which is threatening to expose a whole array of other institutions and their secrets.

The choice to be more transparent in government is being made in a small number of locations. It takes a critical mass to reach a "tipping point." Once there is a critical mass of leaders for such transparency, there will be significant changes in the way government is managed, how employees perceive themselves, and their contribution to the public good and renewed trust by the taxpayers. *The Transparent Accountability Paradigm* encourages taxpayers to ask government to demonstrate its impact and justify the use of tax resources. It asks for honesty and effectiveness from government and clarity of expectations from an engaged citizenry. Why do we settle for so little?

Chapter 4
Intrinsic Goodness
and Stewardship

The biggest barrier to accountability for government programs is the widely held concept of "intrinsic goodness," which assumes:

- programs are good,
- there is no need to measure performance, and
- they deserve enhanced funding because they are good programs.

Measuring performance is considered unnecessary rather than a critical component of managing the program and justifying funding. Advocates for the program believe that in times of limited state budgets (all the time), measuring success would be a waste of time and resources which could be better spent on additional services. The advocates already know the program is successful—by definition of its intrinsic goodness. Consequently, most government programs continue to receive funds, usually at a higher level each year, regardless of their ability to demonstrate a positive impact or outcome for the clients or communities served.

Accountability requires all programs to demonstrate their impact and to share this performance information with the advocates, media, and general public so that everyone knows the return on the taxpayers' investment in taxes. This chapter discusses "intrinsic goodness" and the measurement of stewardship with the Carter-Richmond methodology.

Ethic of Intrinsic Goodness

Once a program has been legislated and funded, the responsibility of a good manager is to deliver services in the most efficient way to assure continued funding. The delivery is the end result. The implicit assumption is that the will of the public is reflected in the legislative process that decided that the program was good and needed to receive funding. The only future debate is the amount of additional funding the program will receive. By definition, a funded program is a good program. Otherwise, it would have never been funded. This mind set is pervasive and numbing because it is so self-serving, self–perpetuating, and almost impossible to reverse. It is extremely difficult to introduce accountability into such an entitlement discussion, since there is no perceived need to discuss impact or return on investment questions. It is perceived by program advocates as disloyal to the program's goodness.

Dr. William Benton, a former Deputy Secretary for the Maryland Department of Human Resources, summarized in his keynote address to the International Council of Social Welfare the "ethic of intrinsic goodness" as a significant barrier to accountability:

> *Since the inception in the United States, personal social services have tended to be encapsulated in an ethic of intrinsic goodness. Perhaps, due to their philanthropic origins, social services have been widely viewed as a symbolic commitment of a society to do good. As a result, the extent of a society's commitment has traditionally been measured in the size of the investment in programs to meet the economic and social needs of deserving individuals, families and communities. That is, the more we would spend on social programs, the better.*

> *The ethic of intrinsic goodness has had a profound effect on the development of personal social services at two levels. First, on an individual level, the notion that personal social services are inherently good has created a corps of professionals whose altruism is unrivaled. Second, at a societal level, the ethic of intrinsic goodness has undoubtedly resulted in an investment of personal social services which is much larger than it might otherwise have been. In spite of its important and beneficial role in the evolution of the personal social services, there are substantial limits to the ethic of intrinsic goodness.*

> *First, the ethic has tended to reduce social policy to arguments of 'more' versus 'less.' Since the ethic of intrinsic goodness accepts the efficacy of social services as an article of faith, the most logical way to make a program better has been to increase our investment in it. As long as additional resources have been forthcoming, the ethic of intrinsic goodness has precluded such*

systematic questioning of the need for human service reform.

Second, the ethic has led to an inordinate investment in 'symbolic' programs. Personal social services have often been established to respond to the needs (real or perceived) with little understanding of the technology involved in effecting the conditions which brought about the service in the first place. Since the ethic of intrinsic goodness views personal social services as worthwhile by definition, their efficacy has been beyond question. Indeed, rigorous evaluation of these programs has tended to be viewed as an attack on the service under review. As a result of the ethic's inability to differentiate between the symbolic and the substantive, credibility on the whole has suffered.

Most critically, the ethic of intrinsic goodness is irrelevant to conditions of scarce and ever-declining resources. The debate over proposals to reduce federal spending for human services is informed not one whit by an ethic which enables us to say only that budget cuts are 'bad' and that if reductions could be avoided that would be 'good' (Benton, 1981, p. 1-2).

The prevalence of the ethic of intrinsic goodness is not limited to social service programs. Advocates for some health services like home and community care services for the elderly are as adamant that it is unnecessary to actually demonstrate effectiveness. Education is another example of assumed success (Green, 2005). And, only recently, is there recognition of the need for faith-based services to document how clients and communities benefit from such investments (Fagan, 2007).

The ethic of intrinsic goodness has severely limited the collection of impact or outcome information for most programs. Generally, programs collect and share input (funding) and output (services delivered, clients served) information but rarely impact or outcome information. When outcome data are requested, they are generally collected as part of special research evaluations. These evaluations are time limited and are seldom used to make future key funding decisions although they may result in program policy or structural improvements.

For ten years (1974-1984), I was Director of Planning and Evaluation for the Michigan Department of Social Services. I conducted many such studies and was able to appreciate the value and limitations of this type of information. I have summarized ways to maximize the utilization of these findings (Carter, 1994). Program evaluation attempts to use the scientific methodology to study the efficiency and effectiveness of programs. Program evaluation has limitations imposed by the agency and/or environment that reduce the use of scientific methodology. In order to infer a cause-effect relationship and, thus, prove that a service caused a desired client outcome, the program research design must include:

- random assignment of subjects into
- experimental and control groups and have
- a large enough sample to draw reliable statistical inferences from
- data having high validity and reliability.

There are several different scientific research designs that vary in their ability to draw inferences about cause-effect relationships. Donald Campbell and Julius Stanley (1963) detailed these experimental and quasi-experimental designs. Different approaches to evaluation use these designs and, thus, vary in their ability to draw inferences about cause and effect.

Few of the four conditions necessary for a true experimental research design exist in most evaluations conducted within public agencies. In addition to the limits of conducting scientific experiments, there are other timing and resource factors restricting the collection of outcome information in this context:

- Program evaluations usually take two to three years to complete. The most pressing policy questions usually cannot wait such a long time to be answered by an extended evaluation process.
- Program evaluations are expensive and most public agencies perceive this as too costly.
- Program evaluation samples are usually drawn from a small number of offices, workers, or clients and the findings are open to the criticism of misrepresenting the larger group.
- Scientific findings are often overridden by the persuasiveness of an opposing interpretation based on agency

culture and information with high face validity but inadequate factual basis.

• Program evaluations usually focus on a one-point-in-time analysis and this interpretation lacks the history of prevailing perceptions of program managers and legislators.

It is difficult to change a current understanding of a cause-effect relationship with a one-point-in-time analysis. Conventional "wisdom" trumps evaluation findings especially if they dramatically alter current understanding of a controversial issue. Seldom are evaluation findings so compelling as to change attitudes and preconceived beliefs.

Given these limitations, it is important not to depend on a single evaluation to override conventional "wisdom," but instead, to institutionalize the collection of effectiveness measures (outcomes) just as efficiency measures (inputs and outputs) have been collected routinely on every case. If collected regularly, the results will be available on a continuous basis and will improve the opportunity for managers to monitor outcomes as a necessary component of good management decision making. Over time, these outcome results will become the new conventional "wisdom."

Measuring Stewardship

Stewardship is the responsible caring for others and their resources. Historically, stewards were handlers of luggage and served as personal staff for wealthy families. Today, on cruise ships, the cabin stewards serve as personal staff for guests. A more common use of the word "steward" refers to the responsibility of government or faith-based program staff members to always act on behalf of the best interests of their customers. Good stewards would, for example, use the resources available to them to provide the greatest assistance. Good stewards are able to document the use of resources entrusted to them. The Carter-Richmond approach is a simple set of nine questions which reflect the key dimensions of accountability inherent in good stewardship.

The first seven questions were initially described in *The Accountable Agency* (Carter, 1983) and the final two have been added by Fred Richmond, CEO, Center for Applied Management Practices,

Inc. Most public programs (federal, state, and local); faith-based agencies; and foundation sponsored grants for social services, health, safety, and education programs do not routinely account for their stewardship at this basic level. The first seven questions will be considered separately from the final two, which focus on return-on-investment as a topic for the next chapter.

The nine questions are:

1. How many clients are you serving?
2. Who are they?
3. What services do you give them?
4. What does it cost?
5. What does it cost per service delivered?
6. What happens to the client or community as a result of the service?
7. What does it cost per outcome?
8. What is the value of a successful outcome?
9. What is the return-on-investment?

Most programs can answer the first five but seldom the others, which focus on the long term results. The following example, prepared by Fred Richmond, illustrates answers for the first seven questions for an employment program for a low-income individual. The next chapter will explore the final two ROI questions with an example from an asthma management program prepared by Mr. Richmond.

Example of The Carter-Richmond Methodology

1. *How many clients are you serving?* 100
2. *Who are they?* Single unemployed women ages 21-34 who are seeking employment and have at least one child under the age of 12.
3. *What services do you give them?* A package of job readiness training, job placement, and 90-day follow-up services after job placement.
4. *What does it cost?* $100,000
5. *What does it cost per service delivered?* $100,000/100 = $1,000/job readiness/training/placement package or $1,000/client.
6. *What happens to the clients as a result of the service?* 10 clients, or 10% of the program participants, will obtain a full-time job above minimum wage with employer-provided benefits.

7.   *What does it cost per outcome?* $100,000/10 clients = $10,000/outcome

The outcome is a full-time job above minimum wage with employer-provided benefits.

The answer to the seven questions is a simple way to measure stewardship. These seven questions have been used extensively by the Department of Community Services within the Department of Health and Human Services. They are explicitly embedded within the Results Oriented Management and Accountability (ROMA) required reporting system to receive Community Services Block Grant funding ($700 million for 2010) to reduce poverty (http://www.appliedmgt.com/). The questions are also embedded in the grant application process by the Department of Housing and Urban Development (HUD) to:

- increase homeownership opportunities,
- promote decent affordable housing,
- strengthen distressed communities,
- ensure equal opportunity in housing, and
- embrace high standards of ethics, management, and accountability, and promote participation of grassroots faith-based and other community based organizations.

The extensive use of these questions within HUD is the result of strong leadership by Fred Richmond and Barbara Dorf, Director of Departmental Grants Management and Oversight within HUD. Barbara has worked for HUD for over 30 years and has won several awards for her accomplishments, including a 2007 National Public Service Award presented by the American Society for Public Administration and the National Academy of Public Administration. Fred Richmond and Barbara Dorf have also developed an e-Logic model that greatly simplifies the process of collecting and using the nine questions outlined in the Carter-Richmond Methodology. In short, the nine questions are helpful in the management of several federal programs.

One of the biggest barriers to adopting this approach is to gain the support of the program managers to collect and use outcome performance information. It will be the focus of the next section. In the next chapter, I will discuss two approaches to summarize the value of successful programs: cost-benefit analysis and return-on-investment.

Outcomes

Question six (what happens as a result of the services?) is the most important dimension of accountability. It refers to the outcome or impact of the program on the clients after they have completed the program. Simply raising the question of outcome is viewed by program advocates as questioning one's moral commitment to the program. There are many examples of appropriate outcomes which generally fall into specific categories of client satisfaction, recidivism rates, prevention rates, and status on select outcome events (in school, obtain GED, employed, in training program). The Urban Institute (1981) provides suggested outcome examples for various social programs such as delinquency prevention, foster care, child protective services, day care, work incentive program, adult choice services, marital counseling, and vocational rehabilitation services. The Center for What Works (Urban Institute) created the Outcome Indicators Project (http://www.urban.org/center/cnp/Projects/outcomeindicators.cfm),which provides suggested outcomes across 14 specific programs including: adult education and literacy, advocacy, affordable housing, assisted living, business assistance, community organizing, emergency shelters, employment training, health risk reduction, performing arts, prisoner re-entry, transitional housing, youth mentoring, and youth tutoring programs.

Outcome indicators for Maxey Boys Training School (Bureau of Juvenile Justice, 2005), a juvenile delinquency prevention residential treatment program in Michigan, include:

- 70-85% (1997-2003) of youth are free of felony arrests 12 months after release from the program;
- 61-69% (1997-2003) of youth are free of felony arrest 24 months after release from the program;
- 37-51% (1997-1999) are free of felony arrest 60 months after release from the program; and
- 63-69% (1997-1999) of youth are free of incarceration in Michigan adult prisons 60 months after release from the program.

A residential treatment program for troubled youth at The Pressley Ridge (Fabry, 1994) in Pittsburgh, Pennsylvania, uses the following outcome indicators:

- 66-85% (1986-1993) of kids are living in foster care, with family or independently five years after release from the program;
- 56-63% (1986-1993) of kids earned a high school diploma or GED five years after release from the program;
- 46-68% (1986-1993) of kids are going to school or working five years after release from the program; and
- 43-53% (1986-1993) of kids had negative police contact (no arrests) within five years after release from the program.

The key to selecting the best outcome is to envision the best impact on the client or community after the service has been completed. The outcome timeframe may vary by service based on the expectation of the program's intervention. In the case of Maxey Boy's Training School, the program provided an intensive 24-hours-a-day treatment for an average of one year and had a long outcome follow-up period of five years. Most social service interventions are not as intense and, thus, the impact of the program on the client may have a shorter timeframe. Head Start has an extensive outcome follow-up timeframe because the program expects early intervention to affect academic success during the first several years of schooling.

Some program managers have difficulty accepting an outcome that happens after a client is no longer a client. They feel that it is unfair to judge them on the basis of what happens after the service was delivered. They believe that they no longer have any control over the results because many other factors become influential in determining the outcome. General Motors, on the other hand, places importance on repeat sales of its cars because this outcome demonstrates that customers experienced the car over a period of time and ultimately chose to repurchase a new model based on their prior experience. Repeat sales take place long after the original experience with the product.

In Lansing, Michigan, there used to be a big billboard for Davenport College of Business (since 2000, Davenport University), a small community college specializing in clerical, computer, and administrative training. Its outcome, however, is the percent of graduates who obtain employment. The college's principal billboard focused on the 95% employment outcome for its graduates. Davenport clearly understood that it wasn't good enough for students to be trained. Students ultimately need employment as a result of the skills obtained in training. Davenport College structured itself so that it was in constant communication with local employers to assure that, once trained, its graduates would be sought by local businesses for careers with them. Davenport focused on jobs as outcomes, rather than training as outcomes. This emphasis placed a large responsibility on the institution to be teaching appropriate skills. This educational organization actively solicited input from future employers of its graduates to help anticipate new curriculum and teachers capable of creating the appropriate skill set necessary for each company's success. Davenport College recognized the value in tracking outcomes after graduation to determine that the school was achieving success and can use this same information to assure potential students that their investments will pay off for them.

Some publicly funded program managers see this tracking of graduates over time as a very expensive administrative task of following a highly transient client population that may or may not want to cooperate with them. It is difficult, but this type of follow-up information may uncover opportunities to improve on current programs or provide other needed services based on feedback from these graduates. All major universities have established alumni associations to track their graduates and/or dropouts so that they can solicit alumni contributions for the latest fundraising expansion programs. The universities have figured out a way to track graduates for fundraising purposes but not for purposes of knowing if the education they received resulted in a job as a measure of the university's effectiveness. I received my doctorate from Michigan State University in 1975. I have had several jobs in my career and have moved several times within the mid-west region. MSU has successfully tracked me for the past 30 years without any effort on my part to keep the university informed about how to reach me. MSU has the technology and the determination to accomplish this outcome.

Explicit client outcomes need to be established for all programs. It has been done in rehabilitation centers, employment training programs, hospitals, and in many other service areas. Without outcomes, there is little true accountability. With outcomes, there is the opportunity to know the success rate and to use the information to continuously improve a program. Some managers resist sharing outcomes and cost information with legislators, the media, and the public. Some managers fear that the public would be alarmed if outcomes are low and the costs are high. However, such information could also lead to a better appreciation of how rare and difficult it is to accomplish the outcomes. We have this appreciation about how rare, difficult, and expensive it is to develop a successful baseball player. The public may be disappointed initially with the performance information, but will ultimately become more knowledgeable and realistic about what is possible.

Winning the Minds and Hearts of Program Managers

The program manager is the key to collecting and using outcome information and then to disclose these findings to all stakeholders so that trust can be restored, in part, to government.

There is nothing magical or particularly difficult about establishing a client outcome approach to management. It requires a program manager to understand the legislative and historical intent and to articulate this intent into measurable outcomes for the clients of the program. Legislative intent is often deliberately vague. This provides little direction but great latitude to define appropriate outcomes. No one is in a better place to define program outcomes than the program manager.

The collection of outcome information is no different from the collection of any other type of program information. Program management:

- decides what data it wants collected,
- develops a form to capture the information,
- writes manual or policy instructions detailing how to fill out the form,
- collects the data and stores it in a computer,
- summarizes and distributes the information,
- gives staff members feedback on their accomplishments,
- analyzes the outcome data and explains why some offices are more successful than others, and
- tries to understand how to make the poor performing units more like the high performing units.

Program managers have followed this same process hundreds of times in developing other dimensions of their programs. They are experts in this process.

Some program managers object to the measurement of outcomes and present seven delay or prevention tactics, which will now be described along with a proposed counter-strategy. Initially, I believed that these tactics were unique to opponents of outcomes. Now, I believe that they may be more general tactics to resist any management initiative.

1. *My clients each have unique needs.* This objection is used to convince the manager that the client and program complexities prevent any generalization about expected outcomes. Each client is so unique that there is no one measure that could accurately capture their idiosyncratic outcomes. The key counter-strategy is to be patient, persistent, and to set timeframes to come up with the best possible outcome measures. None will be perfect, but some will be developed. Consensus is not necessary for decision-making to take place.

2. *There are multiple outcomes for clients.* This is a variation of the first tactic. It generally takes the form of endless attempts to reach philosophical or professional consensus on the appropriate outcome for clients. The debate takes place among program staff and is impossible to resolve. The counter-strategy is to not attempt to resolve the debate. Instead, be willing to accept more than one outcome. For example, foster care has several legitimate outcomes for different types of clients. The outcomes could include return home, placement with the other parent if there is a divorce, placement with a relative, release for adoption, petition to terminate parental rights, and other (release to another county or state).

3. *I do not agree with the outcome.* This is one of the more difficult tactics because program managers believe that unless they believe in the outcome, they cannot be personally motivated nor responsible for the success of the program. The counter-strategy is to have a strong commitment from top management that does not require the program manager to believe but simply to do what agency leadership has asked—namely, announce an outcome, measure it, and hold staff accountable for improving the outcome level.

4. *But I want the outcome measure to be perfect. Why do it if I cannot do it right?* This is probably the most difficult ob-

jection, because it appeals to the illusion of perfection as if there is perfection in any area of work or personal life. Who can be against doing something perfectly? Unfortunately this objection usually means that there should be a long drawn out process that may include such activities as:

a.   An extensive review and critique of all outcome measures that have ever been used to assess the effectiveness of the program,

b.   High consensus of stakeholders on which measure is best,

c.   Several years of testing the measure to assure its high validity and reliability, and

d.   Several years of experience on a pilot basis to be completely sure that it is the most appropriate assessment tool.

This set of delay tactics is designed to test perseverance. A counter-strategy is to acknowledge the need to select the right measures of outcomes, but to set realistic deadlines for introducing these measures into an on-going routine of collecting all other information for program management.

5.   *Once a client is no longer a client, I do not have a way to stay in touch regarding follow-up on outcomes.* This is a simple problem to resolve. Have clients agree as part of the initial intake process that they will cooperate after they have completed the program with suggestions on how the program helped them achieve their goals. There are logistic problems of remaining in contact with the clients (current address and phone number) while they are in the program or they have graduated from the program. It is the same logistic problems facing all college alumni associations tracking their graduates.

6.   *Health Information Privacy and Protection Act (HIPPA) and other confidentiality laws and telecommunication regulations prevent me from contacting a client who is no longer a customer.* Confidentiality and privacy laws are primarily designed to protect clients from inappropriate release of personal information to an unknown source. All such laws have provisions for the client to direct the agency to release such information for a specific reason. This re-

lease process can be easily accomplished for purposes of collecting most client outcome information. For example, when I am screened for an X-ray, I give permission to the X-ray company to share the results with my physician. Similar arrangements can be devised for clients to provide permission to release subsequent outcome information after they are no longer enrolled in a program. In some select cases, confidentiality and privacy acts do create barriers to obtaining the best outcome measures. For example, a recidivism outcome measure for a drug abuse prevention program may be re-admission to a drug rehabilitation treatment center. The treatment center may refuse to release the information regardless of the previous wishes of the client. Such cases are rare and would require the selection of an alternative measure of outcomes.

7. *My program's funding source only allows me to bill for services while the client is receiving services, not after their case has been closed.* Build into the budget the necessary funds to follow up with the client after they are no longer a client. As an alternative, find the funds from an alternative source or convince the funding source that your program could be so much more effective if you knew the factors most responsible for positive outcomes. Some faith-based foundations now include a portion of their grants for the explicit purpose of measuring program outcomes. The Heritage Foundation estimates that the costs for an evaluation component are typically between 7-12% of the program's budget, but may be less after the first year (Fagan, 2007, p. 10).

I previously believed that these seven barriers were unique objections to outcomes as the basis of good management decisions. I now believe these objections are part of a broader issue of obtaining the cooperation of staff for all managers. Ferdinand Fournies, a management consultant, wrote a book entitled, *Why Employees Don't Do What They Are Suppose to Do and What To Do About It* (1999). Fournies recognizes the reasons why any initiative is resisted or not implemented. Among the reasons he describes as to why employees don't do what they are supposed to do before work begins are the following:

1. *They do not know what they are supposed to do.*
2. *They don't know how to do it.*
3. *They don't know why they should do it.*
4. *They think your way will not work.*
5. *They think their way is better.*
6. *They think something else is more important.*
7. *They anticipate future negative consequences.*
8. *Personal problems.*
9. *Personal limits.*
10. *Obstacles beyond their control.*
11. *No one could do it.*

To assure that employees do what they are supposed to do before the work begins, managers should:

1. *Let them know what they are supposed to do.*
2. *Find out if they know how to do it.*
3. *Let them know why they should do it.*
4. *Convince them that your way will work.*
5. *If their way is not better, explain convincingly why it is not better.*
6. *Let them know the work priorities.*
7. *Convince them that anticipated future negative consequences for attempting to perform will not occur.*
8. *Work around personal problems or give the work to someone else.*
9. *Verify that the work is not beyond their personal limits.*
10. *Verify that there are no obstacles beyond their control.*
11. *Verify that it can be done.*

Fournies has a similar list for following up once work has begun. Effective managers find a way to get staff cooperation for implementing any new concept including the collection and use of outcome measures.

Rarely does one encounter a program manager who is "wired" for outcomes as a critical component of managing. Such managers cannot imagine being effective without such feedback. I will introduce two such managers, Vergil Pinckney and Clark Luster, in Chapter 6. This type of manager "gets it." They embrace the fundamental concept that managers and staff need to know their impact on clients to recognize the program components that work and those that do not work. Without the feedback they would not be challenged and would not find work to be meaningful.

The ethic of intrinsic goodness limits the Carter seven questions of accountability to the first five as the basis for funding and management. The final two questions of outcomes are unnecessary and threatening to those managers who embrace the ethic of intrinsic goodness. However, the final two provide answers about the program's impact and ways to improve the program's effectiveness. The next chapter discusses return-on-investment, which illustrates how program managers have combined cost and outcome information to demonstrate the value of their programs.

Chapter 5
Return on Investment

Program managers have justified the value of their programs for initial and subsequent funding. They have approached this challenge primarily through a cost-benefit analysis whereby the investment in the program can be considered a benefit to the larger society. This has largely been accomplished through a cost avoidance approach that suggests that a preventive program can defer future costs. For example, a child abuse prevention program can defer future expenses for other costs associated with likely delinquency, welfare, and health care related expenses.

Mental health specialists refer to this approach as a medical cost off-set, which is defined by the American Psychological Association (APA, 2006) as occurring "if medical utilization decreases as a result of mental health intervention. A total off-set occurs when general health care savings exceed the cost of mental health treatment effectively resulting in the treatment paying for itself." APA summarized the supportive research literature for mental health services utilization by indicating that:

- Mental health patients typically over-utilize medical services, and, if effectively treated for mental health illnesses, will reduce their use of other health services.
- Outpatient mental health services can off-set the cost of more expensive inpatient care.
- A study by Kaiser Permanente, a large California-based Health Maintenance Organization, found that patients who received psychotherapy showed a 77.9% decrease in average length of stay in a hospital, a 66.7% decrease in frequency of hospitalization, a 48.6% decrease in the number of prescriptions written, a 47.1% decrease in physician office visits, a 45.3% decrease in emergency room visits, and a 31.2% decrease in telephone contacts.

A second example of the cost-benefit analysis is a simple, but highly effective, program used by some hospitals to reduce avoidable infections resulting from care delivered in intensive care units. Avoidable deaths due to infection or any other error is one of the best benchmarks for any health system. Johns Hopkins developed a simple five-step process to reduce such infections in its hospital intensive care units. The five-step process when using a central venous catheter included:

1. wash hands with soap,
2. clean patient's skin with chlorhexidine antiseptic,
3. put sterile drapes over the entire patient,
4. wear sterile mask, hat, gown and gloves, and
5. put a sterile dressing over the catheter site.

Johns Hopkins tested this approach in Michigan (Pronovost, et al., 2006; Gawande, 2007, and Brody, 2008) through a partnership with the Keystone Foundation, a quality research organization within the Michigan Health and Hospital Association. One hundred and eight hospital intensive care units were encouraged to follow these steps over an 18-month period. This resulted in a reduction of catheter related infections from 4% to almost zero. This project avoided over 1,500 deaths and saved nearly $200 million. The project expenses were $500,000. The cost avoidance was 400 times the investment. This is truly a remarkable investment. The Keystone Foundation is now attempting this same approach in surgical units and ultimately in emergency rooms.

The third example is called ROI (return on investment). ROI has been used extensively in the private sector to assess the expected financial rewards expected from a current or proposed initiative. It is a measure of risk-reward and is often used to justify new ventures. For example, if a corporation is considering launching a new product, the management will estimate the costs to develop and market the item and then project the necessary profits to recoup or exceed its investment. The ROI is traditionally expressed as a ratio of profits to costs ($5:$1) so that it is easy to observe the expected trade-off involved. This approach has only recently been considered as an appropriate measure of value for public sector human services programs, which are often designed to serve the public good regardless of their return on investment. Schools, fire safety, and police are three good examples of organizations that serve the public regardless of ROI considerations.

Before 1985, hospitals were considered financially viable as long as they had retained earnings (more revenue than expenses). Hospitals kept two separate accounting systems—one for expenses and one for revenue. They did not know which diagnosis and treatment expenses resulted in what revenue. As long as there was more revenue than expense, there was no need to know the ROI for each diagnosis. This all changed in 1985 when Medicare, a major payment source for hospitals, decided to change its reimbursement formula from a unique cost per hospital to a standard cost per diagnosis. Standard costs were identified by DRGs (diagnosis related groups) so that all hospitals received the same amount for the same procedure. Medicare had created a need for hospitals to know their costs by diagnosis. The hospitals needed to calculate their ROI per diagnosis.

Fred Richmond

Fred Richmond, President of the Center for Applied Management Practices, Inc. (2007), has developed examples of ROI calculations. The following is an example he has provided of calculating an ROI for an asthma management program.

Return-On-Investment
Asthma Management Program
Coatesville Family Center—Chester County, PA

In 1995, the Coatesville Family Center's staff nurse began to implement a health promotion program to families with children who suffer from asthma. Through this program, children were routinely monitored and families received instruction and support in asthma management techniques. As a result, asthma treatment shifted from crisis care to prevention.

Over the one-year period from mid-1995 through 1996, 57 children participated in the Asthma Management Program. Program statistics before and after initiation of the program are identified below.

Outcomes

1. Emergency room visits were reduced from 5 to 2 for an annual cost savings of $1,350 per child, per year.
2. Crisis physician office visits were reduced from 5 to 2 for an annual cost savings of $114 per child, per year.
3. Annual savings per child resulting from a shift in crisis care to preventive care is $1,464.
4. The cost of the Family Center Asthma Management Program is $252 per child annually. This generates a savings of $1,464 in crisis care costs per child; or a net savings of $1,212 per child annually.
5. Gross savings in physician and hospital costs = $83,448.

6.   Net savings, physician and hospital costs minus nursing costs = $69,084.

Every $1 spent on preventive asthma care management results in saving of $5.80 ($1,464/$252=$5.80) in crisis/emergency services for a 580% return on investment (ROI).

A more conservative and often used approach to calculating the ROI for business purposes is to divide the investment costs by the net profits/savings (profits-costs). In this particular example, the ROI would be 4.81 ($1,464 - $252 / $252) or a 481% net return for the initial investment.

This ROI calculation does not consider other benefits, such as:

- reduction in school absenteeism,
- ability to do homework,
- increased likelihood of child not repeating grade,
- mother returned to work force,
- improved physical and mental well-being of child, and
- improved physical and mental well-being of family.

Mr. Richmond also created ROI estimates for case management, as well as working with HUD to calculate an ROI for many of its programs. He (2007, Slide 31) cautions program managers to recognize that:

> *Some programs may lend themselves to Return-On-Investment analysis better than others such as employment and training, Weatherization, LIHEAP, and economic development where the monetary value of the outcome(s) can be more easily derived. For programs and services such as homeless assistance, domestic violence, food and nutrition and early intervention, it may be harder or more complicated to establish a monetary value of the outcome.*

Conclusion

Regardless of the approach to value (cost avoidance, cost-benefit, ROI) program managers would benefit from constructing a way to demonstrate to their funding sources the return on their investments. There are many creative approaches to establishing the value of injuries or lifetime earnings for purposes of resolving auto accident liability cases. Lawyers and insurance companies have created financial values for resolving such litigation. If return on investment calculations cannot be accomplished in financial consequences, then it may be attainable through non-financial results such as increased safety, reduction in child or domestic abuse, and less crime.

Return on investment is important because it requires government to establish a value to clients and communities for the investment of tax dollars. ROI requires the stewards of public funds to justify continued trust by taxpayers who seldom have been told how their tax investment has improved the lives of citizens or communities. Taxpayers continue to be asked to make more of a commitment as an ongoing expense with no known results. Government is selling "an invisible product." The public may not know how to assess a reasonable outcome and must trust government just like they trust their doctor, lawyer, accountant, and mechanic who also sell "an invisible product." However, with most of these other trust relationships, we, as consumers, have the option of selecting an alternative professional to trust. With government, this is seldom the situation. However, when there is such an option, as with the Postal Service, such competitive options probably have resulted in increasing the service quality of the Postal Service. For example, my post office in East Lansing is now open in the evening to provide service at a more convenient time for working citizens.

ROI, however defined, is an opportunity to instill trust that someone in government is "watching the store" and cares enough to define the current accomplishment level of programs and how they are contributing to improving the lives of citizens and communities. Government leaders should not be concerned about a low ROI. Many citizens assume it to be low and would be suspicious if it was high. Finally, ROI provides the basis of pride and self-esteem for government staff members that are robbed of knowing how good they are at improving the lives of citizens and communities. Left to their own devices, government staff tend to underestimate their impact.

Chapter 6
Program Managers
Vergil and Clark

Vergil Pinckney and Clark Luster are two program managers who understood the value of management by outcomes. They illustrate how and why they chose this approach to stewardship.

Vergil Pinckney, Maxey Boys Training School

I met Vergil Pinckney in 1975 when I was the Director of Planning and Evaluation for the Michigan Department of Social Services, a statewide welfare agency. Vergil was the Director of Institutional Services, which included the Maxey Boys Training School for approximately 600 delinquent teenage boys who received treatment for 1-2 years in an institutional setting. The Maxey mission was to provide delinquency prevention training and education for youth who were removed from their homes and families and had become wards of the state. The expected positive outcomes were that the graduates would return to the community to live a delinquency-free and productive lifestyle. These delinquents were highly likely to continue their criminal behavior and possibly spend time in the Michigan prison system. Maxey Boys Training School staff monitored several factors while a delinquent was receiving services. These included:

- changes in attitudes and values,
- educational achievement,
- assault behavior on other residents or staff,
- truancy and crimes committed while in treatment, and
- length of stay in treatment.

Vergil also collected outcome information after the youth were released from Maxey. He monitored them for 12 months after release regarding arrests and productivity (work, school, or training) and then tracked them for six years to see if they entered the Michigan prison system. Vergil wanted to know if he and his staff were successful. The only way to know was to follow them after they were released from his program.

No one required Vergil to find out. Vergil was wired to know the results of his efforts. No one paid him to collect this information.

He flew under the "radar screen" of state agency bureaucracy. No one stopped him. Most did not even know he was doing this type of follow-up. Vergil's follow-up process was simple. His secretary and a full-time analyst contacted the county community service worker assigned to assist the youth to transition back into a delinquency-free and productive lifestyle. The interview with the worker included questions about the youth's criminal arrest behavior and participation in school, work, or training. They tracked 4,000 graduates released from 1974-1982, and were able to obtain information on 98% of them within three months of release and 90% within 12 months of release from Maxey Boys Training School. Over this timeframe (1974-1982), the results (Carter, 1984) indicated that:

- 29-30% were arrested after three months,
- 45-55% were arrested after 12 months,
- 55-65% were productive (work, school, or training) after three months, and
- 20-50% of 1974-75 graduates spent some time incarcerated in Michigan prisons over the subsequent six years from 1977-1982.

Vergil shared the outcome information with his staff every six months. The report was broken down by the ten different treatment centers so that each team would have a score of success. He had a statistical summary, but also a short vignette about each specific graduate. An example would be that Tommy Jones was attending auto mechanics training in Howell and has not been arrested during the past six months for anything more serious than a speeding ticket. These stories became known as Vergil stories. They were eagerly awaited by staff members that were very curious about the specific details within each story. There was also a healthy element of competition between the treatment centers, each of which contended that they cared for the highest level of difficult youth.

Vergil used the outcome data to reinforce or alter his current practices (Carter, 1983, p. 50-51):

- *The productivity status (school, training, or work) at three months is the best predictor of re-arrest. As a result of knowing this, we have emphasized our efforts to increase educational achievement and/or work skills while the*

*youth is in care. This has been our best intervention strat-
egy to ensure a delinquency-free life style.*

- *We use the fact that over 40% of the youth will spend time
  in the Michigan prison system as a deterrent. We tell the
  delinquents that unless they get some type of education
  and/or skill training while at Maxey, they have a much
  greater chance of ending up in prison.*
- *Outcome information allows us to defend our programs
  in budget appropriations hearings with data that clearly
  show our effectiveness. This approach keeps us "on top"
  of the program and enables us to provide the best type of
  accountability. We are not as vulnerable to impulsive decisions or recommendations by budget analysts because we
  have better data than most programs by which to argue
  for continued funding. There is always a risk, however,
  with collecting outcome data. The risk is that you don't
  know how it is going to come out or how it is going to be
  interpreted. This is true of all information, but it is particularly true of outcome data. Over the years, however, the
  range is relatively small and there are few really surprising deviations from the rates which were experienced in
  the first few years.*
- *The outcome measures are not perfect. However, they are
  the best estimators at this time. Not everyone is content
  with them, and, occasionally the rate of expected outcome
  or the wording needs to be renegotiated. It is important
  that managers not try to establish the "perfect" outcome
  measure but only the best ones because there are no perfect measures everyone will agree with.*
- *One of the difficulties of client outcome findings is that
  you have no other state to compare yourself. You end up
  comparing your achievements against last year's achievements. Until there are more agencies developing this kind
  of information, I do not know how effective my programs
  are in a comparative basis.*

Vergil always contended that he was the best program manager
in the country of residential treatment programs for delinquent
youth. He knew he was the best because he knew that he was
the only program manager who collected outcome information.
He knew that no one could refute his claim of being the best. In
subsequent years, similar programs in other states replicated
and improved on his outcome monitoring system. Vergil was correct that when such comparative outcome information became
available, Maxey's outcomes were similar or better.

One of the unique characteristics of outcome data is that the outcome levels settle into a relatively narrow range. For example, with the productivity measure (school, work, or training) after the months of release from the program, the range of outcomes was approximately 60% for any year from 1978-1983. It was within 7% either up or down from 60%. This is a relatively stable statistic regardless of the changes that may be taking place in the mix of delinquents, staff, or programming. The stability of outcome levels is remarkable, and it reflects the difficulty and challenge of creating successful initiatives. It is just like baseball batting averages, which stay in a relatively narrow and low range (the exceptional player will hit the ball safely and get on base one out of three times at bat). Low but stable outcomes in baseball have existed for over 100 years regardless of the changes in salaries, training, equipment, steroids, stadium designs, or the introduction of artificial lighting for night games. Outcomes are humbling because they remind us how difficult it is to attain historical levels that clearly establish the limits of our best efforts even at a relatively simple task of hitting a baseball safely.

Vergil used outcome information to argue for additional funding for his programs. I recall watching him during the annual budget appropriations hearings in Lansing, Michigan. The legislators were always impressed that he even had such information. The legislators did not know what to do with the outcome information. Should they be impressed with this level of outcome or be outraged by it? They did not know where to begin. They were unprepared for his level of understanding about the way his program affected the young delinquents. No other program managers had outcome information. Vergil stood out because the other managers could only provide counts of clients and services delivered and a testimonial from a selected client who had a positive outcome and spoke on behalf of continuing the funding for the program.

There were many private or religious alternative residential treatment options to Maxey Training School available in Michigan, such as Starr Commonwealth and Highfields. That program competed with Maxey for court treatment placements of delinquent youth. Vergil set the bar in terms of the expected outcome levels and costs per outcome in order to maintain the leadership role of Maxey Boys Training Schools. Soon, all competitors were measuring themselves against the criteria and standard set by Vergil. His initiative raised the quality of care across all provider groups because of the active use of outcome data to measure program success.

Vergil Pinckney retired from state employment in the early 1980s. His legacy continues. His commitment to outcomes has also been continued by the program managers who have replaced him. Over the past 25 years (1982-2007), there have been some changes to the outcome measures. Arrests are now only for felonies—the most serious type of crime. Incarceration in Michigan prison is now tracked every 12, 24, and 60 months. The productivity measures (school, work, or training) are no longer tracked because of an Auditor General finding that criticized the measure as a subjective opinion of the community placement workers. The outcomes (Bureau of Juvenile Justice, 2005) over the past seven years (1997-2003) indicate:

- 15-30% were arrested for a felony 12 months after release,
- 31-49% were arrested for a felony 24 months after release,
- 49-63% were arrested for a felony 60 months after release,
- 4-7% were incarcerated 12 months after release,
- 9-23% were incarcerated 24 months after release, and
- 31-37% were incarcerated 60 months after release.

The arrest information collected earlier is not comparable to the felony arrest data now being used. However, the incarceration information is very similar. The incarceration rate (after six years) was 45% for 1974 graduates and 37% for 1997 graduates (after five years).

Vergil was a pioneer in operating a government program through collecting and using client outcomes to best manage a program. He institutionalized the concept and the process is still being used decades later. Other programs within Michigan and in other states became aware of Vergil's outcome management practices and explored how to test and improve on them in their state. Pressley Ridge Schools in Pittsburgh, Pennsylvania, was one program that enhanced and improved upon Vergil's original efforts.

Clark Luster, Pressley Ridge

Clark Luster was the executive director of Pressley Ridge from 1975-2002. Presley Ridge is located in Pittsburgh, Pennsylvania, and provides an extensive array of children services—primarily foster care, adoption, residential treatment programs, and community-based family services. Although Pressley Ridge began in Pittsburgh, it has expanded its impact by providing similar services in Delaware, Maryland, Virginia, and West Virginia, as well as other international sites. The budget in 2005 was $56.2 million. The "kids" are predominantly 7-17 years of age and the average length of time in programs is nine months. Pressley Ridge refers to their "kids" rather than "youths" or "clients." Its motto is "once a Pressley Ridge kid, always a Pressley Ridge kid."

Pressley Ridge has its roots in two Presbyterian orphanages: The Protestant Home for Children, founded in 1832, and the Pittsburgh and Allegheny Home for the Friendless, incorporated in 1861. These two orphanages merged in 1969. Currently, Pressley Ridge serves more than 1,500 kids and their families. The programs are funded through 170 government agencies with Medicaid being the largest source of funding (Gannon, 2002).

Clark Luster was an amazing manager and created, along with his staff and supporters, a remarkable set of achievements with a particularly strong focus on outcomes as the basis of good management decisions. Luster was obsessed with outcomes and contended that monitoring outcomes was the only way to continue to improve the institution's programs.

I met Clark Luster in 1983 just after my book, *The Accountable Agency*, was published. He incorporated the Vergil stories into the Pressley Ridge management system and began an extensive outcome monitoring approach that was much more systematic, comprehensive, and accurate than Maxey Boys Training School's initiative.

Bernie Fabry worked for Clark Luster as the project director for the *Follow-up Project 1993 Report* (Fabry, 1994), which illustrates the value of collecting and using outcome information. Outcome information was collected for eight years (1986-1993) for each cohort for one year after they completed services with Pressley Ridge. This reinforced the stability of the outcome levels over time and demonstrated a reliable way to collect accurate information by using collaborating sources to verify outcomes. Fabry considered four outcome areas:

1. where kids live,
2. where kids go to school,
3. how kids play, and
4. how kids feel about their lives.

Over the eight years, outcome information was collected on 1,179 kids. Various informants were contacted regarding the status of the kid:

> *In most cases two or even three people were able to describe how a given kid was doing. In those cases one person was considered the primary informant, and the information obtained from other people was used to verify the primary informant's statement. Whenever possible a kid was used as the primary informant and other people such as parents or Pressley Ridge staff were used as the secondary informants* (Fabry, 1994, p. 15).

The structure of the telephone interview across the four outcomes included the following questions:

1. *Living Situation* (Where does the youth live now? Has the youth received any outpatient or in-home therapeutic support? Is the youth married? Has the youth fathered or bore a child?)
2. *Work/School Situation* (What is the youth's educational placement? Is the youth working?)
3. *Playing* (Has the youth used drugs or alcohol in the last year? Has the youth been stealing in the last year? Has the youth been involved in physical aggression? Has the youth been in contact with the police for problems? How does the youth spend leisure/recreation time? Who does the youth talk with, visit or go out with?)
4. *Feelings* (How happy is the youth with the living situation? How happy is the youth with the work/school situation? Overall, how happy is the youth with life? Overall, how good or bad was Pressley Ridge for the youth?).

The answers to these questions allowed interviewers to create Vergil stories about the lives of kids like Tom presented below. In many ways, these stories have proven to be more helpful for

Pressley Ridge staff, Board members, media, and funding sources.

> *Tom came to our program on 3/17/91 at the age of 15 from a residential treatment center. Tom was discharged from our program on 9/1/91 at the age of 16 years to a residential school. Tom is now 18 years old. After leaving your program, Tom was placed in a residential school and was released early due to good behavior. He was then placed in a group home. While at the group home, he became involved with a vocational program. He currently lives with his mom and is attending GED classes. He is not married and has no children. So far, Tom has done well staying out of trouble and being successful in his placements after your program* (Fabry, 1994. P. 1).

The statistical results for youth after one year of release from Pressley Ridge programs indicate that between 1986-1993:

- 60-77% of youth are living in foster care, with family or independently,
- 53-65% of youth had earned a high school diploma or GED or were in educational placements less restrictive then the Pressley Ridge program from which they had been discharged a year earlier,
- 64-77% of youth were in school or working at least on a regular part-time basis,
- 33-63% of youth had no contact with the police during the year following discharge from Pressley Ridge,
- 84-89% of kids were satisfied with their various situations (living, school/work life), and
- 87-90% of the kids or families felt Pressley Ridge did some or a lot of good.

The outcomes generally stay within a narrow range with outcome levels varying up or down a few percentage points from the previous year. Seldom does the outcome data for one year spike relative to other years. This consistency of the outcome data is very common if the outcome definitions and process of collecting the information remain largely unchanged.

In 1989, Clark Luster began a longitudinal outcome study in which the outcome information was collected on the same cohort of kids from 1989-1993. He followed the same kids for five consecutive years to see if the outcome levels changed over time for these kids. This is remarkable because most programs never make this type of investment. It provides a rare glimpse into the long-range impact of programs. The results indicated that over this five-year period, of time, the kids experienced improvements in living situation and educational placement, a stable level of having had no police contact, and a decreasing involvement with school or work. The specific findings were:

- 66% of kids in 1989 versus 85% in 1993 were in an acceptable living situation (foster care, with family, or independently),
- 56% of kids in 1989 versus 63% in 1993 had attained an acceptable educational goal (earned a diploma/G.E.D. or attend a less restrictive placement),
- 68% of the kids in 1989 versus 46% in 1993 were going to school or working, and
- 47% of the kids had no police contact in both 1989 and 1993.

Pressley Ridge staff members were very explicit that these relatively positive results are, in part, a result of their inability to contact all kids in this cohort. The kids not reached in this report probably bias the trends because the "strong anecdotal data" suggests that these kids are not doing well, and if they could have been found might have skewed the results. The original universe of kids decreased about 5% each year because of an inability to contact them for various reasons. This same challenge exists for all longitudinal studies. In general, the trend information over a five-year period is extremely helpful for understanding the long-range outcomes for the kids. It is much harder to assign a cause-effect relationship between the Pressley Ridge experience or any other experience and their subsequent quality of life across these four broad dimensions. Longitudinal studies probably do not need to be repeated on a regular basis because the trends are probably stable and unlikely to change. However, these trends are often only obvious by obtaining and analyzing this type of outcome information on the same cohort over a long period of time.

The Pressley Ridge Web site includes a section on research and evaluation, and it reflects an unusual focus on outcomes and the use of this kind of information for assuring the continuing improvement in its programs:

Why do we measure outcomes?

When Pressley Ridge began studying the outcomes of our services in the early 1980s, no one else was. It was a risky concept at the time. We were opening ourselves up to the scrutiny of many. We started studying outcome measures because we made a commitment to kids and families that we would keep in touch with them for up to 2 years after they were discharged (Once a Pressley Ridge kid, always a Pressley Ridge kid). Naturally, we wanted to examine the impact of keeping in touch, and so the annual follow-up study was born.

Today, we still hold true to this value. We find kids up to two years after they have been discharged, interview kids and their families, compile the data, and pass it on to programs for their interpretation. These interviews are used as reality checks for our services. By examining this data, we can ask important questions about the impact and comprehensiveness of our services and make plans for the future.

Measuring outcomes is a key part of all our services. Our outcomes have helped Pressley Ridge compete for contracts, change program operations, lead new service developments, and shape child and family service policies. More importantly, we believe monitoring our outcomes has improved the lives of kids and their families.

Outcomes: What We Measure

We've studied a core set of outcomes over the years. Below is a quick list:

- Severity and type of problems
- School attendance and graduation
- Employment status
- Restrictiveness of home
- Type of school placement
- Involvement in the legal system
- Pregnancy and parenthood
- Use of drugs, alcohol and tobacco
- Aggression and harm
- Family problems
- Leisure activities

- *Satisfaction with school, life and work*
- *Satisfaction with our services*

We also examine length of stay, types of services provided, cost of services and numerous demographics (e.g., age, race, gender, diagnosis, problems at entry).

We determine what outcomes people are interested in by surveying hundreds of stakeholders both my mail and in person. It is interesting that other agencies have done the same and validated that these outcomes are most often the ones that stakeholders are most interested in knowing about.

Pressley-Ridge recently released a one-year follow-up study of telephone interviews with 1,984 youth or its caregivers for the years 2001-2005. The outcome results were similar to previous studies (Trunzo, undated).

Vergil Pinckney and Clark Luster are excellent examples of how to collect and use outcome information to be accountable, improve programs, and be transparent in sharing these results with a broad set of stakeholders.

Chapter 7
Lessons in Transparency

This chapter provides an example of transparency as Michigan nursing homes publicly shared the family satisfaction level and the public health inspectors' perception of care in nursing homes. This initiative provides insight into the decision to be transparent, the process, and the consequences of such openness. There are risks and rewards involved with transparency as there are with secrecy.

The Consumer Guide to Michigan Nursing Homes (The Guide) was created by three trade associations representing the majority of nursing homes. *The Guide* included:

- name and address of all 450 nursing homes arranged by county,
- information on Medicaid and Medicare eligibility for coverage of nursing home,
- criteria to select a quality nursing home,
- history of average family satisfaction survey results, and
- history of annual inspection deficiency citations.

Trade associations are similar to government because they represent members who pay dues (taxes) to belong. Trade associations, government, and any other organization are suspect when publicly sharing the success of their efforts. It is very difficult to validate one's own success level. It is easily perceived as self-serving. Ideally, the preferred approach is to have a credible third-party (i.e., J.D. Powers and Associates, *Consumer Reports*) report about an organization's effectiveness.

One of the ways to measure results or impact of any intervention is to ask clients their evaluation of one's efforts. This can be done during or after the period of time they are receiving services. This information provides valuable feedback regarding how the program helped the consumer.

From 1984-2007, I worked for the Health Care Association of Michigan (HCAM), a nursing home trade association representing 250 of the 450 homes in Michigan. These homes provided care 24 hours a day for 25,000 residents throughout the state. A typical resident is an 81-year-old female with multiple health and mental challenges that require daily care and supervision.

Incontinency, dementia, and wandering are common. In the early 1990s, HCAM initiated *The Guide* to publicly disclose, by individual home, the satisfaction level of families who currently have selected nursing home care as the most appropriate option for a relative. The family was selected as a "proxy" for the resident since many residents were mentally confused and their responses would be considered unreliable in many cases. The questions for the family satisfaction survey were gathered from 300 families with relatives in Michigan nursing homes and were tested for reliability by a research professor from Western Michigan University (Reding, 1999).

This chapter reviews the methodology, findings, uses, and cost to conduct satisfaction surveys as an outcome measure for nursing home care and explore issues relating to the sharing of results with the public as a commitment to transparency. Public trust and support is based, in part, on the willingness of providers and government to share results openly and honestly.

Original Intent

Michigan nursing home providers have experienced a long history of aggressive regulatory enforcement by government inspectors. The culture within the state regulatory agency was perceived by nursing home operators to be very punitive. Michigan's average deficiencies found during an annual inspection per nursing home were twice the national average. The Michigan homes were perceived as low quality within the state by the professional advocacy organizations, the Health Care Finance Administration (HCFA—the federal agency which oversees the Medicaid and Medicare programs), the press, and the general public. At the same time, the families who selected nursing home care often reported high satisfaction with the care that was being provided.

In 1995, HCAM's Board of Directors moved from a defensive to an offensive approach to public image, legislative agenda, and to improved care. The HCAM Board agreed to a long-term strategy to define our "guiding principles." The resulting ten principles were passed by the Board on January 17, 1995. They largely focused on customer satisfaction and established the basis for *The Guide*. The ten principles are:

1.   *Substandard care shall not be tolerated. Providers and families share with the State the responsibility to protect and promote the health, safety and welfare of our cus-*

tomers. *HCAM stands ready to assist any member who requests assistance in addressing quality of care issues.*

2. *Customer satisfaction is the most important basis for defining quality. Our customers are the residents and their families.*

3. *Customer-satisfaction-driven criteria should replace the current government regulatory model for assuring high quality care and resident satisfaction.*

4. *The customers' need for long term care services should be assessed and the necessary resources (public and private) committed to meeting these needs. The State has a responsibility to insure appropriate resources to enable providers to meet the goal of furnishing quality services to our customers.*

5. *Competition should be encouraged among providers to deliver cost effective, high quality services along the entire continuum of care (sub-acute ... home and community based care). Regulatory mechanisms should not restrict these market forces from assuring the highest level of customer satisfaction. Providers need flexibility to deliver services effectively and efficiently. Customers demand and appreciate such flexibility in meeting their unique needs.*

6. *Customers need to be informed about the costs and outcomes of LTC services so that they can make the most informed choice possible.*

7. *Customers should have the right to choose the most appropriate setting for the delivery of LTC services and these options should be encouraged by public policy. To ensure that customers have access to the most appropriate level of care, there should be a "level playing field" wherein providers of similar services have equal access to markets and are regulated and reimbursed similarly.*

8. *Broad brush legislation to address isolated behaviors is inappropriate, particularly when available remedies have not been exhausted.*

9. *Any legislative changes should be based on sound information with assurances of enhanced quality of care and customer-driven satisfaction.*

10. *Uniform standards should be promoted. State regulation should be no more stringent than existing parallel federal requirements.*

The original intent of *The Guide* was to:

- publicize the high satisfaction among consumers,
- provide a second and more important benchmark for quality (e.g., family satisfaction),
- provide visible evidence that member homes sought and used consumer input to improve the quality of care in their homes, and
- publicly share valuable comparable performance information so that consumers could make better decisions about future placement in specific nursing homes.

The Guide would provide nursing home operators recommendations from families on how to improve care at specific homes. In addition, *The Guide* would change the public and legislators' perception of nursing homes as consumer satisfaction oriented and committed to self-improvement as a result of publicly sharing the results of the family satisfaction surveys. Finally, if *The Guide* was successful at changing the perception of legislators, we anticipated legislative support for a more timely, consistent, and fair regulatory process. This is exactly what happened after the release of the first *Guide* in 1999. In 2000, the legislature passed a law that mandated the development and use of clinical practice guidelines for nursing homes so that both providers and state agency regulators would share a common definition of best care practices. These guidelines reduced the degree to which state regulatory inspectors could use their subjective opinion of best care practices. This, in turn, reduced the conflict level between providers and regulators.

The Pilot and First Edition

Homes were skeptical about publicly releasing performance information. They did not know what their specific performance level would be with a new family satisfaction survey instrument and subsequent score. In 1995, 50 random HCAM homes were selected to pilot a newly designed family satisfaction questionnaire and process. The individual facility results were only shared with the specific homes. Only the statewide information across the 50 homes was shared with the general public. No scores were released for any given home. This random sample provided perspective for all member homes. The average satisfaction level indicated that 85% of families were satisfied. There was a 47% completion rate among the families who were sent a survey. The cost to complete the trial run was $30,000.

All 450 nursing homes were invited to participate in the family satisfaction survey which was completed in 1998 and *The Guide* (HCAM, 1999) was released in January 1999. The content of the 207-page report largely focused on listing all the nursing homes in terms of address, city, number of beds, payments accepted (Medicaid, Medicare, and private pay), family satisfaction score, and results of the most recent annual inspection by the Department of Consumer and Industry Services. It also included important information to help families understand the hospital discharge planning process, Medicaid and Medicare eligibility criteria and covered services, criteria to assess a nursing home for quality and how to interpret the inspection findings, and advice on long term care (LTC) insurance. The need for this information was suggested by two focus groups each comprised of 20 families who recently placed their relatives in a nursing facility. *The Guide* was sponsored by of all three trade organizations: HCAM, Michigan Association of Homes and Service for the Aging and the Michigan County Medical Care Facilities Council. Nursing home membership in the three trade associations represented 350 of the 450 homes in Michigan. There were 306 of 450 homes that chose to participate in the family satisfaction portion of the first edition. The average family satisfaction level remained at 85%.

The Guide received endorsements from key legislators and state agency directors, and received extensive positive coverage by the editorial boards of the major newspapers. Here is an excerpt from an editorial in the *Detroit Free Press*, Michigan's largest newspaper (Detroit Free Press, 1999):

> *The industry has much to gain in consumer confidence from being aggressively open about facilities and personnel.* The Consumer Guide to Michigan Nursing Homes *is an easy-to-use book and Web site compiled by the Health Care Association of Michigan along with the Michigan County Medical Care Facilities Council and the Michigan Association of Homes and Services for the Aging. It contains all the questions you need to ask plus a listing of all Michigan nursing homes in a straightforward table showing capacity, services, family satisfaction rating and the most recent inspection report* (p. 14A).

The Guide was distributed to 6,000 various consumers including: 450 nursing homes, 384 public libraries, 30 major newspapers, 200 hospitals, 100 state agencies, 20 state ombudsmen, 4,000 individuals, 50 state nursing home trade groups, and 568 others.

The Guide was available on the HCAM web site (http://www. hcam.org). There were 8,000 unique visitors to the page where *The Guide* appeared for the first edition and almost 6,000 for the first six months of the second edition. The entire *Guide* could be downloaded from the Web site. The total cost for the first edition was $182,000.

Feedback

The major newspapers provided positive coverage of *The Guide*, especially in the first year. The primary focus of subsequent articles was to list the nursing home ranking for the homes in each home's hometown newspaper. Reporters also were interested if facilities chose not to participate and often called the homes to inquire about their reasons for not participating. Their answers became part of the news story. The main reason for not participating was that they already had a process to gather family satisfaction information. In subsequent updated editions (2001, 2003, 2005, 2007), it became harder to interest newspaper reporters to cover this subject.

The vast majority of placements to nursing homes come from hospitals. The discharge planners in hospitals received a copy of *The Guide*. A survey was sent by HCAM to discharge planners on July 21, 2000 asking them to assess its usefulness. One hundred and eighty hospitals received surveys. Thirty-eight responded. The vast majority (85%) of surveys from the discharge planners used it at least once and many had used it repeatedly. Of the 32 discharge planners who had used *The Guide*, 88% rated its overall effectiveness as "helpful" or "very helpful" in their job. The most common reason for using it was to help families select a facility outside the geographic service area for the hospital.

Individual nursing homes received the results of the family satisfaction surveys, which included answers to specific questions and any additional comments from respondents. Most homes found that the comments were the most helpful component.

Such comments provided specific recommendations about how to improve care. Some nursing homes used the feedback to:

- measure the effectiveness and subsequent salary bonus of the administrator,
- to make recommended improvements to care, and
- to inform current or future customers about their nursing home's performance level on family satisfaction and the results of annual inspections, especially in comparison with statewide averages.

Subsequent Editions and Trends

The subsequent editions were similar to the 1998 first edition. Updated information was included for the policy changes regarding Medicaid and Medicare eligibility and any new regulatory requirements. Otherwise, *The Guide* remained largely unchanged in style and format and distribution. The following trends provide an important and consistent set of findings, which confirms the reliability of the survey instrument and the process of obtaining the satisfaction and OBRA survey information.

There was a decline in facility participation in the family satisfaction study over the period from 1998-2006. This was troubling. In part, the decline was due to a number of factors:

- 28 homes closed over the six-year period (1998-2004),
- bankruptcies during this period resulted in a group of homes sold to new owners who had major financial distractions, which prevented participation in the satisfaction study, and
- chain organizations that decided not to participate, in part, because they conduct their own satisfaction studies and did not perceive the benefits of The *Guide* in the larger political context.

The average family satisfaction level moved from 85% to 91%, largely as a result of a more accurate measurement of satisfaction level. The cost to complete subsequent editions from 1996-2006 was approximately $832,000.

Eighty-four percent of the families reported being satisfied with the care received by family members in the 1996 pilot of 50 homes (Great Lakes Marketing, 1996). Subsequent surveys indicated a slightly higher percent of satisfied customers (86% in 1998, 89% in 2000, 91% in 2002). The 1996 survey included responses from 2,410 families and subsequent surveys each included responses from over 12,000 families each (13,882 in 1998, 12,423 in 2000, and 12,873 in 2002). The satisfaction level of families of nursing home residents increased over time. Probably half of the increase was due to a change in the calculation of the satisfaction level to exclude the respondents who did not answer the specific question: "How satisfied are you overall with the services you are receiving from this facility?"

The percent of extremely satisfied family members increased from 38% in 1996 to 52% in 2002. The group of extremely satisfied customers is very predictive of other measures of quality: high staff satisfaction, lower survey citations, lower agency pool usage and lower staff turnover.

Size of a nursing home makes a difference in family satisfaction levels. The smaller the facility, the more families report being satisfied. Homes of 50 or less beds have the highest satisfaction levels. The very largest homes (more than 200 beds), however, provide a more satisfying environment of care than the 151-200 bed nursing home. This is hard to explain. Possibly, the very large home is broken up into more manageable "neighborhoods" or defined units which results in better perceived care by family members.

The more rural the location of the nursing facility, the higher the satisfaction of resident families. The lowest satisfaction averages were in the southeast region (Detroit) and the highest were in the Upper Peninsula of northern Michigan.

The family satisfaction questionnaire does provide an opportunity for families to comment. There was an average of one comment per respondent. There were over 30,000 comments over the several editions. There were both positive and negative comments even if the total satisfaction level was high. We contracted with Wayne State University's Institute of Gerontology to analyze family comments from a representative sample of five homes with a total of 194 family comments.

There were about an equal number of positive and negative comments, and they fell into the following general categories:

- Facilities (10%),
- Staff (16%),
- Quality of Care (59%),
- General (11%), and
- Other (5%).

In the Quality of Care category, 33% of the comments were positive and 67% were negative. The positive comments fell into six categories:

1. communication with residents and families,
2. overall satisfaction with care/services,
3. easing burden of family/guardians,
4. personal hygiene,
5. medical therapy/treatment, and
6. food activities.

The negative comments fell into nine categories:

1. overall neglect/lack of care,
2. neglect of personal hygiene,
3. improper medical care,
4. lack of activities and services,
5. missing personal items,
6. problems with food,
7. lack of communication,
8. understaffed and ill-trained, and
9. poor response to/unaware of patient needs/issues

We were unable to prioritize recommendations from the family comments. In short, many things are important to families and quality is at the top of that agenda.

Lessons in Transparency

As previously mentioned, the original intent of *The Guide* was to:

1. publicize the high satisfaction among customers of nursing homes,
2. provide a second and more important benchmark for quality (i.e., family satisfaction rather than inspection citations),
3. assure the public that nursing homes sought and used consumer input to improve quality, and
4. publicly share performance data to encourage competitive forces and improve quality.

Most of the four intentions have been met to some degree.

We did not expect to learn so much about providing transparency to various stakeholders. We naïvely anticipated much greater support from the media and the consumer advocacy groups like AARP. *The Guide* was designed to assist the consumer with performance data to make the best choice of nursing home care, but the consumer advocacy groups were suspect of such transparency from trade associations representing nursing homes. We learned several lessons about the various fears of any organization that decides to increase its transparency. These fears include the fear of:

- low results,
- high results,
- misinterpreting results,
- litigation, and
- not understanding how to use results as a way to improve care.

Fear of Low Results

The fear of low results is a frequent and powerful obstacle for public reports of program outcomes. Fear of personal embarrassment is reasonable because there are risks and potential negative consequences to sharing the results of one's efforts.

It is important to recognize the basis of this fear and to implement strategies to alleviate this concern to the extent possible. In the case of *The Guide*, we conducted a trial run of 50 homes so that the owner/operators could see the range of satisfaction levels. Most homes had conducted their own family satisfaction surveys. Some large chains had been collecting similar family satisfaction information for decades but had never shared the data publicly. All had their own survey questionnaire, which looked remarkably similar to surveys being used by other nursing homes. The range of satisfaction levels for the 50 pilot homes was 49% to 100%. The average was 85%. Once the range was known, most homes realized that they could accept sharing this outcome information with the press and the larger public. They were willing to take the chance of embarrassment from a low satisfaction score because the value to them was greater than the risk. In addition, the survey would be repeated every two years so there was the opportunity to improve their family satisfaction scores. Thus, the risk to participate was time limited. However, once they agreed to participate, the satisfaction results were used in *The Guide.*

Fear of High Results

There is a fear that high results will be perceived as unbelievable by providers, the general public, and certainly by professional advocacy groups like the Office of Services for the Aging or AARP. Satisfaction levels across all health care providers are high. Providers know this as does AARP. A review of the research on satisfaction levels (AARP, 2002) with health providers across all age groups indicates:

> *Consumers' perception of health care quality stands in stark contrast to the views of technical experts who warn of deficiencies. For example, although it is known that many people, including Medicare beneficiaries, do not receive appropriate care, the vast majority of consumers across all age groups are very satisfied with the health care quality they receive* (p. 105).

AARP recognizes the low health literacy among seniors and, thus, they are unaware of the shortcomings in the health care system. Nonetheless, there is high satisfaction among customer families for the care they receive in nursing homes. This has been reinforced by many such reports across several states.

The difficulty of many provider groups to accept high satisfaction levels has been a frequent experience for me. There are several barriers to such acceptance. Staff members of service organizations are often primarily focused on deficiencies in care and limitations on their ability to meet their own agency's standards and regulations. Thus, they are acutely aware of their shortcomings and unable to appreciate the larger picture of the difficulties of accomplishing high quality of care expectations. The consumers of care, on the other hand, are often more realistic about the efforts of the provider community and are very appreciative of the help offered. This recognition is reflected in the high satisfaction scores they give providers.

Misinterpreting Results

A third fear is how the outcomes will be interpreted by those skeptical of an organization reporting its own success level even if the measurement is conducted by an independent third party. In the case of *The Guide*, we contracted with a third party to conduct the family satisfaction survey. The firm was Great Lakes Marketing, a research company in Toledo, Ohio, which had been conducting this type of research for Health Care and Retirement Corporation, a national chain of nursing homes, for ten years. Great Lakes Marketing also did satisfaction surveys for hospitals and day care centers.

It is reasonable to expect such skepticism. However, I seriously underestimated the extent of the negative response from the anti-nursing home professional advocacy community representatives like the Office of Services for the Aging, Nursing Home Ombudsman Program, Citizens for Better Care, and AARP. They largely promoted the concept that there could only be low satisfaction among families with relatives in nursing homes as they primarily heard from the 6% who were "extremely dissatisfied" with nursing home care. Their preference was to advocate against nursing homes and in favor of care for the elderly provided at home.

One of the most vocal of these professional advocates was Michael Conners, who previously worked as staff of Citizens for Better Care, a consumer-based long term care advocacy organization headquartered in Detroit, Michigan. Mr. Conners wrote a 15-page critique of the first *Guide* and sent it to the new Attorney General demanding that she investigate the findings and prevent continued publication.

I received a call from the Attorney General's office to meet with Jennifer Granholm, the Attorney General. She would later become the Governor. She wanted to talk about *The Guide.* I initially believed she would be impressed that a provider organization would be so transparent with satisfaction information and provide a useful tool for consumers to make informed decisions about selecting a preferred nursing home for themselves or a relative. I had even hoped she would endorse *The Guide* and encourage its distribution and use. I was too optimistic, naïve, and disappointed. It was not going to happen.

She was concerned about the accuracy of the regulatory information provided by the state agency's professional staff members that annually inspect each home and assesses its compliance with regulation requirements. She asked us to check on the accuracy of the citation information. She shared with me a copy of Mike Conners' letter to her.

On the first point of accuracy, she had a legitimate and helpful criticism. We had made errors. We interpreted deficiency information from the state agency to represent results from annual inspections. Instead, we had been given a combination of annual visits and complaint visits. The former is a thorough review across 318 potential deficiencies and the latter is only a review based on a consumer complaint. We had reported in *The Guide* that the deficiency information was from annual visits. Some homes were listed as having fewer citations because the score reflected a complaint investigation rather than the annual review. Mr. Connors was correct that we had seriously misrepresented the citation levels for these homes. The deficiencies were much larger at the time of the annual survey than the scores of a complaint investigation. We found that 12% of the homes had been assigned lower complaint scores than annual inspection scores. In some cases, it was dramatically different giving the advantage to the home to appear to be in much more compliance.

All of the homes had a chance to review this information before *The Guide* was sent to press. None of the poor performing homes alerted us to this discrepancy in their favor. This is an important lesson in checking the accuracy of the outcome information and to have a healthy skepticism about the willingness of providers to self-report accurately. We were embarrassed. We recognized our errors and corrected them on our Web site. Unfortunately the 6,000 published printed copies had already been released. We agreed to have the Attorney General's office review a draft of subsequent guides before they were released in order to have some independent assurance that the deficiency findings were accurate. In retrospect, we learned from our mistakes and subsequent editions were more accurate. The Attorney General's oversight also provided an assurance level that we appreciated.

We were too eager to release the first edition of *The Guide*. One probably cannot be too careful about the accuracy of outcome information, especially with the first edition when the interest level and visibility are the highest and one's critics most suspicious. Transparency initiatives need to create a historical track record of reliable and consistent outcomes. Once this is established, the opposition will have more difficulty in making its case against a program.

The Attorney General never did endorse *The Guide* with a public statement of support. We asked her but she politely said "she was not at that point yet" of endorsing it. She was early into her first term as Attorney General. She worked with us to provide a better guide for consumers. I respected her for her decision to seek a better product rather than create a legal confrontation opposing the publication.

Fear of Litigation

The fourth fear was that trial lawyers who were prosecuting nursing home operators for patient abuse or wrongful deaths would use the satisfaction data as part of their cases against specific nursing homes. This fear is a good example of unwarranted concerns that prevent transparency to the public and future consumers. This fear never became a reality after ten years of releasing the results of family satisfaction surveys.

Fear is part of the risk of transparency. Once publicly released, there is no way to protect against the inappropriate use of the information. Not being transparent is also a big risk as the Catholic Church and Anderson accounting firm discovered.

Not Knowing What Caused Satisfaction

The fifth lesson we learned was that our member homes did not know what factors caused high satisfaction and thus, did not know how to make improvement in their care delivery system. One of the benefits of satisfaction or any outcome information is to improve care. Many of the nursing home operators analyzed the consumer satisfaction results for their facilities to address problems families had identified. The most successful homes were unable to identify the causal factors explaining their high performance.

There were 20 homes identified in the first edition that received a 100% satisfaction level. There was a 47% average return rate of families who received the satisfaction survey. These outstanding homes were asked to share their best practices with their colleagues at a HCAM training session. Many were unaware of what made them unique. They were uncomfortable in presenting themselves as superior operators and were anxious about speaking in public to their peers. The outcome data clearly stated that they were better, but they neither believed it nor were able to articulate the reasons for their high performance level. Ten of the 20 top homes were willing to share their practices. Randy Jordan was one of them. Randy was a second generation owner/operator of a 105-bed nursing home in a rural community.

Randy Jordan had grown up caring for the elderly as an employee of his family's nursing home and he had recently purchased it from them to become the owner/operator. Mr. Jordan was unaware of how his style of care assured high quality and high family satisfaction. He simply agreed to talk about his typical day as an administrator of a typical-sized nursing home in a rural setting. His leadership style was to simply focus on resident care by visiting every resident every day to observe care and to ask if there were ways to improve the experience of every resident. He made his "rounds" as a physician would make rounds in a hospital by assessing every patient for any changes in his or her health conditions and to make appropriate changes as necessary. He kept a little notebook about the size a reporter would use to write down the changes, and then spent the balance of the day making those changes happen. He would cross off each task as they were completed. He then went home and returned the next day to follow the same routine. He assumed all good administrators followed about the same process.

His peers listened and were impressed. They were stunned. Most knew they did not focus as he did on this highly successful approach to care. The other nine presenters each summarized his or her approach and the combined set of 38 recommended practices provided a rich set of suggestions for improving care and family satisfaction with care.

These lessons in transparency provide some understanding and appreciation for the difficulties and rewards of communicating satisfaction and regulatory deficiency information across a wide spectrum of nursing home shareholders. Many of the lessons are likely to apply to other attempts at transparency. Some of the areas of concern for the sponsoring agency could have been anticipated. Some were totaling unexpected.

The next chapter focuses on the last lesson regarding the use of outcome information like satisfaction and attempts to explain some of the causal factors of satisfaction for nursing homes. The approach, however, is applicable to any agency interested in identifying the causes of outcomes. The chapter is called "Connecting the Dots."

Chapter 8
Connecting the Dots

Several decades ago, there was a company that specialized in "connecting the dots" for one particular U.S. intelligence agency. The company scanned Russian newspapers, magazines, and other public documents to identify trends or unusual circumstances occurring in Russia that might be of potential interest. One of the analysts had observed a winning high school soccer team in a remote part of Russia. This scenario peaked his interest and ultimately led to aerial photographs taken from a satellite. It showed the construction of a nuclear power plant. The analyst had connected the dots:

- newspaper article about a winning high school soccer team.
- soccer players have athletic parents.
- construction workers would be athletic parents.
- construction work must be taking place in this remote area of Russia.
- confirmation via satellite pictures of construction of nuclear power plant.

This is a brilliant example of "connecting the dots." This chapter provides insight into how to connect the dots to identify which factors are most responsible for program outcomes. Defining, collecting, and sharing outcome information is a very necessary beginning point. Managers need to understand how programs can maximize their performance levels by analyzing the causal factors affecting outcomes and then experimenting with subsequent changes in these programs. "Connecting the dots" refers to the documentation and explanation of how these causal factors affect outcomes.

The General Accountability Office (Finch, 1995), in an assessment of the Government Performance and Results Act, summarized this need to connect the dots in testimony before the House Subcommittee on Government Management, Information and Technology:

> *Our work has shown that if planning and performance management are going to provide information that is both useful and used, they must be integrated with daily operations in the agencies...*

> *Even the best performance information is of limited value if it is not used to identify performance gaps, set improvement targets and improve results. Our work on leading organizations in the private sector and in state and foreign governments has shown that these organizations recognize that it is not enough just to measure outcomes. Such organizations recognize that they also need to continuously assess their core processes that contribute to achieving their desired outcomes* (p. 9).

Ten years later, in 2004, the GAO (1995) found that:

> *While the percentage of federal managers who report having performance measures for their programs has increased over time, their use of performance information in making key management decisions, such as new program approaches or changing work processes, has not* (p. 2).

There has been a remarkably stable use of performance measurement information by federal program managers. From 1997 to 2003, 51-66% of federal managers use performance data across five key decision areas:

1. setting program priorities,
2. allocating resources,
3. adopting new program approaches or changing work processes,
4. setting individual job expectations for their staff, and
5. rewarding staff they manage or supervise.

In 2005, GAO recognized this utilization level of performance information and purposefully selected five federal agencies (Departments of Commerce, Labor, Transportation, Veteran Affairs, and the Small Business Administration) to identify examples of using performance measures. GAO did not attempt to verify that the use of these measures ultimately resulted in improved outcomes. Nonetheless, GAO has provided a helpful approach to categorizing uses and identifying common management practices within these agencies. Four uses of performance information for management decision-making included:

1. Identify problems and take corrective action.
2. Develop strategy and allocate resources.

3. Recognize and reward performance.
4. Identify and share effective approaches.

The five practices to enhance the use of performance measures are:

1. Demonstrate management commitment.
2. Align agency-wide goals, objectives, and measures.
3. Improve the usefulness of performance information.
4. Develop capacity to use performance information.
5. Communicate performance information frequently and effectively.

One of the examples the GAO (General Accountability Office, 2005) found was from the National Traffic Safety Administration. It illustrates how the enforcement of seat belt laws led to a significant decrease in accident fatalities.

Over the past 20 years, the National Highway Traffic Safety Administration (NHTSA) has used performance information to identify, develop and share effective program strategies that increase safety belt usage, and as a result contributed to an increased use of seat belt usage nationally from 11% in 1985 to 80% in 2004. With a mission to save lives and prevent injuries, NHTSA's evaluation office analyzes information provided by the annual National Occupant Protection Usage Survey, in which safety belt use is directly observed at locations across the country, and the Fatality Analysis Reporting System, a database of all fatal crashes in the United States. From its analysis, NHTSA estimated that safety belts are 50% effective at preventing fatalities of front seat occupants in crashes in which these motorists would otherwise die. In an effort to increase usage nationally, NHTSA conducted several small studies in the 1980s and 1990s on how to best increase safety belt usage. NHTSA's research showed that educating the public on the safety benefits of seat belts was not very effective and that laws requiring seat belt use, while somewhat effective, only increased usage by 40%. One of NHTSA's studies, "Buckle Up America," revealed that active enforcement combined with media campaigns highlighting enforcement, as opposed to safety, could increase usage incrementally by 4-8% a year.

However, NHTSA officials said these studies alone did not influence states to change their expenditures with regard to safety belt use. Building on the findings of these studies, NHTSA then developed and piloted the Click It or Ticket safety belt campaign, which included both a paid media enforcement message along with periods of active police enforcement of safety belt use. The campaign, co-sponsored by the Airbag and Safety Belt Safety Campaign of the National Safety Council, was piloted in three states. Double digit increases in safety belt use were seen in all three states, demonstrating the effectiveness of this strategy in changing motorists' safety belt use behavior. Ultimately, performance information documenting the program's effectiveness in multiple states began to persuade officials from other states to adopt the program. By 2003, 43 states, the District of Columbia and Puerto Rico had participated in the twice yearly national Click It or Ticket campaign. As a result, the national average for safety belt use is up to 80%. NHTSA is now focusing on identifying and developing strategies to target specific segments of the population found to have the lowest safety belt usage rate, such as drivers of pickup trucks (p.6).

This example of identifying factors causing fatalities (not using a seat belt) in order to reduce fatalities is particularly imaginative because the initiative did not attempt to limit accidents but rather to decrease fatalities once an accident has occurred. The National Highway Traffic Safety Administration (NHTSA) did not attempt to resolve the much more difficult causes of accidents (e.g., inexperienced younger drivers, alcohol or drug use while driving, speeding, cell-phone use while driving). Rather, NHTSA focused on ways to improved safety when an accident occurs. NHTSA approached an important dimension it could impact. It approached obliquely the problem of fatalities and reduced dramatically the number of fatalities and identified the sub-set of drivers who have low safety belt use. This example takes place over a twenty-year period of studying the causes of traffic fatalities. In retrospect, it appears to be a simple story of cause and effect.

How to Connect the Dots

"Connecting the dots" discovers and analyzes factors that cause an outcome. It provides an approach to identify and prioritize the reasons an outcome occurs. It requires a healthy curiosity and willingness to investigate the components of a program and why some combination of factors is more effective than others.

Head Start originated from a healthy curiosity about the factors most predictive of academic success. That program's initial assessment determined that the most important factor was the quality of the child's early relationship with an adult (usually the mother). Management built the Head Start program from this understanding of the factors causing success in school. Research and understanding of the causal factors may lead one to factors beyond the components of a current program. This, in turn, may result in rethinking the way one can influence these factors currently outside his or her control.

Most program managers do not know how to connect the dots and may not be motivated to make the effort. Why? Ferdinand Fournies (1999), a management consultant, has outlined the reasons why employees do not do what they are expected to do at work. Fournies provides a valuable starting point. Three reasons, in particular, include:

1. They do not know what they are suppose to know (about connecting the dots.
2. They don't know how to do it (connect the dots).
3. They do not know why they should do it (connect the dots).

Fournies' four recommended solutions include:

1. Let them know what they are supposed to do (connect the dots).
2. Find out if they know how to do it (connect the dots).
3. Let them know why they should do it (connect the dots).
4. If they do not know how to do it, then provide the training so that they can do it (connect the dots).

These are my ten principles of how to connect the dots.

1. "Connecting the dots" is simply telling the story about how a program works to accomplish outcomes.
2. The story is filled with facts of varying accuracy and sources from formal research findings to anecdotal experiences.

3. It will be a story that will change as each part of a story is assessed. But ultimately, each story will have a core set of factors that explains the greatest amount of the outcome.

4. The story needs to be understandable to a relatively uninformed audience and should focus on the key or core set of causal factors. There is a tremendous and powerful tendency for the story-teller to initially include unnecessary details of individual client case experiences. It is very difficult to step back from such detail.

5. The story should be set in the context of current funding, regulation, and other limitations. The focus should not be on how the program could have higher outcomes with more funding and less federal reporting and regulation. This is a separate story.

6. Let the data, facts, and reality tell the story rather than imposing the facts to reinforce the historical bias of the program. Be open to revisions to the story based on an assessment of the program components responsible for the outcomes.

7. Expect to find that many program components do not have a direct or indirect relationship to the outcomes. Factors beyond the program may have the greatest impact on outcomes. For example, most of my students at Albion College (an expensive, private, small liberal arts undergraduate school in Michigan) grew up in families that valued higher education and made learning much more relevant than students from families that did not value higher education as much. Over 80% of the graduates of Albion College extended their education to graduate school in law, medicine, or business. They were motivated and prepared to learn. My role as professor was a minor factor in their learning. They were prepared to learn regardless of the professor.

8. Look outside the program components for important causal factors. These will provide valuable direction to focus program resources to reinforce these causal factors.

9. Seldom will a story ever have scientific proof of the causal relationship between the factors and the outcomes. Most explanations do not include such scientific rigor.

10. Managers should explore many alternative stories until they are convinced that the remaining version is their best understanding of the core factors causing outcomes.

Ruby Payne (2003), a research sociologist, creates a story about the factors she believes are responsible for an individual to emerge out of poverty. The same factors enable a middle-class person to enter the wealthy class. Payne believes that the individual must master the new set of rules for the class they are entering. She then presents the rules for the three classes and emphasizes the role of parents and schools to prepare the students for this reality-based transition. Ruby Payne created her story over a 24-year period of studying poverty. She used multiple sources to document the individual parts of the story. Her work is an excellent example of connecting the dots. The guiding principles of how to connect the dots will become more evident with a more concrete example of determining the causal factors leading to quality care in nursing homes.

What Causes Nursing Home Quality?

The following story of what factors cause nursing home quality is an illustration of how to connect the dots. It took me 24 years of working with nursing home owners, administrators, medical staff, regulators, families of residents, residents, media, funding sources, legislators, and advocate organizations. I was the Vice-President for Reimbursement and then served as President/CEO (1984-2006) for the Health Care Association of Michigan (HCAM), a trade organization representing 250 nursing homes.

The sources of the story included:

- family satisfaction surveys of nursing home care, including 30,999 families over a ten-year period (1996-2005),
- deficiency citation results from the Department of Community Health's annual inspection visits to 450 nursing homes for compliance with 318 federal regulations,
- historical trends in Medicaid and Medicare trends in costs and rates,
- nursing home employee salary and benefits surveys conducted by HCAM,
- telephone interviews regarding longevity of administrators and Directors of Nursing at the 50 homes that were identified as high quality providers,
- 24 years of daily interaction with a wide array of nursing home stakeholders plus visits to over 100 nursing homes, and

- research and public policy publications from the American Health Care Association, Centers for Medicare and Medicaid systems, and the General Accountability Office.

There are other stories explaining quality of care in nursing homes that focus on other factors than the ones presented in this story. However, these are the five factors that I believe are the most important. It is not an exhaustive list of factors.

Start with the Story

The first factor necessary for high nursing home quality is a strong commitment to a sustained strategy of high quality. There is a system of expectations that explicitly identifies how care will be delivered, the staff members that are responsible, and the assurance that the necessary steps are completed. This system is usually evident in manuals and management reports.

The second factor is a small rural community where the nursing home is located. Such a location provides staff with a stable employer and the opportunity to care for neighbors, friends, and relatives. This personal connection between staff and residents is extremely valuable as a continuous motivator for high quality.

The third factor is frequent community involvement by staff, family, volunteers, media, visitors, nursing home board members, community leaders, and vendors. This high visibility is a powerful force in establishing and enforcing the community's expectation of quality. If anything negative happens at the nursing home, it is transparent to the entire community, which knows almost immediately and applies informal pressure to self-correct and be accountable. It is a built-in quality control process that is much more effective than annual inspections or complaint investigations by the Department of Community Health oversight staff.

The fourth factor is the commitment level of leadership as reflected in the longevity of the individuals who serve as administrator and director of nursing.

The fifth factor is that health care benefits for staff and their family encourages all staff to remain committed to the residents of the nursing home. This provides a stable set of care givers—a dimension of high value to both residents and their families.

The story was told in five short paragraphs. This type of clear thinking requires program managers to explain why successful outcomes happen. This type of logic and curiosity are character-istics of the best managers.

Compile the Supportive Information

The story dictates the information needed to test the validity of interpretations. It is better to tell a story first because it forces one to be clear about the relationship between the key causal factors and the outcomes. If one starts with the available data, your ability to understand the causes will be limited. It is far bet-ter to have a clear story without all the backup supportive proof than a story based on available but irrelevant factors.

The outcome information is a good starting point. In this ex-ample, there were two outcome measures: family satisfaction and deficiency citations. Family satisfaction was measured by survey questionnaire responses from family members who had a relative in a nursing home. The question they responded to was: "How satisfied are you overall with the services you are receiving from the nursing home?" If they responded extremely satisfied or moderately satisfied, they were considered satisfied. Deficiency citations were compiled from the most recent annual on-site review by a set of professional staff (nurses, social work-ers, pharmacists, dieticians, therapists) from the Department of Community Health who followed extensive federal procedures to determine compliance with 318 Omnibus Budget Reconciliation Act (OBRA) regulations reflecting the provision of quality care. Such inspections average 3-4 days at the nursing home. The measure of quality was the number of citations, and there was no attempt to differentiate between the severity of the citation.

Fortunately, family satisfaction and deficiency citations were moderately co-related: that is, one generally found that a home with high family satisfaction also had low deficiency citations. The high quality homes were able to accomplish both outcomes. This relationship between outcomes was evident by simply list-ing all 450 homes in order of high family satisfaction and their citation deficiencies as a result of their most recent annual in-spection. There were 50 homes at the top of the list, and these were considered for our purposes to be the quality homes. We focused our analysis on which causal factors were also charac-teristic of these homes. We were testing out story by looking at the data to support it.

I prefer simple tables that display both the outcome and causal factors measurement. It is displayed as a spreadsheet. It may be initially overwhelming, especially for those who are not comfortable with data and intimidated by numbers and statistics. The hardest part initially is to obtain and display the information in a single table. Usually the data are taken from many different sources and, thus, there are many issues about different time-frames and levels of confidence in the accuracy or completeness of the information. This should not be a deterrent. Once managers have compiled the table, they should simply look at it and visually see if there appears to be much relationship between the outcomes and the causal factors. If the relationships are not relatively evident in simply observing the data, then it is going to be much more difficult to support the story. They must "listen" to the data and allow the data to "talk" to them as if they have no bias about which causal factors are related to the outcomes. They need to become an objective researcher and allow the information to "tell" the story of the relationship between the causes and the outcomes.

Once the story begins to be verified by the data, they should try out their story and supporting information with as many stakeholders as possible to determine if the story seems to fit their interpretation of reality. There will be wide variations in the degree of certainty they have about each causal factor relationship with the outcomes. HCAM had access to a wide set of information on all homes and, thus, was in a unique position to array the data across the universe of nursing homes. We created a list of the 50 best quality homes from the universe of 450 homes. This was not the only information used for our story, but it illustrates one type of analysis which helped to confine parts of our story.

The seven causal factors we assumed were related to quality included:

1. rural/urban location of the nursing home,
2. bed size of the nursing home,
3. Medicaid rate,
4. longevity in current position as administrator and director of nursing,
5. profit/nonprofit ownership of the nursing home,
6. county medical care facility or hospital ownership of the nursing home, and
7. administrator/owner status of administrator. Our story only uses five factors.

TABLE 1

BED SIZE BY FAMILY SATISFACTION LEVEL

BEDSIZE	FAMILY SATISFACTION LEVEL			
	1996	1998	2000	2002
	N=2410	N=13882	N=12423	N=12873
0-50 beds	95%	92%	96%	96%
51-100 beds	87%	90%	91%	93%
101-150 beds	82%	84%	89%	91%
151-200 beds	74%	82%	86%	86%
201+ beds	86%	85%	87%	88%

Great Lakes Marketing (1997, 1999, 2001, 2003).

TABLE 2

URBAN/RURAL BY FAMILY SATISFACTION LEVEL

URBAN/RURAL	FAMILY SATISFACTION LEVEL			
	1996	1998	2000	2002
	N=2,410	N=13,882	N=12,423	N=12,873
Region 1 - Detroit	81%	83%	86%	86%
Region 2	82%	87%	88%	91%
Region 3	89%	88%	92%	93%
Region 4	88%	85%	88%	91%
Region 5 – Upper Peninsula	88%	92%	95%	95%

Great Lakes Marketing (1997, 1999, 2001, 2003).

Small and Rural

We had observed over a ten-year period (1996-2006) that family satisfaction surveys from 30,000 respondents indicated a consistent finding that smaller and rural facilities were perceived to provide higher satisfaction. These two factors were an integral part of our story.

We knew by the family satisfaction demographics that the highest satisfied families had relatives cared for in small (50 beds or less) nursing homes in rural communities. This characterized the findings for ten years across over 30,000 families. These were two of the factors in our story. The Tables below show the satisfaction level by bed size and urban/rural location of the facility. Detroit is the most urban region and the Upper Peninsula is the most rural region.

There are reasons why small and rural facilities provide higher quality care:

1. The care in a smaller home (50 or less beds) is easier to co-ordinate and monitor because there are fewer residents and staff.
2. Staff members are caring for friends, relatives, and neighbors who they grew up within a 30-mile radius of the nursing home before they were admitted to the facility.
3. In small rural communities, everyone quickly knows the good and bad news of what happens in the local schools, churches, neighborhoods, police departments, and nursing homes. This informal communication network is a built-in quality control mechanism that enforces a community cultural expectation level. In many ways, this is a much more powerful motivator than the oversight provided by the annual inspections and episodic complaint investigation by the Department of Community Health staff.
4. Nursing homes in rural communities are often one of the largest, most stable, and best paying opportunities for staff and, thus, longevity and team building is possible.

This type of explanation is derived from many conversations and experience with the small rural nursing home operators, staff, and community stakeholders.

Longevity of Management

The third factor that appears to be related to quality of care is the longevity of the administrator and the director of nursing. These two positions supervise the balance of the other staff and provide the leadership and coordination necessary for a systematic monitoring of care and the resolution of appropriate solutions to problems.

Table 3

HEALTH INSURANCE COVERAGE

HEALTH INSURANCE	CMCF	ALL OTHER NURSING HOMES
Percentage of Health Premium Paid by Employer	93.45%	56.09%
Percentage of Family Health Premium Paid by Employer	75.65%	39.02%

Health Care Association of Michigan (April 2003).

Community Involvement and Family Health Benefits

These two factors are characteristic of County Medical Care Facilities (CMCF), which represent a disproportionate number of top 50 quality homes. They only represent 10% of all nursing homes in Michigan but represent 45% of all homes in the top 50. There is something special going on with County Medical Care Facilities. They provide more community ownership and involvement and pay staff benefits that include family health care coverage (not just coverage for the employee). CMCFs are owned by counties, which as county employers, are able to offer a more attractive benefit package for all county employees, including the staff of the CMCFs. They receive a higher Medicaid reimbursement rate (an average of $35 more per day) and, thus, they can afford to, and do, pay for family health benefits. Medicaid is the payment source for 70% of the residents of nursing homes.

The higher Medicaid rate does not necessarily assure higher quality of care. A comparison of all CMCFs with all other nursing homes indicates that the additional Medicaid funds are more likely to be used to enhance health care benefits to include the family. This is reflected in the following information prepared by HCAM in 2003.

The value of investing in fringe benefits to improve quality was reflected in the research of Farida Ejaz, a senior research scientist at the Benjamin Rose Institute in Cleveland and Jane Karnes Straker, a senior researcher at Miami University, in their analysis of responses from 40,000 nursing home families and resident satisfaction surveys in 2001 and 2002:

Higher spending on fringe benefits for direct care staff was linked with higher resident satisfaction. Perhaps better benefits make staff happier, which in turn, could affect residents' satisfaction. Spending more on temporary workers—a fairly common practice—was linked with lower resident satisfaction; this could indicate that temporary staff members don't have enough time to get to know residents (Hosteller, 2007).

Finally, some CMCFs have a local millage tax for new construction and operating expenses. In short, local taxpayers supplement the cost to operate this county facility and, thus, are motivated to be more involved with the level of care. All CMCFs also have a Board comprised of two Governor-appointed representatives plus the County Director of the Department of Human Services to oversee the operations of the nursing home. These two factors encourage community involvement. We were unable to document this higher community involvement. We do know that CMCFs, as a group, have other indicators of high quality such as lower average citation deficiencies (4.5 vs. 9.37 for 2002) and higher staffing level (3.8 hours vs. 3.21 hours per resident for 2002) than statewide averages for all homes. This concludes the documentation of the story.

Implications of the Story

Once managers have created their story and compiled and analyzed their supportive information, they should consider the implications of this explanation for improving their program's services and investments in the future.

In this example of the causes of quality, our analysis indicated that the highest quality homes were located in small facilities in rural areas. The assumption is that the greatest concentration of poor performing homes are probably in the large facilities in urban settings like Detroit, Flint, and Grand Rapids where there is a less committed labor force who are also not from the neighborhood of the facility and, thus, are not caring for neighbors, friends, and relatives.

Downsize

The first implication is that large urban homes should be physically downsized into smaller homes under 50 beds or even ten-bed designs like the "Green Houses" originated by Dr. Bill Thomas. Presbyterian Village in Redford, a suburb outside Detroit, has built such structures to test this concept. These smaller homes could be located in inner-city neighborhoods with a homogeneous ethnic and religious culture of commitment to caring for each other. These types of neighborhoods can be found within large cities like Detroit such as Hamtramac, a Polish community. This type of shared values among neighbors creates the same built-in quality control mechanism that characterizes the rural communities.

A large facility in an urban area, especially with a declining population base and a high Medicaid occupancy level, will probably not be able to financially rebuild a 200-bed nursing home into four smaller 50-bed homes. However, an incentive program was adopted by the Medicaid program to encourage such a change. Michigan has initiated such a concept to build these types of homes. The name of the program is FIDS (Facility Innovative Design System). So far, the prototypes have not been built in the inner cities, but they have been constructed in rural or suburban areas.

Large urban nursing homes (100-300 beds), nonetheless, could establish "neighborhoods" within the facility. They would be separate wings, floors, or clusters of residents to approximate a more defined community. The same staff can be assigned to the residents of such a neighborhood to assure continuity of care. Unfortunately, the basis for creating such neighborhoods is currently based on the clustering or residents by diagnosis and acuity level of residents (Alzheimer's, independent, behavioral, high acuity patients). This type of clustering is convenient for staging purposes and is often the preferred clustering by residents because each does not want to be intermingled with residents with higher acuity levels than their own acuity level. Many residents want to be segregated. The concept of neighborhoods and their value to residents of nursing homes is important to improving care in large urban homes. The central idea is to have residents share their lives with the same neighbors and staff in order to create meaningful relationships.

Autumn Woods is a 330-bed nursing home in Warren, Michigan, a suburb of Detroit. Libby Wolfe has been the administrator for more than 20 years. She has established many strategies to maintain quality. Among them:

- The home is broken down into separate "neighborhoods."
- She purchased a bus to transport staff to/from work.
- She has an extensive award and recognition process for rewarding staff who provide exceptional service.
- She installed video cameras throughout the public areas to monitor staff and visitor behavior when she is at her own home during off hours. She believes that video over-sight acts as a deterrent for any current or potential new staff from deviating from quality expectations when supervisors are not physically present.

Increase Community Involvement

All homes should expand their community presence at the nursing homes in order to take advantage of the benefits of the quality control contribution that results from having community members recognize, observe, and monitor the quality of care being provided. Such involvement could include:

- expanding visiting hours so they are convenient for family and relatives of residents,
- increasing the number of special events when visitors are invited to attend a function or celebration at the nursing home,
- increasing the number of volunteers who provide companionship and entertainment for the residents (e.g., church choirs presenting Christmas carols, humane society arranging for pets or other animals to visit, master gardeners helping to plant plants and flowers),
- increasing the coverage of local media to cover special features of the nursing home such as physical therapy to rehabilitate and send home short-term residents recovering from hip surgery, and
- encouraging high school students to adopt a grandparent resident to visit on a regular basis.

Provide Family Health Benefits

All employers should expand the provision of health benefits for the entire family of staff members. This would be an incentive for the employees to commit to a long career with the nursing home. Other incentives may include career enhancement opportunities to educate and train Certified Nurse Assistants (CNA) to become a Licensed Practical Nurse (LPN) or a Registered Nurse (RN). CNAs provide 90% of the direct care for nursing home residents. Many are single mothers with limited education and employment skills. They would appreciate any scholarship help to promote their future employment opportunities.

Since Medicaid funds 70% of the residents of nursing homes, the Medicaid reimbursement system could provide special provider rate increases to urban homes that initiate programs to enhance the stability of the staff and assure a consistent set of caregivers. As an alternative, nursing home operators could assist CNAs to qualify for publicly-funded programs like tax credits, food stamps, child care, and transportation. Any help to stabilize and improve their family life can translate into more attention and energy available for reliable resident care.

Encourage Longevity and Leadership

The final implication is that the leadership and longevity of the administrator and director of nursing is very important for attaining quality care coordination and performance. Owners should build into the compensation system high rewards and continuous recognition of the commitment of these two key positions. They set the example for the balance of the staff.

Conclusion

This chapter described a management strategy called "connecting the dots" to help managers tell their story of how specific causal factors explain their program's successful outcomes. The story will continuously evolve as they explore new causal factors and their relationship to their program's outcomes.

It is important to eliminate factors that do not impact outcomes. Many factors assumed by program policy and practice to be relevant to outcomes mislead managers and create a false story which needs to be assessed by looking at the supportive information. Myths and traditions within programs are powerful obstacles, which should not be underestimated.

Chapter 9
Enhancing the
Public Good

The reason for taxes is to fund public services that otherwise would not be available to assure collective benefits such as education, safety (fire and police), and economic infrastructure (roads, bridges, energy). These services operationalize "the public good." Taxpayers are busy with their private lives and elect political representatives to monitor the use of their tax dollars (37% of earned wages) and to enhance the public good by passing necessary legislation and assuring effective government programs. Essentially, politicians are portfolio managers. However, taxpayers, unlike investors, do not receive an annual performance report regarding their tax investment. There is no comprehensive report back to the investors on the impact of tax contributions on the improvement in the lives of citizens or communities (the public good).

There are ways to measure the public good. Oregon, for example, has set three dimensions of the public good: quality jobs; safe, caring and engaged communities; and healthy sustainable surroundings. Oregon has identified 91 benchmarks across seven broad categories: economy, education, civic engagement, social support, public safety, community development, and environment. The state government has been monitoring these benchmarks since 1992 through its Progress Board. Benchmarks are stable and remain largely unchanged regardless of political leadership. Examples of these benchmarks include:

- national rank among states of cost of doing business,
- per capita personal income,
- unemployment rate,
- percent of children entering school ready to learn,
- percent of eighth graders who achieve established skill levels (reading and math),
- state general obligation bond rating,
- infant mortality rate per 1,000 live births,
- crimes per 1,000 citizens,
- percent of roads and bridges in fair or better conditions,
- *Governing* magazine ranking of public management quality, and
- percent of owner-occupied houses

By monitoring these benchmarks, the citizens of Oregon know if progress is being made on these important measures of the public good. Each year, these benchmarks are updated and assessed in terms of progress. All benchmark information and agency performance measures are available to everyone via a Web site. Oregon has both accountability and transparency in government. All states need to adopt this benchmarking approach and align state agency performance measures so that these efforts can be linked to specific benchmark progress. This is difficult but essential to transforming the current taxpayer skepticism and cynicism into trust in government.

This initiative is part of a broader set of changes being piloted across the country in federal agencies and a small number of states and local communities. I call this set of changes *The Transparent Accountability Paradigm* shift. Signs of *The Transparent Accountability Paradigm* shift are evident in the Government Performance and Results Act (1993), *Service Efforts and Accomplishments* (Governmental Accounting Standards Board), *Legislating for Results* (National Conference of State Legislatures), Alfred P. Sloan Foundation, Center for What Works (Urban Institute), and two books *Reinventing Government* (Osborne and Gaebler, 1994) and *The Price of Government* (Osborne and Hutchinson, 2004).

The Transparent Accountability Paradigm

The ten dimensions of *The Transparent Accountability Paradigm* include:

1. Taxpayers want a government that works. They want a positive relationship between taxes and tangible program success.
2. Government programs should demonstrate a positive impact on citizens and communities they serve.
3. Government should share results with all stakeholders, including the public.
4. Results should be measurable, simple, realistic, manageable, and easily understood.
5. Results should be the primary basis for important resource decisions.
6. Program managers should maximize results.

7. Program managers should create results measures and obtain the necessary consensus/acceptance from various stakeholders.
8. Government should only fund programs that improve results and remove those that cannot.
9. Voters should elect leaders who demonstrate this level of accountability.
10. Voters should become better educated on the performance of government and communicate directly with their leaders about their "ask" of government.

This new paradigm is largely unknown to the general public, but parts of the paradigm have existed in pockets of interest around the country since the early 1990s. One of the biggest challenges for advocates of this approach to government is to create the grassroots pressure for politicians to adopt *The Transparent Accountability Paradigm* beginning with benchmarking. Both political parties could benefit from this approach. Both will initially resist because they will need to be transparent rather than secretive with a non-partisan scorecard on how successful they are at improving the benchmark measures.

In 2011, there is a heightened frustration of the American public that is reflected in a low approval of political leadership at the national level. This is important because it is one of three conditions that are necessary for any significant change. Resistance to change is lowest when:

*   there is high dissatisfaction with the status quo,
*   a shared vision of an alternative future, and
*   the first steps of action are clear (Lippitt, 1998).

High dissatisfaction with the current political and government performance is shown by a public opinion poll (UPI.com, 2010) indicating that 66% of the public believe the country is going in the wrong direction. *The Transparent Accountability Paradigm* is a vision of the future. It currently is not a shared vision. Benchmarking is one of the first steps of action toward a preferred direction. Lippitt (1998) recognizes the consequences of a newly defined preferred future:

> *Preferred futuring initiates a large paradigm shift, taking us from being powerless victims to being empowered and connected to our deep passions and motivated*

> *to work together to create a future we want. It means*
> *we are responsible and cannot blame others. But there*
> *is a tendency to resist this reality. For many of us, feel-*
> *ing helpless or victimized has been a way of coping with*
> *our sense of powerlessness* (p. 67).

Transparency and Trust

The general public is highly unlikely to understand or take the time to review the 91 Oregon benchmark measures as outcomes for their tax dollars. However, with benchmarking, citizens would know that at least the politicians, government leaders, and school officials are aware of what is expected, the results are being monitored, and are being sent to all stakeholders. The "ask" is clear. Someone is expected to "watch the store." In the end, the general public must "trust" that government is working for its best interests and is a good steward of its tax dollars. If the trust is eroded, then the willingness to increase taxes or continue to pay taxes is also eroded. The public does not currently have the ability to understand government operations or appreciate the complexities of attaining positive outcomes. It is similar to the trust everyone needs to have in their physicians, dentists, lawyers, or mechanics. We need to trust that they know what they are doing and that they have our best interests at heart. We need to trust because it is impossible for the consumer to know what the professionals know.

Trust in any expert is risky and requires some way for the customer to assess whether the expert provides a good outcome.

Some economists have attempted to analyze consumers' decisions to trust. Henry Schneider, a Cornell University economist, conducted an experiment to assess an auto mechanic's diagnosis of two relatively easy problems with his Subaru automobile (Leonhardt, 2007). He loosened the battery cable which could prevent the car from starting, and he emptied most of the coolant from the radiator, which could cause the car to overheat. He then took the car to 40 auto repair shops asking for help in understanding why the car would not always start and was overheating. Twenty-seven of the 40 mechanics identified the disconnected battery as the reason why the Subaru was not starting. Eleven of the 40 mechanics identified the lack of coolant as the likely problem of the overheating. Ten of the mechanics recommended costly and unnecessary repairs like replacing the starter. When asked how to assess a mechanic's assessment of a car, Schneider replied that if one is an uninformed customer, it is very difficult to know if he or she is getting good service. The best way is to rely upon someone who knows enough about cars and car repairs to recommend a good mechanic.

Schneider's experiment illustrates how difficult it is to assess outcomes because of our limited ability to understand the complex world of automobiles and most other encounters we have with other professionals. We are vulnerable due to our low level of knowledge, and must trust experts to be honest, reasonable, fair, and competent in the delivery of their services. This is a fairly common experience across a wide array of purchases, including government services. Most people have a limited ability to assess the quality of government services. Their judgment may be based on personal experience criteria such as courtesy, timeliness, ease of compliance (e.g., Internet or mail purchase of auto license plates or driver license), and predictability e.g., timely garbage pickup). Many citizens' judgment of government agency performance is affected by negative media coverage of misuse of resources (e.g., financial scandals) or incompetence such as the Federal Emergency Management Agency's (FEMA) inability to assist victims of Hurricane Katrina.

The economic value of trust has also been a topic of research for university schools of business. Dyer and Chu (1997) have estimated the value of trust for automakers and their suppliers. Their sample included three U.S. auto manufacturers (General Motors, Ford, and Chrysler), two Japanese firms (Toyota and Nissan), three Korean companies (Hyundai, Daewoo, and Kia), and a representative set of their suppliers. A total of 453 supplier-automaker exchange relationships were assessed from 1992 to 1994. The suppliers of parts had the highest trust level with the Japanese auto manufacturers and subsequently had lower transaction costs for contract negotiations expenditures and increased information sharing. The authors define trust as "one party's confidence that the other party in the exchange relationship will not exploit its vulnerabilities (p. 3)." Trust has three components according to the two researchers—reliability, fairness, and goodwill. These components were determined by interviewing supplier informants who, on average, had been employed by their suppliers for 16 years. They had a long history of working with the automakers. These key informants often were accompanied by other senior executives of their organization. The level of trust was established by three factors:

1. the extent to which the supplier trusted the manufacturer to treat suppliers fairly,
2. the extent to which the automaker has a reputation for trustworthiness (following through on promises and commitments) in the general supplier community, and
3. if given the chance, the extent to which the supplier perceived that the automaker will take unfair advantage of the supplier (reverse trend).

Transaction costs included:

- search costs for gathering information on potential trading partners,
- contracting costs for negotiating an agreement,
- monitoring costs to ensure that each party fulfills their contracted obligations, and
- enforcement costs to assure contract conditions are fulfilled.

The staff costs associated with these functions were used to establish the transaction expenses.

If suppliers had a high trust of the automaker, they were more likely to also propose new product designs and technologies. One supplier executive provided the following example:

> We are much more likely to bring a new product design to [Automaker A3] than to [Automaker A1]. The reason is simple. [Automaker A1] has been known to take our proprietary blueprints and send them to our competitors to see if they can make the part at lower cost. They claim they are simply trying to maintain competitive bidding. But because we can't trust them to treat us fairly, we don't take our new designs to them. We take them to [Automaker A3] where we have a more secure long term future (p. 24).

Trust is not just a concept. It is a powerful way to reduce risk, reduce costs, and to provide a competitive edge not only in automobile manufacturing but in other settings. Nursing home operators have a mutual distrust of government regulators who assess compliance with an extensive array of quality indicators. Both parties are responsible for this level of distrust. In Michigan, the cost to taxpayers (both federal and state taxes) of nursing home care exceeds $2 billion annually. The care for 70% of all nursing home residents is paid by Medicaid. The extensive cost of regulating nursing homes could be reduced if there was an increase in the trust between the provider and regulatory stakeholders.

Harry Beckwith, the author of *Selling the Invisible* (1997), makes a very important point that consumers of a service do not have the ability to assess the service regardless of whether it is provided by a lawyer, a doctor, or a mechanic. They do not have sufficient understanding of the underlying laws, medicine, or their automobile. Consequently, they must trust their lawyer, physician, and mechanic. It is in the nature of the service commodity. It is true across all services, according to Beckwith:

> *In most professional services you are not really selling expertise—because your expertise is assumed, and because your prospect cannot evaluate your expertise anyway. Instead you are selling a relationship. And in most cases, that is where you need the most work. If you are selling a service you are selling a relationship* (p. 42).

This insight provides an important roadmap for both politicians and government leaders who are selling a relationship with the taxpayer, and trust is the most important dimension of the relationship. To earn the citizen's trust, they must be able to honestly answer all questions that challenge this trust. Both must be transparent at all times whatever the consequences are for the individual politician or agency.

How to Lose Trust

The current crisis in trust of the Catholic Church is an excellent example of how to lose trust. The sexual abuse of children by a small percent of priests undermines the credibility of all priests. The hiding of this abuse by the hierarchy of the Church is even more damaging. The Church leadership was aware of the mistreatment of its members (customers) and did not stop this abuse. It risked the safety and mental health of its parishioners so that the institution of the Catholic Church could survive. This was a major mistake, which may result in a serious weakening of the Church's authority and good will into the foreseeable future. The subsequent cost to settle cases against the church has averaged $1 million per case with some as high as $3 million. On January 4, 2011, the Catholic Diocese in Milwaukee, Wisconsin, filed for bankruptcy, becoming the 8th in the United States to do so as a direct result of claims made against its priests for child sexual abuse.

The current crisis in airline security is another example of failing to protect the customer. A letter to the editor of *The Economist* (Donahue, 2002) said it best:

> *The lack of security at airports was a deliberate decision of the airline industry to under invest in safety. Since the industry did not think their aircraft were worth protecting, the airlines should not be surprised at their losses. Terrorism is hardly a new phenomenon. The airlines and their insurers profited from this underinvestment and it is only right that they should share in the losses from this business decision. Protecting firms from their own folly (the socialization of losses, if you will) only fosters an atmosphere where companies take bigger risks if they can pass losses to taxpayers. This was the lesson behind the savings and loan scandal, Credit Lyonnais, and the entire financial industry in Japan. The Bush Administration should not bail out airlines, it should hand them the bill.*

A third example was the failure of Arthur Andersen to accurately reflect the value of Enron to its shareholders. There has been a growing conflict of interest between the accounting gatekeeper function and the need for Arthur Andersen to obtain consulting contracts with the same firms it audits. It is amazing to me how quickly the reputation of Arthur Andersen was lost once it was charged with a single count of obstruction of justice because of allegations that the firm illegally destroyed Enron-related documents. Arthur Andersen is the focus in this case. However, the gatekeeper role is at risk for all accounting companies and stock analysts who provide recommendations to the public on the viability of specific companies. Harvey Pitt was the Chairman of the Securities and Exchange Commission during this period. He was removed from this position because the SEC was, in part, blamed for the failure to prevent the financial consequences to Enron shareholders. This was perceived to be a failure of regulation. Harvey Pitt recognized that regulatory oversight was a second line of attack to assure investor confidence in stock brokerage firms or other financial advisors. The first and most important is the ethical behavior of individual brokers or accountants who must always act in the best interests of the investor. Pitt (2002) observed that:

> *Similar to the securities industry, doctors confront a surfeit of laws, regulations and codes of ethics, designed to make them act the way we expect them to act. But, no matter how many laws, regulations or codes exist doctors must do what is right as a matter of habit and ethic, not because someone's looking over their shoulders. There are so many times when no one looks over a doctor's shoulder, frequently involving life and death situations. When doctor and patient are alone, the patient's last and best refuge is the doctor, not the rulebook. Regulation can't substitute for doctors doing their jobs honestly, in a manner serving the best interests of their patients. So it is for your customers. You're charged with taking care of their financial health* (p.1).

In all three examples (the Catholic Church, airline security, and Arthur Anderson), they have not been truthful to their customers about the true risks involved with their services. These companies lost their "moral compass," which defines what is in the best long term interests of their clients rather than the best short term interests of the corporation. In each case, the institutions were willing to risk the trust level of their client base. This is a simplification, but it helps us to assess the value of transparency and the price of losing trust.

Distrust of Government

Americans have a strong distrust of government (The Council for Excellence in Government, 2004). They perceive government as a combination of politicians and agency bureaucrats. They differentiate between the political process and the agencies that deliver the service. They have an unfavorable opinion of legislators as reflected in the fact that Congress has never received a favorable job performance rating higher than 50% and often considerably lower. Nonetheless, Americans overwhelmingly re-elect incumbents. They also believe government agencies to be inefficient and wasteful although they hold highly positive views of specific federal agencies. Given this historical assessment and contradictions, Americans, nonetheless, want government to do more but do it more efficiently. Distrust of government is based on a widely held negative assessment of both politicians and agency performance. However, the politicians are perceived to be most at fault.

The Council for Excellence in Government is a national, non-profit, non-partisan organization with a dual mission of improving government performance and increasing the trust and participation of citizens in our democracy. The Council compiled the best summary of historical public opinion research findings on trust in government. Some of these findings include:

- Trust in government has declined since the mid-1960s and has remained at this lower level. This loss of trust also characterizes the public's perception of ten major institutions (medicine, education, organized religion, the military, major companies, the press, the Supreme Court, the Executive branch, Congress, and organized labor).
- When asked why the public does not trust government, respondents gave five reasons:

    (1) Eighty-percent said government leaders tell us what they think will get them elected and not what they really believe.
    (2) There is too much political bickering.
    (3) Special interests have too much influence.
    (4) Government is inefficient and wasteful.
    (5) Elected officials are dishonest and lack integrity.

- *While often critical of government performance, the American public continues to expect the federal government to respond to just about every pressing economic and social need. Some scholars have argued that the decline in trust in government may be attributable, at least in part, to the federal government's growth and the extent to which it has failed to solve problems it has taken on* (p. 16).
- The public gives highly favorable ratings to specific federal agencies. The highest is the Postal Service (89%) and the lowest is the Internal Revenue Service (38%).
- The public differentiates between federal, state, and local government and is least trusting of the federal government.
- *Whether the public's perceptions (of the federal government) are accurate or not, poor performance ratings are*

strongly linked to distrust of government. People who believe the government does a good job running its programs are much more likely to express high levels of trust in government than are people who give government low marks for performance (p. 33).

- The public recognizes its responsibility to be more engaged with the political process to improve government performance.
- Public trust in government is similar across demographic characteristics such as sex, age, income, geographic region, and educational level.
- The public has a much higher positive perception that civil servants do the right thing most of the time (67%) versus politicians (16%).
- Fifty-five percent of the public believe government has a positive effect on their lives overall and especially in the areas of public schools, roads and highways, food and drug safety, consumer safety, workplace health and safety, and environmental protection.

Three strong predictors of trust in government according to the study by the Council are:

1. the public's perception of political leaders who do the right thing most of the time,
2. the public's rating of government performance, and
3. the public's sense of being connected to the political component of government.

The Transparent Accountability Paradigm directs government to share its performance (outcomes) with a public that is largely uninformed and, in many ways, unable to make realistic decisions about the performance of politicians or agencies. The public needs to become much better educated in how to assess the outcomes of government programs and to know what are realistic expectations of government. The benchmarks are a beginning set of progress measures. The challenge for government (politicians and agency leaders) is to demonstrate how their programs positively impact these benchmarks.

Some initial steps may include:

- clear and prioritized benchmarks focused on widely shared goals,

- aligning of government programs with specific benchmarks,
- development of a tracking mechanism to establish the relationship between program outcomes and benchmarks,
- sharing results with the public so that success can be understood, appreciated, and improved, and
- encouraging public participation in the political process to connect with citizens in a meaningful way.

This is a big task, and it will require a strong partnership between the professional public policy research community and a focused political leadership. In Michigan, such a community of scholars released *Michigan at the Millennium: A Benchmark and Analysis of its Fiscal and Economic Structure* (Ballard, Courant, Drake, & Gerber, 2003), a report that provides a historical review of important economic trends such as academic achievement levels, expenditures for schools, poverty rates, unemployment rates, percentage changes in toxic substances, crime rates, and income levels. The authors of this 710-page report are researchers from the major universities and public policy organizations. The book has been provided to all legislators since it was published in 2003. The extent to which legislators actually use this type of historical trend analysis for purposes of setting a legislative agenda is unknown.

The larger task of linking benchmarks with programs would be extremely difficult for any set of state agencies, universities, and public policy organizations. The sharing of these results would, I believe, be welcomed by citizens because of their eagerness to be told the truth about their tax investments and to be challenged to collectively solve problems. Many citizens would prefer an effective and transparent government.

The public recognizes its responsibility to become engaged citizens. It does not know how to become more active in a constructive way. It does not feel welcome. It does not feel that its input will be valued by government agencies or its political representatives. Nonetheless, the public recognizes that its voluntary participation with government could have the greatest impact on improving government by:

- increasing the number of voters (73%),
- teaching young people more about government and getting more involved in communities (65%),

- increasing involvement with schools (63%), and
- talking more to elected officials (52%).

In 1999, a public opinion survey for the Center for Excellence in Government found that a respondent's age predicted the sense of feeling close or connected to government. The older the person's age, the more connected he or she felt with government. There is a huge opportunity for both politicians and government agencies to foster ways to improve the sense of being connected to the political process and government.

Government is Largely Invisible

One of the difficulties of engaging and informing the public about how to assess performance and to participate in the political process is that government is mostly invisible to the general public and taxpayer. Schools are probably the most visible, as least for those who have children attending schools. Other visible examples of government include local pickup of trash, snow plowing of roads, fire and police activity, delivery of mail, and road repairs. The vast majority of the public rarely encounters government employees at work unless a citizen is receiving a public service like obtaining license plates for a car or purchasing a hunting license. Government is largely off the personal radar screen for most citizens, and this leads to a very low level of literacy and understanding of even the most elementary information about government services, let alone the outcomes of these programs. For example, only seven percent of Michigan citizens know that Medicaid is, by far, the biggest payment source for residents in nursing homes. Most believe that Medicare is the primary payer because Medicare covers other health care costs for older people.

In 2010, the State of Michigan spent $1 billion on nursing home care for Medicaid recipients. This was matched by $2 billion from the federal government as part of a matching funding program. Most citizens probably do not know how their tax dollars are being used for purposes of elderly care or any other purpose. The combination of low visibility of government services and the low literacy level about even the existence of government programs presents great opportunities and challenges for encouraging the adoption of *The Transparent Accountability Paradigm*. Simply informing citizens about the scope of services, let alone their impact on clients and communities, can have positive or negative consequences in the perceptions of the public.

On the positive side, if the public becomes more aware of the scope of government services, then taxpayers may be more appreciative of the use of their tax contribution. On the other hand, by becoming aware of the scope of services, the taxpayer may become shocked that tax resources are being used for these purposes and that outcomes are either relatively low or do not exist. Regardless of their reaction, citizens need to know how their tax dollars are being used to improve the quality of the lives of individuals and communities.

Experimenting with Transparency

There are many examples of experimenting with transparency. The Whistleblower Protection Act of 1989 provides federal employees the opportunity and protection to expose their agencies' illegal or inappropriate policies and practices to legal authorities. The Sarbanes-Oxley Act of 2002 extended whistleblower protections to corporate employees.

A similar opportunity is available via advocate journalists and reporters. In the health services area, there has been considerable interest and transparency attempts to improve care and better inform stakeholders of variations in quality outcomes and costs. Over the past twenty years, there have been transparency initiatives involving hospitals, health plans, nursing homes, home health agencies, and physicians. The lessons learned from these early projects, summarized by John Colmers (2007), are similar to conclusions from the experience of the Oregon Progress Board and the Governmental Accounting Standards Board:

- Public reporting adds value. For example, public reporting of comparative data on patient satisfaction enhances and reinforces quality improvement efforts already under way, and appears to stimulate quality improvement activities in areas where performance levels are reported to be low.
- Reports must be designed carefully. An emerging body of research indicates that the way information is presented affects how it is interpreted and weighed in decisions.
- Collaboration appears to be essential. The most successful approaches to public reporting and transparency

have resulted from partnerships involving the private and public sectors as well as purchasers and providers.

- Many state and local efforts have proven successful, in part, because the scale is manageable and local sponsors are able to account for factors that affect performance at the regional delivery system.
- The movement toward greater transparency is in its infancy, and research and concurrent evaluation have actively informed the most successful efforts.
- Automated data collection is needed because when data are not routinely and unobtrusively collected as part of the ongoing care process, the result is an additional burden on providers and health plans (p. vi).

Linking Benchmarks to Program Outcomes

Once benchmarks are established, the next step is to align them to the state agencies and their programs and begin to assess their impact on benchmarks. Aligning some programs with specific benchmarks is straightforward—anti-poverty programs with poverty rates, police and prison programs with crime rates, schools with graduation rates. Some programs will not align with any benchmarks. They need to be assessed in terms of their expected outcomes and those results should be shared with the public.

Oregon has been experiencing this alignment difficulty especially with smaller programs within the larger agencies. Many of these programs without links to benchmarks have developed from a base of advocates who believe the program does serve a public good. Program advocates are often not motivated to demonstrate the program's effectiveness because "intrinsic goodness" (of the program) is enough, in their minds. For example, day care programs are good because they provide a safe setting for children. There is no need to establish any outcomes regarding day care (employment of the mother, school readiness for the children) because day care is "intrinsically good." By definition, in the program advocates' mind, the program is justified. It is a circular and moral argument for continuing a program.

Benchmarking is one way to define the most important signs of progress and subsequently what programs are most important for enhancing the public good.

There is probably some level of consensus among politically active Oregon citizens regarding the 91 benchmarks selected to reflect Oregon's definition of the public good. The 91 benchmarks are not prioritized in terms of importance. Within each benchmark, one of the challenges is to analyze the various factors including government programs that cause changes in the various benchmarks (poverty rates, unemployment rates, crime rates, graduation rates). There is considerable debate among experts in each of these benchmark areas about specific causal factors and their relative importance in causing changes to these benchmarks. This type of public policy debate needs to take place in order to understand the payoff of program investments to the investors (taxpayers). This is the way to determine if programs are effective in enhancing the public good. There is much similarity in the benchmark measures among states with benchmarking initiatives.

One of the first steps in linking programs to a specific benchmark is to develop a conceptual logic of expectations so that the explicit causal factors are identified with progress in a specific benchmark. For example, changes in the poverty rate should result from successful programs to increase high school graduation rates; decrease teenage pregnancy; increase the formation of two-parent families; increase school readiness; increase employment skills and experience; improve family functioning; improve health; and increase the availability and use of affordable day care, Medicaid, food stamps, and other support systems. The following Table provides a summary chart of the logic of program expectations for affecting the poverty rate.

TABLE 4

PROGRAMS IMPACTING POVERTY BENCHMARK

CORRELATES OF POVERTY	PROGRAMS IMPACTING CORRELATES
LOW EDUCATIONAL ACHIEVEMENT	• Head Start (improved school readiness) • Effective schools (H.S. graduation rates)
TEENAGE PREGNANCY.	• Safe-sex education programs (reduction in teen pregnancy) • Abstinence programs (reduction in teen pregnancy)
SINGLE MOTHER WITH CHILDREN	• Day care (employment or educational achievement)
INADEQUATE PARENTING SKILLS	• Child abuse and neglect prevention programs (reduction in child abuse)
LOW EMPLOYMENT SKILLS	• Training for employment (employment)
INADEQUATE ENGLISH LANGUAGE COMPETENCY	• Learning English programs (employment)
POOR QUALITY HOUSING	• Energy assistance programs • Home improvement programs
LOW EARNINGS FROM EMPLOYMENT	• Food stamps (improved health) • Medicaid (improved health) • Tax credits (improved earnings) • Finding higher paying employment with benefits (increased earnings and reduced use of subsidies) • TANF

Historically, the poverty rate has remained within a relatively narrow range of 12-18% of individuals from 1965-2009. In the late 1950s, it was 22.4%, or 39.5 million individuals (National Poverty Center, 2011). It has been very difficult to link the success of any given anti-poverty program to changes in the poverty rate, in part, because many of the programs do not prevent poverty or increase the economic mobility of the families in poverty. Many programs provide assistance to simply survive (food, housing, medical care, transportation) during difficult financial periods. The most recent period of economic prosperity (1990s) did coincide with a decrease in the poverty rate. The welfare to work legislation (TANF) did shift recipients of welfare (AFDC) to employment during this period, but did not necessarily transition them out of poverty. The rate of poverty is probably not the best index of movement out of poverty. A preferred measure may be the earned income level of adult children as compared to their parents. This inter-generational metric would reflect the percent of children born in low income families who ultimately are able to earn a level of income to no longer receive various subsidies like food stamps, Medicaid, and energy assistance. This research design of inter-generational mobility has not been applied to families in poverty but has been developed for families with earned income above the poverty level. The results of this type of analysis illustrate the extent to which inter-generational mobility exists throughout various classes within American society. In general, most children remain in the same or similar economic class level of their parents.

The research model has been developed by a cooperative research project funded by a number of large public policy organizations in Washington, D.C. (Pew Charitable Trust, the American Enterprise Institute, The Brookings Institute, The Heritage Foundation and the Urban Institute). The initiative is called The Economic Mobility Project (Isaacs, 2008) and it compares the income of four generations of men born between 1925 and 1974. The son's income is compared to the father's income when they were both in their thirties. Incomes were adjusted for inflation. The comparisons reflect sons with marginally higher average earnings when compared to their fathers. This has been historically the case of upward inter-generational mobility for the average citizen until the most recent comparison, which reflected a decrease in the comparisons of sons in 2004 (average income of $35,010) versus their fathers in 1974 ($40,210). Future analysis of this database will provide a more complete picture of improved inter-generational mobility based on family income comparisons that will reflect the tremendous growth in wives working since 1974 to enhance the family earnings. Two of the benchmark charts from this research effort are included in the next section, which identifies a number of key benchmarks that reflect progress. Unfortunately, this project does not focus on the inter-generational mobility of families in poverty. This type of longitudinal research demonstrates the kind of analysis necessary to appreciate the causal factors of any benchmark.

Eight Important Benchmarks

I have selected eight benchmark charts to provide a focused starting point for monitoring progress. The charts include:

1. International comparison of scores in mathematics, reading, science, and problem solving (2003).
2. High school graduation rates (1998).
3. Female headed household poverty rates (1959-2006).
4. Family income (1947-2006)
5. Parents versus adult children median income levels (1967-2002).
6. A child's chances of getting ahead of his or her parents (1967-2002).
7. International comparison of spending in health care (1980-2004).
8. International comparison of total expenditure on health as a percentage of gross national product (1980-2004).

These benchmarks represent indicators of our standard of living—educational achievement, two-parent families, ability to attain inter-generational increases in earned income levels, and a cost effective health care system. There are many other benchmark measures that could be included on this list. The following charts focus on a few that represent prioritized and significant challenges. The charts illustrate broad historical trends in three important areas of educational achievement, poverty, and health care costs. Two other areas are without charts: infrastructure and energy diversification.

1. U.S. students (15 years of age) score below average on mathematics, reading, science, and problem-solving tests relative to 30 other industrialized counties. If the U.S. is to remain competitive in a global economy, our children need to be better prepared to compete. The average U.S. students' (9, 13, and 17 years of age) scores on academic achievement (reading, mathematics, and science) have not significantly changed from 1970-2004). High school graduation rates are much lower for African Americans and Latino students. Educational achievement remains the most predictive factor of future earning levels.
2. The family poverty rate (percent of all families with earned income below poverty level) has remained within a narrow range of 12-18% since the anti-poverty programs were introduced in the 1960s. Two of the best predictors of poverty are low educational achievement and single mother households. "In 2006, for the first time in U.S. history, a majority of all live births to women under 30 (50.4 percent) were out of wedlock. Nearly 80 percent of births among black women were

CHART 1

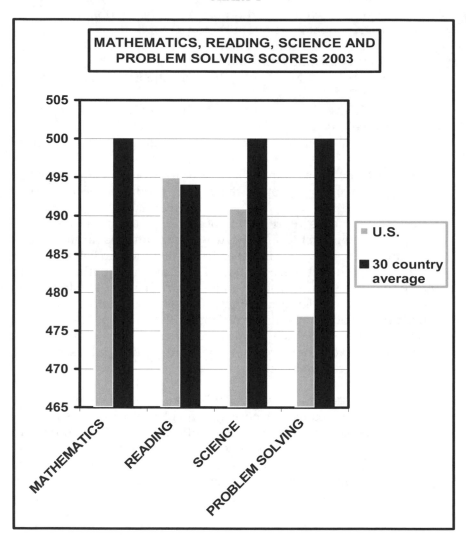

National Center for Education Statistics (2007). *Digest of Education Statistics: 2007.*
Table 389.

CHART 2

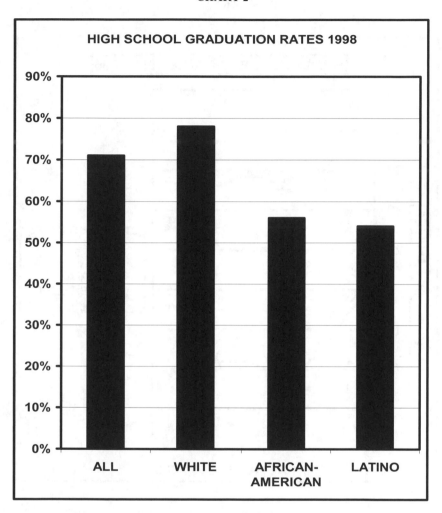

HIGH SCHOOL GRADUATION RATES 1998

Greene (2002). *High School Graduation Rates in the United States*. New York: The Manhattan Institute.

CHART 3

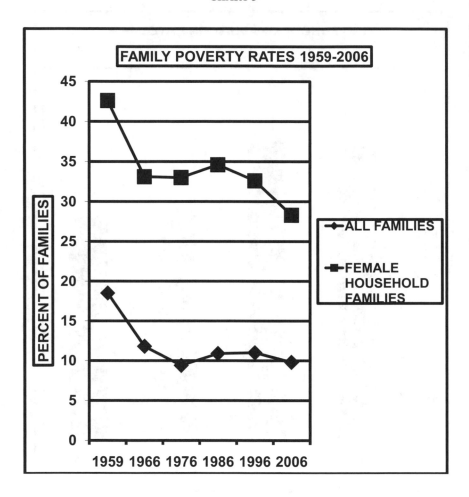

U.S. Census Bureau (2008). Historical Poverty Tables – Table 13.

CHART 4

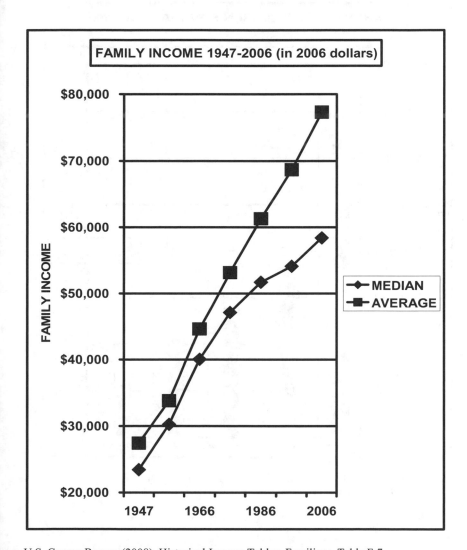

FAMILY INCOME 1947-2006 (in 2006 dollars)

U.S. Census Bureau (2008). Historical Income Tables, Families – Table F-7.

CHART 5

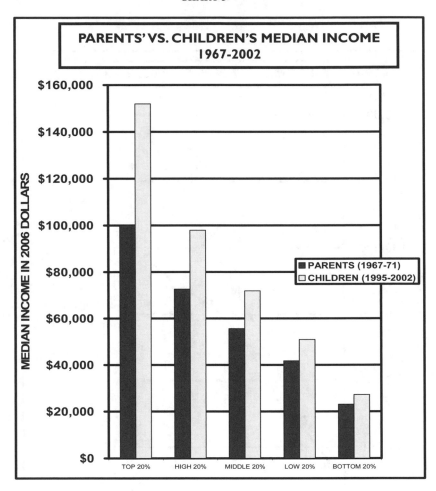

Isaacs (2008). *Economic Mobility of Families Across Generations* (Figure 1). Washington, D.C.: The Brookings Institute.

CHART 6

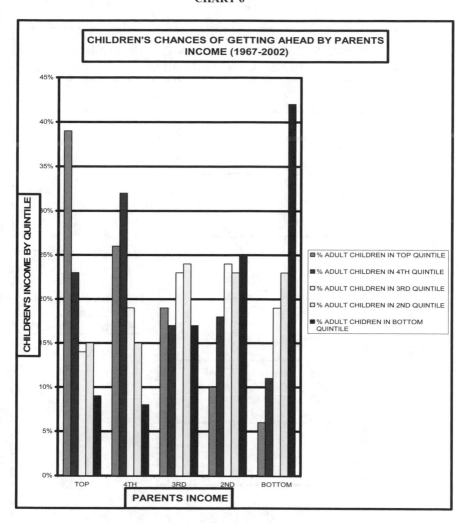

Isaacs (2008). *Economic Mobility of Families Across Generations* (Figure 4).
Washington: D.C.: The Brookings Institute.

CHART 7

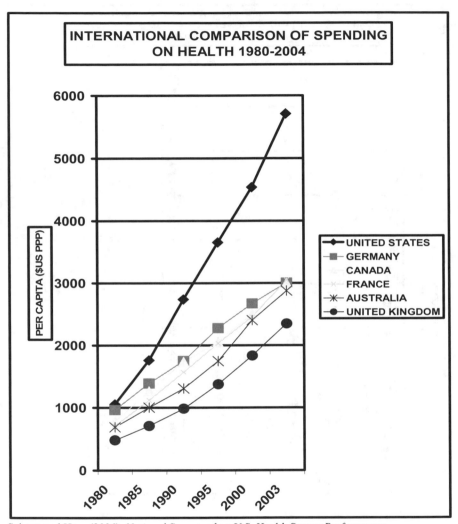

Schoen and How (2006). *National Scorecard on U.S. Health System Performance*:
Complete Chartpack (Slide 58). New York: The Commonwealth Fund.

CHART 8

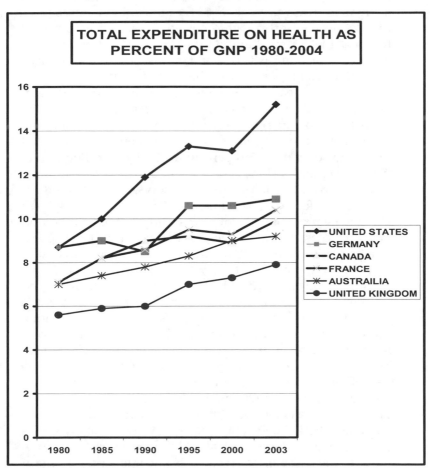

Commonwealth Fund (2006). *National Scorecard on U.S. Health Performance:*
Complete Chartpack (Slide 58). New York: The Commonwealth Fund.

out of wedlock (Herbert, 2008)." Once a teenage girl decides to begin her own family prior to graduating from high school, the probability of a lifetime in poverty greatly increases. It is easier to achieve earned income above the poverty level if there are two wage earners in a family. Many families at middle-income levels need to have two wage earners simply to retain their current standard of living. This trend in two-wage-earning families is one of the most significant changes in the U.S. labor market over the past 50 years.

3. The U.S. health care system outcomes (life expectancy, mortality amenable to health care intervention, infant mortality) often fall below many other industrialized nations in spite of the fact that our approach is more expensive as reflected in total expenditures and percent of gross domestic product (Shoen, Davis, K., How, and Schoenbaum, 2006). Administrative overhead costs plus unnecessary optional testing are two reasons for excessive expenses. The U.S. health system challenges are to provide lower cost, improve outcomes, and improve access to care coverage. However, improving access to a cost inefficient system is not likely to lower the cost of care but rather increase the cost by expanding covered lives even in a preventive model. There are many recommended solutions to the unnecessary expenditures. But as are witnessing in 2011, there is strong resistance to implementing these recommendations from vested interest groups who financially benefit from such inefficiencies, and efforts were being made to repeal many reforms that were enacted as part of the Patient Protection and Affordable Care Act signed into law by President Obama in March of 2010.

4. The fourth area is the viability of the economic infrastructure including the levee system, roads, bridges, railroad tracks and equipment, and electrical grid. All are important conditions for the transportation of goods and sustaining economic growth. I am not aware of a summary database to monitor the status of the various current infrastructures and the risk assessment of unnecessary and avoidable failures. The consequences of under-investing in infrastructural projects only become obvious once the failure has occurred. Many such failures were predicted but there was strong resistance to fund such public investments.

5. Finally, the fifth area is developing renewable energy sources such as wind, solar, and nuclear options, and conserving the use of fossil fuels that pollute the air and water. There is no single database to create a benchmark for this issue. The creation of alternative sources of renewable energy is a nec-

essary initiative to assure future generations the opportunity to live in a healthier world. Individual commitments to this approach are detailed by Pollan (2008).

Conclusion

Benchmarks measure the "public good" and make government visible and focused. Benchmarks should be developed by input from many citizens, prioritized, shared, and updated, with progress reported at least annually. This chapter reviews ways for government to embrace this approach to accountability. Several example states like Oregon present processes successfully used to implement benchmarking measures.

Now is an appropriate time to introduce transformational change by adopting *The Transparent Accountability Paradigm* because three important conditions exist for defining a preferred future (Lippitt, 1998) for the United States:

1. There is high discontent by citizens with the status quo (high unemployment, low high school graduation rates, high health care costs, decreasing mean-income levels, zero interest rates, high home foreclosure rates).

2. There is a clear vision of the future with benchmarking and *The Transparent Accountability Paradigm.*

3. There are first steps proposed in the last chapter.

The discontent reflects the lack of trust in government. Trust in government is based on the belief that the best interest of the public is also shared by its leaders. Trust in government is particularly hard to earn because government is largely invisible and often only becomes visible during a crisis such as the 9-11 attack, response to Hurricane Katrina, the Gulf of Mexico oil spill in 2010, and the financial disaster of 2008. These examples are vivid illustrations of the failure of government oversight and regulation to protect the public. Benchmarking makes government visible and the "ask" of government clear so that government stays focused on outcomes to improve the public good.

Trust is fragile and can be easily eroded. The chapter describes several institutions (Catholic Church, airlines because of 9-11, banks and brokerage firms because of financial crisis) that have lost significant levels of trust by failing to represent the best interests of their members. They also experienced huge expenses as a result of subsequent litigation and the loss of future revenues. In addition, there will be large re-investment necessary to recover the trust.

The public sees government as a combination of political leadership and federal agencies. Both components need to be trustworthy. When asked why they distrust government, the public identifies five reasons:

1. Political leaders misrepresent their views to get elected.
2. Political leaders are dishonest and lack integrity.
3. Political leaders are not interested in resolving differences.
4. Special interests have too much influence.
5. Government agencies are inefficient and wasteful.

Some of the necessary steps to get focused on improving the public good are outlined in the chapter and include creating clear and prioritized benchmarks, aligning government programs with benchmarks, tracking client outcomes to demonstrate effective programs, public sharing of results, and encouraging active participation by citizens. Although several benchmarks are provided as examples, it is only necessary to prioritize the top three in order to demonstrate movement to a preferred future. It is impossible at one time to provide the focus and resources for improvement across all benchmarks. Three that would make the greatest differences in the public good would be, in my opinion, reducing unemployment, increasing the percentage of the population with college degrees, and decreasing health care costs. These three challenges all have solutions, and all solutions have vested interest groups that support or oppose these solutions. The role of citizens is to forcefully ask legislators to reach agreement on how to most effectively improve the public good (benchmarks). Their job is to move the bar, not to explain why it cannot be moved.

Chapter 10
Answers to Key Questions

This chapter answers eight key questions:

1. Why are legislators reluctant to require government to be accountable?
2. Has the Government Performance and Results Act (GPRA) of 1993, which required the collection of performance measures, increased accountability and transparency?
3. Do agencies that value and use outcome information increase their outcome levels of performance?
4. What role should the media play in promoting government accountability and transparency?
5. What is the value and best use of client success stories?
6. Will outcome information limit the use of political party agendas as the basis of funding programs?
7. What is the appropriate timeframe to collect outcome information after a client has completed a program?
8. Could an outcome-based accountability approach to the SEC have prevented Bernie Madoff from using a Ponzi scheme to destroy $50 billion in savings from various investors?

1. Why are legislators reluctant to require government to be accountable?

One might think that legislators would be interested in defining expected outcomes for legislation, especially the passage of a statute that creates a program and is subsequently funded. This is almost never the case. To pass legislation, so many stakeholders need to agree that vagueness is necessary to gain consensus. This way, everyone can have their own outcome expectation, and the critical debate on a consensus outcome never happens. Thus, most programs are based on laws with no outcomes. Laws are necessary to establish programs and appropriate funds to operate them. To pass a law at the federal, state, or local level, it is necessary to gain consensus from a diverse group of legislators representing many interest groups. To pass a law, it is necessary to maximize the number of legislators who could benefit from offering their support.

To accomplish this, it is customary to be vague and undefined in terms of the population at risk (who would be covered under the law), what services or intervention strategy will be provided, and what client outcomes will result. The vague language allows each legislator to promise benefits to his or her constituents, or at least to promise that no harm will come to them. In return, the legislator gets future favors from the initiators of the law. The initiators get a new interest group. The interest group gets the law to use as the basis for lobbying for an appropriation to implement the law. The law authorizing a program does not typically include clearly defined client outcomes. If money is appropriated through the budget appropriations process, there may be some general understanding between the appropriations committee chairman and the program administrator as to subsequent client outcomes.

Once a program is established, however, it develops its own vested interest groups and takes on a legitimacy and protected status that prevents any serious review of its effectiveness. The history of sunset legislation is a good example of the difficulty of making programs accountable after they have been in existence for some time. Common Cause (1978), a nonprofit government watchdog organization, summarizes the history of perpetuating programs:

> *It is true that legislatures already have the power to terminate existing programs and agencies, but they seldom exercise that power. There is a grain of truth in the saying that "old agencies never die. They don't even fade away." Programs and agencies tend to proliferate. Evaluation reports generally sit on the shelf. The reasons are not mysterious—program evaluation and legislative oversight are difficult, time consuming tasks. It is easy to put them aside. Most legislators look ahead rather than behind. They are extremely busy and can always justify doing something other than oversight. Proposing legislation is more glamorous than reviewing existing laws (p. 1).*

The first opportunity for accountability is lost when laws without client outcomes are passed. It becomes increasingly more difficult once these laws are enacted. The Domestic Violence program is a typical example of a program based on a law that has not specified all the client outcomes. This program was established by Michigan law to serve those individuals (mostly women) who are victims of physical or mental abuse. More specifically, the program was designed to provide a physically safe shelter for women who were at risk of future abuse by their spouses. Although counseling was provided, there were no client-outcome measures for this service. The only outcome delineated by the program staff concerned the safety of the client while housed in the shelter (generally for no more than two weeks).

An appropriate outcome measure for counseling may be the return to a safe home environment where domestic violence is not repeated. This would be a recidivism measure. Many abused women return to an abusive home. The counseling outcome measure should be the percent of shelter clients who are subsequently abused. Physical safety while in the domestic violence shelter is a legitimate short term outcome. This is a self-fulfilling definition of success—the shelter provides safety; if safety is provided, then it is a success. If this is the only outcome, then the shelter should not be funded to provide counseling because there is no agreed-upon outcome for such counseling. Nonetheless, the appropriations committees continue to provide state funds for shelters. Legislators must take responsibility for passing laws specifying client outcomes. As long as laws remain vague, it is very difficult, if not impossible, to ensure public agency accountability.

I am not optimistic that legislators will explicitly designate client outcomes in legislation. They will probably argue that this is clearly an executive branch responsibility, and that the legislature's responsibility is simply to convey the intent of the law with the specifics to be worked out later by the department that receives the appropriated funds to operate the program. The problem is that there are many intents, and each is represented by a different vested interest group. Subsequently, the client outcomes seldom get established. The irony, of course, is that the initial failure to reach consensus before passage returns to plague legislators if they attempt to then hold an agency accountable. Laws can be made very explicit in requiring complete accountability by mandating the collection of client results information.

If there are no outcomes in law for a given program, legislators have the opportunity every year to review the program's performance and determine if it should continue to be funded and at what level. Thus, they have an annual opportunity to establish or clarify outcome expectations during the appropriations process. They almost never do. At some point in the appropriations process, the program representative meets with the appropriations committee or funding authority to review the request. The committee is generally comprised of representatives of the legislature. Both the House and Senate have such committees, and both must agree on spending levels prior to the passage of the appropriations bill. These meetings are open to the public and are attended by the program managers, top department administrators, and special interest groups, in addition to the legislators and their aides. The chairperson of the committee has generally been involved for several years with the programs whose budgets are being reviewed. As a result, he or she has a major advantage in understanding the budget for these programs. In addition, his or her aides have considerable power to influence decisions based on the information they provide to the chairperson. Often a session begins with an overview by the program manager or department administrator. Such an overview may or may not include client outcomes; generally it does not. Rather, it focuses on how many clients are being provided what services at what cost. Only intermittently does a legislator ask about the results on clients. Then the program manager generally answers with vague responses and anecdotal experiences. Any recent newspaper article (especially front page of a major newspaper) may be an issue and may receive an inordinate amount of discussion at such public hearings.

The best annual opportunity for public accountability is through the budget appropriations process during which state and federal funds are negotiated between state agencies and legislative representatives (of the public). The focus of the appropriations process is on the number of clients served, the kinds of services provided, and the costs. These are important dimensions but clearly secondary to the key issue of client outcomes.

The role of the legislature is to establish laws and to ensure that the executive branch meets the intent of the law in executing the various programs that implement the law. The role of the legislature is then to hold the executive branch responsible and accountable for outcomes and process measures. It is the legitimate role for the executive branch to decide how to implement a mandate. This is the exact point at which neither the legislative nor the executive branch is willing to finalize the debate about how to measure the intent of legislation. There are as many intents as there are legislators on the appropriations committee. This debate must end in order to get on with the collection of measurable outcomes so that accountability can take place. As long as the debate goes on, there is no final agreement on expected results.

The executive branch, represented by the agency director, is probably in the best position to interpret the intent, establish measurements of expected performance results, and inform legislators on the appropriations committee that this is the department's interpretation of the legislative intent. Furthermore, the agency director should then inform these same legislators that such a decision also requires a commitment in resources to measure these outcomes and to report them back to the appropriations committee in subsequent hearings.

One of the best times to establish a commitment is at the beginning of a new governor's term of office. This allows the necessary two or three years of stability needed to put into effect the measurement of outcomes.

The current legislative appropriations hearings process is complex. Each of the legislators serving on the appropriations committee generally has a special interest program that needs his or her support during the course of the hearings. When this program is up for review, the legislator will become particularly attentive and may provide testimony to the committee regarding the importance of the program. This is the nature of the political process, and it also is the fundamental difficulty in lobbying for accountability. There is no vested interest group for better accountability. There are, however, many lobbying groups who have a strong interest in a program regardless of how accountable it is. More typically, only the chairperson, his or her staff, the department administration, and specific lobbyists are aware of most of the facts or the issues of the total budget. Other legislators do not have time to become knowledgeable about how every program operates; let alone what the outcome measure needs to be for accountability.

Members of the appropriations committees need to be better informed in order to have complete accountability. Each year, each department attempts to brief new and old members of the appropriations committees on the operations of the department. However, this is only a superficial review, at best. As long as there is no pressure on legislators to be accountable, there will be no pressure on state agencies to be accountable. The best way to establish state agency accountability is to limit or eliminate programs that cannot establish and measure client outcomes. This would be a bold and unprecedented action by legislators. This is unlikely to happen until the general public and the taxpayer demand it.

The legislators who are most important for true accountability are the chairpersons of the appropriations committees. The next most important are their staff members. Taxpayers must make personal contact with their legislators. Responsible legislators respond to letters, newspaper articles, and phone calls from members of their constituency. Individual citizens can make a difference by simply sending a letter to their representatives asking that he or she ensure that state agencies are held accountable by knowing what impact these services are having on clients. These citizens should demand that they be kept informed of his or her personal efforts to ensure that all tax dollars are being spent appropriately.

Legislators seldom get such letters and when they do, they will reply with a very general response that they, of course, agree with the writer and are looking out for the best interests of the taxpayer. Constituents should not settle for this type of response, and should ask their legislators specifically about *The Transparent Accountability Paradigm* and that he or she report back on how well the state agencies are performing by providing relevant benchmarks on progress. This will make a point. If a legislator receives ten such requests in a single year, he or she will be aware that constituents are monitoring his or her performance as their representative. This contact with legislators will have a very effective collective result in raising their public accountability consciousness.

The democratic legislative process is very time-consuming and detailed in its day-to-day operation. Good lobbyists spend most of their time providing valuable information to legislators. They stay abreast of the current laws, policies, and practices in their specific areas. They spend time, effort, and money to get to know the legislators personally. They provide convincing alternative arguments to legislators who rely upon them to provide quick and thorough analyses of the issues as they relate to the organization the lobbyist represents. In many cases, lobbyists appreciate the transparency and meaning of every vote involved in passing or defeating legislation. They act as paid extended staff of their clients and many legislators.

In contrast, the general public only realizes the implications of a law after it has been passed and has an effect on them personally. This is why a legislator pays so much attention to an unsolicited letter. They don't get that many of them, and view them as the potential tip of the iceberg. If they get ten or more of them on the same topic, they become very aware of the underlying issue. Unfortunately, most legislators do not have an effective mechanism of staying in touch with their constituents. It is most often a hit or miss proposition based on being as available as possible for local events or speaking engagements.

It is important for taxpayers to understand that they can create an external environment for better accountability. The way to ensure that legislators will consider outcome information in appropriating resources is to have a strong, effective lobbyist representing this perspective. In many states, there are a few public interest organizations (i.e., Common Cause, OMB Watch) that focus on representing taxpayers by advocating for outcome information as critical information for good decision-making during the appropriations process.

2. Has the Government Performance and Results Act (GPRA) of 1993, which required the collection of performance measures, increased accountability and transparency?

GPRA was important federal legislation for mandating performance measures, including program outcomes. After 18 years, however, there are only anecdotal examples of how these federal agencies have used these outcome measures to improve performance. There are significant examples of poor performance with such federal programs as the Federal Emergency Management Agency (FEMA) in 2006 following Hurricane Katrina in New Orleans and Mississippi. GPRA did not guarantee that FEMA would respond appropriately to this type of challenge.

The media, legislators, and the general public are largely unaware that performance information is mandated by GPRA and would probably be disappointed by the GAO finding that managers have not used the outcome information to improve programs. GRPA, for most managers of federal programs, is unfortunately only another reporting requirement for continued funding. The intent of GPRA was to force federal agency funding to be based, in large part, on performance measures. GPRA has not changed the need to include outcomes in appropriations bills and then make future funding decisions based on prior year's performance levels. David Osborne, co-author of *Reinventing Government,* understood this and reflected it in his testimony regarding GPRA in 1993:

> *Some of the lessons from abroad and from State and local government tell us that unless a legislature puts performance targets in its appropriation, they will never be taken seriously. You must force legislators who are appropriating money to define the outcomes that they want, and I don't think that is mandated in S.20...Unless it is done, the performance reports will sit on the shelf* (Osborne, D., 1993, p. 58).

Mr. Osborne, I believe, is correct—legislators need to designate outcome expectations for government programs and include them as part of the appropriations process at the federal state, and local levels. Improvements in programs must be linked to funding. Today, most programs receive continued or increased funding with remarkably little serious review of impact on clients or communities. GRPA has increased federal performance reporting requirements, but there is only limited evidence that most federal agency directors embrace using outcome information for purposes of making important personnel and resource decisions.

Barbara Dorf, a senior manager with the Housing and Urban Development Agency (HUD), is an exception. She mandates the collection of the Carter seven questions of accountability, as well as an estimated return on investment for many programs funded by HUD grants. The answers are available on a HUD Web site and she plans to use this information for making future grant award decisions. Barbara Dorf is a rare example of a federal bureaucrat who truly embraces the spirit of accountability mandated by GRPA.

3. Do agencies that value and use outcome information increase their outcome levels of performance?

Yes, but there are upper limits to agency program performance levels, just like in baseball. No matter how well a program is managed and how much resources are available, there are natural ceilings of excellence. Most outcome measures stay within a relatively narrow range. Fifty- to seventy-percent of Vergil's graduates of Maxey Boys Training School successfully avoided entering Michigan's adult prison within five years of release from the residential delinquency prevention program. Pressley Ridge graduates also experienced a relatively narrow range of success across a variety of measures across several years. Almost all programs have such bands of outcome success levels. It is remarkably similar to all sports outcome statistics. Regardless of the amount of money and resources available to sports franchises, the ceilings on success levels remain about the same.

No one realistically expects baseball players to attain Ted Williams' record year batting average of .406 (4+ hits out of every ten times at bat), let alone consistently stay at such a level over the course of several years or a career. Baseball team owners have extensive resources available to them to improve the batting performance levels of the team players. Regardless of these resources, they are unable to move above a relatively narrow band of success (.250-.350) with highly talented athletes. The 2007 steroid controversy was raised, in part, because Barry Bonds and Mark Maguire were approaching the home run record at an unprecedented rate of home runs late in their career when other baseball players historically waned in their final years. The suspicion of steroid use to enhance performance had credibility because of the long historical database that questioned the likelihood that players would increase their home run performance as they aged. The same is true in corporate success as measured by profit margins, return on investment, or yearly growth. Occasionally, a company like Microsoft may exceed expectations, but these high growth firms ultimately return to success levels of average companies. The best managed programs will achieve at the high levels of a limited band of success. It is important to know these bands and recognize when a program is achieving at the highest known level of success. There are limits to the American Dream that all things are possible.

4. What role should the media play in promoting government accountability and transparency?

The media (press, newspapers, radio, TV, and the Internet) could play a valuable role in covering government accountability and transparency. Many news programs like *Meet the Press, The News Hour* and *All Things Considered* probably perceive that they are performing this function of exposing poorly performing government programs (e.g., FEMA and its parent agency, the Homeland Security Administration) and disingenuous politicians. A major barrier to any focused and disciplined approach to any topic is the relatively short attention span of typical viewers who primarily want to be entertained as opposed to be educated.

The media could be enticed into coverage of the topic of accountability and transparency if the information is presented to them in the format that they can use given their programming format. This is the same challenge facing all advocates of a particular perspective. For example, during the election cycle for politicians, some media coverage includes checking facts presented by various candidates. The approach uses the University of Pennsylvania Annenberg Center's factcheck.org for this purpose. This is an excellent use of university resources to assure accurate information is used in political campaigns. Another important contribution by universities would be their objective review of the cost-effectiveness of current or proposed government programs.

The public receives information from many different sources—newspapers, magazines, books, ratio, television, friends/family, and the Internet. With the tremendous number of television channels and access to the Internet, the public has the opportunity to be influenced by a wide array of information and misinformation. Many people choose to receive information and opinions from specialized outlets (e.g., Rush Limbaugh radio show) targeted to their own set of values. They seek programming that reinforces their perspective. This tendency has probably always been the case. Most people do not want a balanced perspective. They want to have their current perspective validated and enhanced. Traditional news vehicles like newspapers, radio, and television have biases toward themes that allegedly increased their appeal and profitability. These biases include preferences for stories on:

- damage to the environment,
- sex, death, and scandal,
- government incompetence,
- big business greed,
- winning sports dynasties or underdog teams, and
- local human interest stories.

This formula for success is now being challenged as readership of newspapers has been steadily declining about 5% a year for the past several years, and the news audience for the three primary TV networks is splintering into the array of options available to viewers of cable TV and the Internet.

The news coverage of Hurricane Katrina in 2005 is a good example of the role of the media and how it needs to change to focus on transparency and accountability. Katrina largely destroyed New Orleans. The media focused on the Federal Emergency Management Agency's (FEMA) inability to evacuate stranded victims. This focus on FEMA missed the more important story of how the damage from Katrina could have been minimized by adequate infrastructure investments in levies that would have been adequate to withstand a hurricane of this magnitude. The damage to New Orleans was the result of a failure to invest in an adequate infrastructure, which should be high on the list of benchmarks that prioritizes taxpayers' expectations of government and politicians. The media missed the big picture for the short-term small picture of FEMA's inadequate response to damage that could have been avoided.

Federal and state public agencies like FEMA are often considered to be worthy of news coverage when there is a serious negative outcome. The media coverage of the 2007 fall fires in southern California did include positive coverage of FEMA's efforts as a result of this disaster. FEMA was portrayed as having learned useful lessons from the Katrina experience. This is a valuable lesson in how to clearly demonstrate outcomes to the media and public in the natural flow of events already being covered as opposed to a formal report on benchmarking and program outcomes.

The media prefer scandals and examples of how government has not performed effectively. In contrast, positive government outcomes have little appeal to news reporters. The following conversation provided great clarity for me about this bias. I called a *Detroit Free Press* political reporter because I was teaching an evaluation course for a Master's in Public Administration program of Western Michigan University. I wanted the reporter to come to my class to provide his perspective on the positive outcomes expected of public agencies. He refused to come. He said that positive outcomes are not newsworthy. The public expects the programs to be effective. What is newsworthy is when a public agency screws up; when there is a scandal or malfeasance or misuse of public funds. I asked him if he could ever envision a circumstance where he would write a story about a positive outcome of a public agency. He said "yes." And then he went on to describe a potential circumstance of a prison riot where the prison was burning and a state employee rescued prisoners at great personal risk. Even with this example, he qualified such coverage as a "maybe."

The opportunity to utilize these new communication options is available to all advocates of any perspective including accountability and transparency as vehicles to increase trust in government. There is no need to convince that reporter of the value of government. It is possible and, in some cases preferable, to go directly to the citizens. Cable television and the Internet provide an unprecedented opportunity for news, gossip, and everything in between. They are significant opportunities to better inform the critical mass of stakeholders necessary for any significant change in government accountability or the use of tax dollars.

At the local level in East Lansing, we have a cable channel that covers the City Council. A couple of meetings each year focus on the city's budget, which detail where the money is spent—schools, public works, and public safety. However, what we never get is how well the city is doing in delivering these services—crime rate, MEAP scores, cleanliness of streets, etc. There is no City Council meeting televised that shows the relative effectiveness of these services with comparable cities in Michigan or nationally. This would be a valuable way to provide balance to the sense of being a captive taxpayer with no choices except to pay more or less taxes.

5. What is the value and best use of client success stories?

Personal success stories are real examples of how programs can change the lives of clients and communities. The stories are filled with unexpected links between the many factors that cause change. The stories remind staff and stakeholders about the consequences of programs. There are many uses for success stories. Pressley Ridge used success stories from the follow-up interviews with graduates of Pressley Ridge to continuously train board members about the value of its intervention strategies and how individual kids were helped by the organization. Many programs use success stories to persuade legislators and faith-based foundations to continue or increase funding for their agencies. Staff members appreciate knowing these outcomes not just in terms of aggregate statistics, but rather on the specifics for unique clients they have helped. The stories provide valuable feedback to staff members who otherwise would never know the consequences of their efforts. There is a need to analyze these stories to profile the service combinations which cause success and to provide feedback for program design changes to benefit future clients.

In the absence of outcome information, program staff members tend to underestimate their success rates and are much harder on themselves than the outcome data demonstrates. I suspect that staff members are focused and trained to detect client problems and apply an unrealistic level of expectations for their clients' success. The clients, on the other hand, are much more reasonable in their expectations and appreciate the help more than the staff realizes. In short, clients are satisfied with their level of benefits from the programs, but staff members are not. Outcome information provides staff members valuable information about the results of their efforts.

A very practical way to understand the impact of programs is to create a "focus group" of previous clients. They are invited to share their experience of the program by answering a series of questions like:

- How did you hear about the program?
- What did you value the most about the program?
- How did the program help you?
- What would you recommend to improve the program?
- What factors outside the program were most influential in helping you attain your success? (e.g., friends, relatives, churches, and opportunities).

The "focus group" should be limited to 8-10 clients and all should be encouraged to participate. The sponsor of the focus group could be the agency in charge of the program or a neutral organization with no vested interest in a particular set of answers. This is a listening opportunity to hear from a group of previous clients. This feedback can provide valuable insights into how to improve a program. Previous clients are generally not shy about revealing their experience with a program. In some cases, it may be several months or years before it is evident to a client how a program had affected their lives.

HCAM used focus groups of families who had a relative as a resident in a nursing home. The purpose of the focus group was to get family feedback on *The Consumer Guide to Michigan Nursing Homes.* The families recommended ways to improve an earlier draft by enlarging the section on general information about Medicaid and Medicare eligibility criteria and coverage. They appreciated the comprehensive listing of all nursing homes by address and phone numbers so they could easily compare options available in their county. They also clearly indicated that they did not understand Omnibus Budget Reconciliation Act (OBRA) regulatory deficiency citations and did not want to understand this level of government oversight. Instead, they wanted a shortcut to knowing which deficiency was a "red flag" for poor quality care. They were most interested in how satisfied the families were with care and if they would recommend this nursing home to others.

An unexpected insight was their observation about the preoccupation of the nursing home staff with the perceptions of regulations rather than client and family perceptions of care. This feedback was helpful in regaining the most important focus on the customer.

6. Will outcome information limit the use of political party agendas as the basis of funding programs?

At this time, when there is heightened accountability and transparency in other institutions (airline security, churches, corporations, banks, and accounting firms), in the political arena, re-election trumps everything else—including program performance measures like impact and outcomes. Politicians learn early on that they are indebted to their political party for initial support and endorsement and ongoing direction during their political life as a candidate and a member of the legislative body. Political leadership sets the agenda and voting options for legislators to assure the best likelihood of continued or future power for their political party. This allegiance by individual politicians to the political party far outweighs any allegiance to their constituents. By representing the party's best interests, legislators believe that they are also representing the best interests of their constituents. The reason why the party has the highest priority is that political power is a zero-sum game. If one is in the majority, he or she has power. If one is in the minority, he or she has significantly less power.

Nationally, voters are either Republican (29%) or Democrat (31%) and the rest are independents, according to a Gallup poll (FoxNews.com, 2011). Many voters vote for a particular party rather than a candidate and, thus, believe in the dominance of the party over the individual politician. Thus, there is support for the practice of using the party caucus to be the dominant factor in determining political legislative votes including budget appropriations bills.

This approach to politics will continue until there is a critical mass of taxpayer constituents who can demand that political leaders use program outcome information as the basis for funding government programs. This is not a partisan issue. It is an issue of being good stewards of taxpayer resources. There will always be different political strategies preferred by Republican or Democratic administrations. Regardless of political sponsorship, the same question needs to be answered: did the investment in the program result in changes to the benchmarks? If the program outcomes indicate success, then the benchmark indicators should also reflect some indication of improvement. The need for accountability and transparency should transcend political party affiliation.

7. What is the appropriate timeframe to collect outcome information after a client has completed a program?

The appropriate timeframe for collecting outcome information depends upon the program's expected outcome. If an employment program expects that a successful graduate will obtain a job, then the appropriate timeframe could be set for three, six, or 12 months after release from the program. If the employment program expects the graduate to obtain and stay at this employment position for at least six months, then the follow-up timeframe would be six months after obtaining employment. A program like Head Start expects that the early intervention should prepare young children to be successful in school several years after completion of the program. Five years would be an appropriate timeframe to collect outcome information on Head Start children. Programs, like most other causal factors (e.g. parents, school, religion, peer groups, siblings) generally have a diminishing influence and ability to affect clients. The stronger the initial influence of any causal factor, the greater the likelihood that this factor will have an impact into the future. A residential program like Maxey Boys Training School has 24 hours a day for one-two years to have a strong imprint on young delinquent boys. Thus, a five-year timeframe to expect an outcome is appropriate. Most programs have much less opportunity to impact lives of clients and the contact with the client may only amount to a few hours per month for less than a year. A one year follow-up outcome timeframe after program completion is probably appropriate for most agencies.

There is always a difficulty in establishing a specific timeframe for an outcome as different clients have different imprints from a program's intervention and unexpected consequences may only become evident many years later. Nonetheless, most programs can obtain valuable information about their impact on the lives of clients and communities by collecting and analyzing outcome information regardless of the timeframe for collecting this information.

8. Could an outcome-based accountability approach to the SEC have prevented Bernie Madoff from using a Ponzi scheme to destroy $50 billion in savings from various investors?

Yes. The Securities and Exchange Commission (SEC) was provided credible and specific allegations of suspicious financial practices of Bernie Madoff. SEC chairman, Christopher Cox, acknowledged multiple agency failures for at least a decade to thoroughly investigate Madoff's operations (Berenson and Henriques, 2008). Madoff kept several sets of books, falsified documents, and lied to regulators. He outmaneuvered SEC investigators and misled investors who trusted him with their life savings. SEC needs to become more aggressive at detecting all forms of financial products that mislead investors (e.g., rating agency claims of risk, advertisement by brokers and investment advisors, return on investment estimates, system-wide risks from bundling mortgage loans into collateralized debt obligations, solvency of reinsurance companies to avoid a repeat of the circumstances that necessitated the bailout of AIG, credit default swaps, and performance measures for 401K plans).

The SEC needs an aggressive consumer advocate chair that will develop a *Consumer Reports*-type rating system at the point of purchase for all financial products. The SEC's aggressiveness level to detect misleading products needs to be greater than the financial firms' deception tactics. If individual brokers like Madoff are willing to lie, deceive, and steal billions of dollars, then the SEC staff auditors need to excel in detecting and protecting investors.

Bernie Madoff is the perfect example of an investment manager who was entrusted with individual life savings, charitable endowment funds, and pension funds. He was a member of exclusive golf courses and was actively engaged in philanthropic efforts to help various Jewish charities and educational institutions. He was trusted. He also was able to provide unusually high (10-18%) and consistent annual returns on his investments for decades. There were no down years like most investment options. He turned down some investors who wanted to place their savings with his firm. There was a sense of exclusivity about investing with his firm. Current investors with Mr. Madoff often recommended their friends as potential investors. Many of the investors shared a common Jewish culture, which reinforced their level of trust in Mr. Madoff and allowed him to be vague about how he actually was able to attain such a remarkable level of success. It was too good to be true, but everyone was winning.

Mr. Madoff was arrested on December 11, 2008 and charged with securities fraud. He estimated a loss of $50 billion to investors over many years. He had structured a Ponzi scheme based on using new investor funds to provide current investors with enhanced returns. This scheme can only survive if there are sufficient new funds available to continue the illusion of returns. In 2008, there were more clients leaving Mr. Madoff's investment firm than new clients. This run on the banks and other riskier investments was the result of dramatically lower housing values and high home foreclosure rates. Investors sought the security of U.S. Treasury bonds.

He used many strategies to establish and reinforce trust. He managed investor trust over several decades. These strategies are important because they illustrate the conditions under which otherwise reasonable people suspend an objective risk assessment by substituting proxy measures such as recommendations by friends or family. Often these proxy measures are highly reliable and used for successfully assessing other risks. The Madoff strategies for establishing trust included:

- the public disclosure of positive returns for investors for decades in both good and bad market cycles,
- the regular provision of printed documents for every client in order for them to track their personal account earnings,
- the prompt return of all funds to any client choosing to close their account or withdraw any funds at any time,
- the provision to Security and Exchange Commission auditors of sufficient information to prevent any sanctions, penalties, or negative consequences to his firm,

- high visibility and engagement in Jewish philanthropic fundraising and educational institutions in New York, Palm Beach, and Minneapolis,
- a charming, engaging, articulate, and self-confident personality who easily solicited investment funds from personal friends, acquaintances, and business associates who were willing to provide him with investment funds,
- the hiring of family members (brother, children, and their spouses) to expand his growth opportunities in countries throughout the world. This provided Madoff with an image as a family venture, another dimension of trust,
- a client list of prominent investors, who included highly visible and successful entrepreneurs and artists like Steven Spielberg, Mortimer Zuckerman (owner of The Daily News), Carl and Ruth Shapiro (owners of a sports team), and Jeffrey Katzenberg (artist), prominent Jewish charities and institutions of higher learning such as Yeshiva University and Tufts University, large investment funds such as the Abu Dhabi investment authority—a sovereign wealth fund in the Middle East—and numerous feeder investment funds. This array of investors provided an exclusive Hollywood-like dimension to the Bernie Madoff investment firm.

Bernie Madoff cultivated the appearance of trust by using very successful strategies to steal $50 billion from smart investors. There was no easily available benchmark for these investors to assess their investment firm because the Securities and Exchange Commission did not pursue investigating the firm even though it had credible allegations of potential fraud. The most obvious benchmark for savvy investors was the unusually high performance level of Madoff's investments in bad economic times when most investment firms were reporting much lower returns.

With fraudulent schemes, it is almost impossible to apply the usual checks and balances that ultimately uncover the deception. However, all investors with Madoff knew at some level that they were participating in a strategy that was very beneficial to them personally and chose to continue to believe in this unlikely scenario. When Madoff was confronted with questions about how he had been able to achieve more consistent returns than other investment firms, he became defensive and abrupt with the person questioning his explanation. Nonetheless, Madoff was successful because his Ponzi scheme required all the participants to continue to accept the basis of the scheme. It only was exposed when the money ran out and investors could not redeem their investment.

Madoff symbolizes the largest loss of savings in history by a high-risk investor community and a willing complicit set of investors who also hoped to gain financially. Thomas Freidman (2008), columnist for the *New York Times,* summarized it best:

> *I have no sympathy for Madoff. But the fact is his alleged Ponzi scheme was only slightly more outrageous than the legal scheme that Wall Street was running, fueled by cheap credit, low standards and high greed. What do you call giving a worker who makes only $14,000 a year a nothing-down and nothing-to-pay mortgage to buy a $750,000 home and then bundling that mortgage with 100 others into bonds—which Moody's and Standard and Poor's rate AAA—and then selling them to banks and pension funds the world over? That is what our financial industry was doing. If that isn't a pyramid scheme, what is?*

Similar strategies for cultivating trust have been provided throughout this book to illustrate how such deception is often undetected by stakeholders in government, schools, corporations and religious institutions. Stakeholders need to be much more aware of the basis for trust and to require all organizations to provide the necessary transparency and accountability to assure trust.

Chapter 11
Next Steps

This book describes a new social contract between citizens and government. It replaces the current system of government as an investment manager who never shares the results from his investment choices on behalf of the customer, the taxpayer. It replaces the current invisible government with a transparent sharing of progress measures. The benchmarks are defined by the public rather than negotiated by legislators who represent the best interests of political parties rather than the best interests of their constituents. The new contract is called *The Transparent Accountability Paradigm* and includes the following ten components:

1. Taxpayers want a government that works. They want a positive relationship between taxes and tangible program success.
2. Government programs should demonstrate a positive impact on citizens and communities they serve.
3. Government should share results with all stakeholders, including the public.
4. Results should be measurable, simple, realistic, manageable, and easily understood.
5. Results should be the primary basis for important resource decisions.
6. Program managers should maximize results.
7. Program managers should create results measures and obtain the necessary consensus/acceptance from various stakeholders.
8. Government should only fund programs that improve results and remove those that cannot.
9. Voters should elect leaders who demonstrate this level of accountability.
10. Voters should become better educated on the performance of government and communicate directly with their leaders about their "ask" of government.

Components of the new contract have emerged from a number of federal, state, and local initiatives to improve government performance by using an outcome-based accountability and transparency approach. A similar contract is being created between nonprofit organizations and their funding sources. Many of these demonstration pilots were voluntary experiments, requested by funders, or mandated by government.

This book provides an overview of these projects over a 30-year period from 1981-2010. During this timeframe, there have been several different Presidents from different political parties and major shifts in the control of the Senate and the House. The shift to outcome-based accountability and transparency has been uneven, relentless, and incomplete as there are only pockets of examples that meet the characteristics of *The Transparent Accountability Paradigm*. During the 1980s, most of the early experimentation was taking place in human services client outcome monitoring programs in state agencies (Pennsylvania, Texas, Michigan, and Colorado) and some local municipalities. The Urban Institute was the primary research and public policy coordinating agency for the state initiatives and the General Accounting Standards Board (GASB) for the city projects. Both the Urban Institute and GASB provided valuable leadership during this initial period and throughout the subsequent years. During President Clinton's administration (1993-2000), the focus shifted to the federal level with the passage of the Government Performance and Review Act (1993) and the General Accounting Office (GAO) in Washington, D.C. became much more visible in providing reports to Congress on federal agency performance. The GAO works for Congress as an independent, nonpartisan agency that investigates how the federal government spends taxpayer dollars. In 2004, the agency changed its name to the General Accountability Office.

During President Bush's administration (2001-2008), there was not much interest in outcomes except in the education reform legislation, No Child Left Behind, which established national learning achievement standards, required compliance testing, penalties for low progress results, and public disclosure of progress. This was clearly an attempt to measure outcomes. There was considerable controversy and opposition from school administrators and teacher unions concerning the difficulties in meeting the required accountability expectations. President Bush was also heavily criticized by the failure of the Federal Emergency Management Agency to effectively respond to the devastating consequences of Hurricane Katrina and the Security and Exchange Commission's failure to prevent the collapse of the housing and mortgage markets that led to the larger financial crisis in 2008. The Bush administration coordinated a taxpayer bailout of banks and insurance companies by significantly increasing the national debt to avoid another Great Depression. Both the responses to Hurricane Katrina and the financial crisis increased the public's perception that government is unable to protect its citizens and prevent major losses of lives, property, and savings.

President Obama, in his second day in office, pledged to provide a transparent government. He has initiated several projects that are largely unnoticed by the general public and apparently are of little interest to the media. His directives to the federal agencies reflect a commitment to targeted transparency that is helpful for consumers at the point of purchase. This is encouraging, and hopefully the new agency of consumer protection for financial services will reflect a focus on reducing risks for investors. His major legislation has been an economic stimulus package and an expansion of access to health insurance coverage. Both may have positive outcomes, but there has not been enough time to know the results. A slow recovery with high unemployment levels is expected to continue for many years (Cooper, 2011).

In 2010, there was a large oil spill off the coast of Louisiana as a result of an explosion of a deep-water oil well that spilled oil into the Gulf of Mexico for months until it was finally sealed in August 2010. The oil spill was a serious threat to vegetation, fish, and tourism and once again showed the failure of federal regulation to effectively protect the quality of life for American citizens. A commission that reviewed the causes of the oil spill concluded in January 2011 that all three companies involved in the spill (British Petroleum, Transocean, and Halliburton) took unnecessary risks. All three companies are currently operating oil wells in every offshore field in the world *(Economist,* 2011).

The commission concluded that the poor management and communication within and between these companies demonstrated a systemic failure of the off-shore oil drilling industry and recommended the creation of a new, independent safety regulator. The Obama administration has continued its commitment to off-shore drilling.

One of the most promising opportunities for the current administration is in the educational achievement grants awarded in 2010 to several states for Race to the Top demonstration projects. The outcomes will not be known for several years.

Finally, one of the best appointments of President Obama is Elizabeth Warren as his advisor on regulating financial products like mortgages to better inform and protect consumers from incomplete, confusing, fraudulent, and misleading information from banks, investment brokers, mortgage lenders, and other financial institutions. She best represents a professional transparency advocate with potential power to effectively represent the best interests and protection of consumers. Ms. Warren, a former Harvard law professor, recognized the dangers of the mortgage crisis and, in 2007, recommended the creation of a consumer protection agency for financial products. She led the Congressional watchdog panel charged with overseeing the Troubled Asset Relief Program (TARP). She clearly recognizes the need for accountability and transparency and provides a visible example of a program manager committed to accountability and transparency in government. President Obama validated his commitment to transparency by hiring agency directors and advisors like Elizabeth Warren.

This rich 30-year history provides many examples of how to structure an outcome-based accountability system, how to communicate performance information to citizens, how to engage the public in defining the "ask" of government, and the failure of political parties to set a nonpartisan legislative progress agenda for all Americans. There is no national contract for its citizens. There is only a Republican or Democratic agenda that is not necessarily followed once legislators are elected. A national agenda would be similar to the North Carolina benchmark categories of:

- healthy children and families,
- safe and vibrant communities,
- quality education for all,
- high performance environment,
- prosperous economy, and
- modern infrastructure.

Oregon had a vision similar to North Carolina and reached a consensus of its benchmarks in a simple way: Oregon asked its citizens to define their expectations for progress. It was a way to define its preferred future and to clarify the "ask" of government to help create that future. The vision, Oregon Shines, has been clear and unchanged for twenty years. These priorities are unlikely to change as most citizens want the same outcomes. This is reflected in the similarity across states that have defined their progress criteria.

No state has asked legislators or political parties to agree on the vision. No vision has 100% agreement among its citizens.

Oregon held town hall type meetings with its citizens to define the vision. A similar approach could be used to set a national set of benchmarks by simply asking its citizens to define their preferred future. National research firms that conduct opinion polls on a regular basis select a random sample of approximately 2,800 citizens to get a reliable estimate (+/- 2.5%). Such a study could be conducted relatively easily and without much expense. The results could be the "ask" of government. I suspect the results would be similar to Oregon, North Carolina, Minnesota, Utah, and Virginia's benchmarks.

The list could even be prioritized so that the national expectations of the citizens are crystal clear to the elected leadership. Such a list provides focus for legislators, media, voters, and the public. For this type of direct democracy to be effective, citizens would need some way to know if progress was being reflected in improved benchmarks and, if not, to elect new leaders who could affect the outcomes. Otherwise, as long as progress was reflected in improved benchmarks, the legislators could remain in office. This is basically a Total Quality Management approach to effective political leadership.

Legislators from different parties will advocate for the best programs to achieve benchmark improvements (e.g., less or more government, less or more regulation, less or more free enterprise, public versus charter schools, bigger or smaller class size). However, with a national scorecard, everyone will share the same truth about the progress measures. For example, in educational achievement, the test scores for grade three students in reading, math, and science will either go up or down or remain unchanged. The conclusion will be clear as to the effectiveness of the programs. Such an exercise can be conducted retrospectively by reviewing past educational achievement scores over the past 30 years (see the chart in the previous chapter). The review indicates that there has been almost no change in achievement scores. All the debate and rhetoric regarding teaching strategies (small class size, busing program, teacher salaries and benefit structure, charter schools, No Child Left Behind) had no effect on progress while many other industrialized countries have improved their scores and have higher scores than students in the United States. We have much to learn from such leading countries as Singapore, Canada, Finland and parts of China (Shanghai).

Transparency alone does not lead to progress. Transparency of targeted outcomes is necessary to motivate citizens and leaders to find effective programs. For decades, educators have known the low achievement levels for schools but have not found effective solutions. Demonstration projects of successful education experiments on a large scale (Harlem and Washington, D.C.) may provide the basis for national practices for the entire nation.

The same situation characterizes the U.S. health care system. It is twice as expensive and has lower health outcome levels than many other industrialized countries. The transparency of outcomes has been clear for many years. Effective solutions have been identified—Pronovost, Mayo Clinic, and Intermountain Healthcare are salient examples—but never mandated or voluntarily adopted by health systems throughout the U.S. During the health care reform debate, editors of the *New York Times* proposed a simple way to save tens of billions of Medicare dollars by simply mandating practices used by the Mayo Clinic (April 10, 2010). The most recent health reform legislation, the Patient Protection and Affordable Care Act of 2010, provided an opportunity to implement a strategy to reduce costs and improve patient outcomes. Neither outcome happened. The legislation increased the number of citizens covered by some type of health insurance. There was not sufficient collective political leadership to establish criteria for either cost containment or improved outcomes and there was no clear "ask" of the public to do this.

The public's anger with divisive political dialogue and failure to effectively respond or prevent crisis has dramatically lowered favorable opinion of members of Congress from a 1985 level of 67% to a 2010 level of 25% (Pew, 2010). The reasons given by respondents for such low ratings were:

- not careful with government money,
- influenced by special interests,
- overly concerned about their own careers,
- unwilling to compromise, and
- out of touch with regular Americans.

Other institutions are also receiving low ratings on having "a positive effect on the way things are going in this country." The results indicate the following hierarchy of institutions with a perceived positive effect:

- 71% small businesses
- 68% technology companies
- 63% churches/ religious organizations
- 45% Obama administration
- 33% entertainment
- 32% unions
- 31% federal agencies
- 31% news media
- 25% large corporations
- 25% federal government
- 24% Congress
- 22% banks and financial institutions

This book defines a two-step process for getting the country moving to the preferred future. The two steps include a continuous transparent monitoring of consensus outcomes, and a relentless testing of new programs to find the most effective options that are then mandated at a statewide and ultimately a national level. This is the essence of this book.

Unfortunately, the public has defaulted to the political parties the responsibility to define the preferred future. Politicians are intensely loyal to their political party. They represent the political party. They are elected by their constituents but are indebted to the party. The party does not vote, but the party supplies some of the money to convince constituents to vote. In most cases, politicians are re-elected based on the support of their party's agenda. If a politician chooses not to be loyal to their party, it is highly likely that they will not have alternative financial support to be re-elected.

Political parties are certainly not the only reason many lawmakers have a powerful incentive to vote against the public interest. In fact, the influence of political parties has been waning for several decades, replaced by the influence of powerful special interests.

Since the 1980s, vested interest groups (labor unions, corporations, lawyers, health organizations, single- issue groups) have had a significantly greater impact on the ability of political parties to frame issues and enact legislation. At best, it is a shared power to distribute appropriations and pass legislation. In some cases, like the success of financial institutions to deregulate the government's oversight of the financial markets, it appears as if the vested interest groups have the ability to set and enforce their preferred legislative agenda with huge negative consequences for the public.

One important way vested interest groups contribute to political campaigns is through three different types of Political Action Committees (PACs): Connected PACs (4,600 in 2009) representing businesses, labor unions, trade groups, health organizations; Non-connected PACs (1,594 in 2009) representing groups with ideological missions, single-issues, members of Congress, and other political leaders; and Independent-expenditure only committees, dubbed Super PACs, representing wealthy individuals, corporations, unions, and other groups for direct attack initiatives, but that cannot coordinate their efforts with either candidates or political parties. Super PACs are relatively new entities resulting, in part, from a 2010 Supreme Court ruling that lifted many spending and contribution limits.

The top ten PAC contributors from 1988-2010 illustrate the specific interest groups and their spending:

1. American Federation of State, County and Municipal Employees ($39,947,843)
2. AT&T ($39,772,431)
3. National Association of Realtors ($33,280,206)
4. Goldman Sachs ($29,588,362)
5. American Association for Justice ($29,520,389)
6. International Brotherhood of Electrical Workers ($28,733,734)
7. National Education Association ($28,388,334)
8. Laborers' Union ($26,881,889)
9. Service Employees International Union ($26,719,663)
10. Carpenters and Joiners Union ($25,995,149)

PAC contributions are primarily distributed by 17,000 lobbyists in Washington who meet regularly with government agency and political leaders to represent the preferences of the various vested interest groups. Legislators try to balance the interests of constituents, political parties, and vested interest groups. It is reasonable to conclude that legislators are not representing the best interests of the public as demonstrated by the low favorable rating (26%) and the opinion by 80% of the public that the country is going in the wrong direction.

Successful politicians understand this concept. They quickly see that loyalty to those who fund their campaigns is far more important than whatever the constituents believe or want. Politicians and the media that cover political events believe that politicians have a monopoly on preferred futures and effective ways to get there. They are the only source of defining a preferred future, and voters need to choose from the options generated by politicians. Citizens are limited to being audience members. The media appreciate the debate because there is always a story about the Republican versus the Democratic solution. The benefit for the media is the endless discussion about the next election. Unfortunately, there is no good alternative set of nonpartisan benchmarks and effective programs to affect the progress measures.

However, as this book argues, there is an alternative to this "solution" monopoly. An alternative way for citizens to discuss a preferred future and the best ways to attain that future is to create a set of national benchmarks and best solutions. This forum would be operated like Wikipedia in that once the benchmarks are set, everyone has an opportunity to offer the best solutions and provide the best supporting information to convince other citizens about the value of a given solution. A good example would be the benchmark for health care costs. A solution would be that hospitals follow a five-step process to reduce infections (Pronovost, et al., 2006). This would require the active participation of health providers, research organizations, advocacy forums (e.g., Commonwealth Fund, Henry Kaiser Foundation, and the Robert Wood Johnson Foundation), and health reporters.

This forum would constantly be updated by individual contributions until there is a strong base to support the best solutions to improve any given benchmark. The best solutions could be constantly available for implementation at the local, state, and national level. Such best practice solutions could be submitted from countries around the world (especially those that far exceed U.S. performance levels). Americans are unaware of, and do not quickly adopt, obvious effective solutions like Canada's universal coverage for health insurance and services. It has taken twenty years for the American auto companies to adopt the

Toyota Total Quality Management approach to improving car performance and reliability. The erroneous belief within General Motors that it was the best auto company in the world prevented its management from admitting that there was a better way to build cars. Similar denials by Republican House Speaker John Boehner that America has the best health care system in the world becomes a barrier to adopting best practices from other countries to improve outcomes and become a more cost effective health system.

A Look into the Future (2011-2020)

Oregon and North Carolina have been the leading states in their use of benchmarking performance. Unfortunately, both states have decided to abandon this strategy. North Carolina dropped its funding at the end of 2006 because it did not provide a favorable view of state government. Oregon's benchmarking was not funded for the 2009-10 biennium. The last available North Carolina information is included in Appendix A. Virginia and Utah have recently introduced a benchmarking strategy. The next ten years will probably include an extended period of high unemployment and pressures on state and local governments to reduce expenses, one of which may be to reduce their commitments to benchmarking as a strategic component for investment decision-making. Most of the important benchmarking measures are long-term indicators of broad trends (unemployment rate; poverty rates; obesity levels; and educational achievement scores for reading, math, and science), and they are difficult to affect. It is common to observe only small changes in comparing annual benchmark measures. For example, the mean family income in Michigan for the past 60 years has shown small annual changes, but a consistent pattern of trending down since the 1950s. Nonetheless, some states recognize the importance of benchmarking and are willing to invest in this approach to planning. For example, Michigan, a state with one of the highest unemployment rates, elected a new Governor in 2010, Rick Snyder, who released in January 2011 the MiDashboard, a benchmarking strategy in five key areas.

Although benchmarking takes place in specific states and local communities, there is no national comparison between states. In Chapter Two, I suggested that there was a need for a competition between states that would be like a baseball league where states would compete with each other across a common set of performance measures. This could be created by using the North Carolina benchmark measures and compiling similar statistics for each state and ranking the results so that the highest ranking states are recognized as doing something special to achieve such outstanding outcomes. They, in turn, could share the best practices so that all states could learn from their successes. For example, Massachusetts is considered an excellent state for educational achievements. Such a project may require a partnership with a foundation, a research organization (e.g., Pew Foundation, Urban Institute), and a state coordination entity like the National Committee of State Legislatures or the National Council of States. At the national level, the best benchmarking would be comparisons with other industrialized countries. This would require a similar set of partners and probably heavily rely upon the Office of Coordination and Economic Development (OCED) for much of the information. The result of such a project would compare measures of progress among countries over time.

The citizens of the United States are very familiar with the data that show the US losing ground to competing nations in the area of educational achievement and in health outcomes and cost effectiveness. These are important areas, because they are predictive of future economic challenges for full-employment and quality of life. This has been known for at least ten years. There is no sense of urgency to reverse these trends nor a willingness to make the necessary changes.

This book has outlined a way to transition from the current taxpayers' skepticism and cynicism of politicians and government to a very different world where government is perceived as accountable, transparent, and contributing to the public good. This, in turn, leads to trust in government by taxpayers. Those who believe that this strategy should be part of our preferred future need to help implement this approach at the local, state, or federal level. Transparent and outcome-based accountability in government and nonprofit organizations is possible and does exist in a small number of cities, states, and within the federal government. These initiatives have made major contributions to developing the most effective ways to implement this preferred future. They provide a broad outline to guide all citizens. The details are available but are not widely known to the mainstream media and general public. An excellent example is the United Way (Hatry, van Houten, Plantz, & Greenway, 1996; United Way, 2000; United Way, 2011).

There is no grand scheme or strategic plan to implement *The Transparent Accountability Paradigm.* There are individual initiatives by taxpayers, citizens, voters, cities, states, and the federal government. It is the collective effort that will enhance the public good. There are many resources available at each level of change. Some of these examples have been illustrated in various chapters of this book.

At the federal government level, the necessary legislation was enacted in 1993—the Government Performance and Review Act (GPRA) and it has been implemented. However, the annual performance reporting results have not been covered by the media and have not been used by politicians as the basis for appropriation levels. The general public is unaware that the legislation even exists. In the case of GPRA, the passage of the legislation has not led to a commitment to use the outcome information to determine funding. The "political will" does not exist to use performance data to make funding decisions. The legislation has basically resulted in more reporting requirements and not better informed decision-making or better use of program resources.

More visibility and engagement by citizens and government agencies have characterized the benchmarking initiatives at the state level and at the local community level. Such projects focus on historical changes to stable benchmark measures and attempt to identify programs that enhance the benchmarks. Once government can link specific program outcomes to improvements in benchmarks, then legislators can begin basing funding decisions on this type of information. There also will be important financial incentives for legislators, program advocates, and the press to cover such issues and educate the public investors regarding the results of their taxes.

Vergil Pinckney, Clark Luster, the Health Care Association of Michigan, and the United Way illustrate how program outcome information can be collected, shared, and used to improve programs. All three were possible without legislation. There are many ways to enhance transparency and accountability without legislative mandate and/or the lengthy process of convincing political leadership that taxpayers should be informed about the effectiveness of the programs they fund.

First, citizens should contact their mayors, state representatives, governors, commissioners, and members of Congress, and ask for their support in implementing this approach to politics and government. They should be clear about their "ask": to create benchmarks, link programs to these benchmarks, and provide program outcomes publicly so that taxpayers can be assured that their investment has resulted in positive impacts on citizens and their communities.

Most politicians will resist this type of commitment because their highest commitment is not to their constituents. It is to their political party and the vested interest groups that enable the political party to remain in power. All major decisions revolve around political party priorities. The power of the political party over legislators is in the distribution of "spoils" to legislators who are committed to the party. The "spoils" include:

- funding of election to office,
- funding for re-election,
- assignment to important committees,
- earmarks, and
- support of the party leadership of a legislator's proposed legislation.

Access to these spoils is dependent upon a legislator's willingness to accept the party's agenda and to cast votes according to the dictates of the party's leadership. If legislators choose not to adhere to the party's agenda, then there will be less of the "spoils" for them in the future.

The political party leadership's primary objective is to promote its party's agenda to assure future party control. If its public policy initiatives resulted in effective programs—outcomes impacting benchmarks—then there would be good reason for voter support. Unfortunately, both parties allege that their programs enhance the public good, are intrinsically good, and do not need to be evaluated by such measures as outcomes and benchmarks to assure the taxpayers that the programs are effective. For these politicians, it is a waste of resources to do so.

It is also a problem for politicians if their programs turn out to be ineffective. For example, the teenage sex abstinence program has been shown to have no impact on subsequent sexual activity for the participants as compared to a control group that did not participate (Trenholm, et al., 2007). Political supporters of this program now have a dilemma. They can:

- continue to fund an ineffective program,
- encourage the program to shift to a more effective approach, or
- not continue to fund the program.

The Transparent Accountability Paradigm focuses on funding effective programs based on outcomes, because this is the basis of good stewardship and Americans basically want their government to be effective. Americans want their government to work. Unfortunately, members of the public are constantly disappointed because their government does not voluntarily disclose an honest picture of the results of their tax investments. By default, the media willingly provide endless anecdotal examples of government not working effectively.

The benchmarks provide measures of progress, especially if they accurately provide a historical trend, so that the public can assess government and society's sense of being on the "right" path. With historical comparison points, it is relatively easy to detect changes in the benchmarks and to identify the impact of any new political initiatives designed to impact these benchmarks.

For example, President Clinton initiated welfare reform in 1996 by requiring employment of welfare recipients as a condition of continued eligibility (Temporary Assistance for Needy Families–TANF). This was presented as an anti-poverty program. Ultimately, this program was expected to lower the poverty rate. The poverty rate, however, has basically stayed in a relatively narrow range of 12-15% before and after the TANF legislation. Probably, there are more poor people working as a result of TANF but they remain in poverty. It is not obvious that such welfare reform has had an effect on the poverty level. TANF probably had an effect on lowering the unemployment rate. This legislation may still be good public policy because it encourages employment as an essential component of entering the middle class and emerging from poverty.

Neither Democrats nor Republicans have done a good job of demonstrating the effectiveness of their programs. There continues to be skepticism about proposed solutions. Many citizens do not understand the research basis for many of the proposed solutions, let alone decipher the "spin" used to interpret the results. University and public policy organizations do not clearly communicate their findings to the general public. Large newspapers have reporters who specialize in areas like science, education, and medicine who translate academic journal articles into useful advice for their readers. Most individuals will choose media options (books, newspapers, TV news channels, Internet sites, blogs, radio, and comedy shows) based on a conservative or liberal political persuasion. They are primarily interested in reinforcing their current preferences. Many voters follow this same commitment to a set of values and programs. All voters, regardless of political affiliation, need to become more aggressive by requesting accountability and transparency for continued support and re-election. The political party that most successfully accomplishes this responsible stewardship has a unique opportunity to appeal and secure the many voters who want solutions to problems like educational achievement, economic opportunity, infrastructure investments, drug-related crimes, teenage pregnancy, and alternative renewable energy sources.

There are many small steps politicians can take to begin this process:

- Politicians can tell the truth rather than be politically correct and "spin" the truth so that it is no longer an accurate description of the issue or event.
- Governors can create a progress board similar to the Oregon model so that benchmarks can be established for measuring the public good. This can be done in all states and should be done at the national level.
- Politicians can require outcomes for all new legislation as a way to begin accountability at the very first point of endorsement—the passing of new laws.
- Politicians and agency directors can require program outcome expectations so that everyone knows what is considered successful. GPRA (1993) was such legislation and it has been irrelevant to subsequent federal spending decisions. It is not sufficient to articulate and require outcome information as a reporting requirement. The decision of refunding programs must use the outcome information as the basis for the decisions. Politicians will not do this unless it is a clear direction from their constituents and from the leadership of their political caucus. A grassroots effort is necessary to continuously "ask" leaders to solve problems or lose voter support at re-election.
- Politicians interested in accountability can access valuable tools from the National Conference of State Legislatures (NCSL) and from the Governmental Accounting Standards Board (GASB). Other states and cities have

already designed model legislation that can be easily replicated and/or customized for all communities. It can be done and has been done with political leadership and a critical mass of interested citizens.

A second approach is to initiate or support transparency and accountability in one's own work environment, among one's friends on Facebook, as a submission to one's favorite blog or other media format. In addition, there are many opportunities for government and nonprofit organization employees and managers to establish this approach within their program area. The major benefit would accrue to workers themselves because they would begin to appreciate their own effectiveness level and how to become better at their job by measuring tangible results. There should be little fear of political consequences since most politicians, unfortunately, do not invest in this type of accountability.

A good example of initiating a transparency and accountability project is the recent interest by some hospitals (e.g., Johns Hopkins, Stanford, and the University of Michigan) to tell patients if there was a medical error in their case. On the average, one in every 100 hospital patients suffers negligent treatment, but only a small fraction press legal claims (Sack, 2008). The motivation for such a change was, in part, the high premiums for malpractice insurance based on a legal strategy of "deny and defend." Dr. Timothy B. McDonald, University of Illinois hospital's chief safety and risk officer, summarized the benefits of this approach: "I think this is the key to patient safety. If you do this with a transparent point of view, you're more likely to figure out what's wrong and put processes in place to improve it" (Sack, 2008. p. A17). The hospitals using this approach have experienced dramatic decreases in litigation expenses.

A third approach is to do something, no matter how small. If there are enough small efforts, there will become a critical mass of citizens (a tipping point) who encourage a new way of thinking and acting. Changing the expectations of government to be more transparent and accountable provides a foundation for larger changes. Doing nothing enables the current dysfunctional government. Like the global warming movement, there are many individuals making small personal changes (e.g., purchasing a small hybrid car) which may lead to increased awareness by others of the need to respond to the threat of global warming. Individual choices make our future one choice at a time. We can begin to make small choices now to create a more accountable and transparent government in the future. And we can accomplish this one person at a time.

North Carolina
Progress Board

North Carolina 20/20
Update Report

Issued by the North Carolina Progress Board
January 31, 2006

North Carolina Progress Board

January 31, 2005

The Honorable Michael Easley
Governor
State Capitol
20302 Mail Service Center
Raleigh, North Carolina 27699-0302

Dear Governor Easley:

Consistent with its statutory obligation to publish a North Carolina 20/20 Update Report this year, the North Carolina Progress Board is proud to issue the attached report.

This report reflects the rapid changes North Carolina is undergoing in its population and economy, and highlights the State's comparative standing in scorecard format for the eight imperatives previously identified as critical to the future wellbeing of the State. We will continue to update it on a regular basis as new data pertaining to our adopted goals and targets becomes available.

Progress has been mixed since we issued the NC 2020 Report in 2001, but, given the economic and fiscal constraints that the State faced, that is not surprising. While in a number of instances the data indicates that North Carolina is not where it would want to be, in those areas the state has emphasized as policy priorities, significant progress has been made (e.g. educational achievement and violent crime reduction).

We would like to express special thanks to the many state agency staff, faculty advisors and other individuals for their positive contributions to this report. The Progress Board hopes that this report will help public officials and citizens alike identify those areas where public policy initiatives are most needed.

As the Progress Board moves into the 21st Century with its newly adopted business model, it stands ready to work with the public and private sectors to collaboratively find creative ways in which to make North Carolina more globally competitive in the 21st Century.

Sincerely,

James Leutze
Interim Executive Director
North Carolina Progress Board

Campus Box 7248, Centennial Campus   919.513.3900 phone   Dr. James R. Leutze
1017 Main Campus Drive   919.513.3790 fax   Interim Executive Director
Suite 3900, Partners 1   www.ncprogress.org
Raleigh, NC 27695-7248

Table of Contents

The Transparent Accountability Paradigm

Preface

The North Carolina Progress Board was created to help anticipate change ... and enhance our state's competitiveness in a rapidly changing world.

North Carolina is undergoing rapid change — in its population, economy and natural resources. Of all the predictions for the future, only one seems certain. More change will come, and it will come with ever-increasing speed. As North Carolinians, our challenge is to anticipate these changes and identify ways to ensure our competitiveness in a rapidly changing world. The North Carolina Progress Board was created to help answer this challenge.

As part of its mission to set strategic targets for the state, and track our progress in achieving those targets, the North Carolina Progress Board presents the *2005 North Carolina 20/20 Update Report*. This report is intended to discharge one of the Progress Board's statutory duties—to report biennially on key performance trends and strategic issues that may shape our state's future. This report provides an interim update of the same indicators reported to General Assembly in 2001 as well as a graphic illustration of our redesigned scorecard system. We believe that the contents of this report, which can be found in more detail (updated with the most current data available) on the North Carolina Progress Portal (www.ncprogress.org), will interest everyone who is committed to making North Carolina the best state in the Southeast and, ultimately, the nation.

Who We Are

The North Carolina Progress Board serves as a strategic compass for our state—identifying critical issues, setting milestones, checking progress and recommending course corrections...

The North Carolina Progress Board serves as an independent proponent for strategic action and accountability. Specifically, our mission is to keep leaders and citizens alike focused on the big picture: the long-term goals and needs of our state and its people. This means serving as a strategic compass—identifying critical issues, setting milestones, checking progress, reporting data, recommending course corrections, and offering imaginative solutions to jumpstart change.

The General Assembly established the North Carolina Progress Board as a permanent entity of state government in 1995. Its 24 members are appointed by the governor, the leadership of the N.C. House and Senate, and the board itself. Over the next six years, the Progress Board worked with citizens, public officials and many others to elaborate on the vision first drafted by the Commission for a Competitive North Carolina. This effort culminated in 2001 with the *North Carolina 20/20 Report*, a comprehensive report describing the challenges facing the state and presenting goals and targets for improvement in eight issue areas.

Throughout this process and even after the release of the *North Carolina 20/20 Report*, the Progress Board sought to involve citizens in debating the state's priorities for the future. We met with community groups and spoke with legislative groups, local leaders and advocacy organizations. Our work showed us the deep commitment North Carolinians have for our state and the perplexity many feel about the state budget. In answer, the Progress Board in 2003 released *Our State, Our Money—A Citizens' Guide to the North Carolina Budget*, a guide explaining how budget decisions are made, sources and uses of money and how citizens can affect the process.

This year, the Progress Board is building the North Carolina Progress Portal, a new website ... with the most current ... public policy data available ...

This year, in addition to publishing the *North Carolina 20/20 Update Report*, the Progress Board is building the North Carolina Progress Portal, a new website designed to link public officials and citizens with the most current and relevant public policy and performance data available, including continual updates of this report. With the creation of this new website, the Progress Board takes another step toward providing citizens and leaders alike with informative and useful tools for decision-making.

North Carolina's Strategic Scorecard

The North Carolina Strategic Scorecard, newly updated, shows in quantifiable terms the direction in which the state is headed for the selected targets. It is designed to illuminate goals, track the progress of existing initiatives, and hold all of us accountable for results.

The North Carolina Strategic Scorecard—with 8 imperatives, 27 long-term goals and 84 strategic targets—is designed to track our progress ... and hold all of us accountable for results

Imperatives and Goals – The Scorecard framework is organized around our enabling statute's eight issues, which we call the imperatives due to their importance to North Carolina's future:

1. Healthy Children and Families
2. Safe and Vibrant Communities
3. Quality Education for All
4. A High-Performance Workforce
5. A Sustainable Environment
6. A Prosperous Economy
7. A Modern Infrastructure
8. Accountable Government

For each of the eight imperatives, we created a vision statement with broad goals for achieving each vision. There are 27 long-term goals (the goals are stated in the Overview sections of each imperative).

Strategic Targets – For each goal, we developed quantitative measures for tracking our progress toward reaching the goal. For each measure, we identified a strategic target for determining where North Carolina should be at the year 2020. We imposed tough criteria for selecting these targets, including credibility, data availability, historical trends and comparative state rankings. The North Carolina Strategic Scorecard now has 84 strategic performance targets for measuring the state's progress, but these targets will no doubt be refined as new data becomes available.

For each target, we note the measure, target, actual performance, national rank, regional rank, definition and data source. In the future, we will assign a letter grade to summarize our state's overall performance ...

Scorecard Format – For each target, we employed a standard format for presenting data. In the left column, we stated the measure, target, actual performance, grade (to be assigned later), national (US) rank, regional (Southeast) rank, target definition and data source. The national rank compares North Carolina to all 50 states (where 1 is the best rank and 50 is the worst) and the regional rank compares our state to the other states of the Southeast Region (where 1 is the best rank and 10 is the worst). In the right column, we briefly described NC's historical performance and competitive ranking for the specific target, provided a chart illustrating the historical performance trend, and (below the chart) presented highlights of supplemental information related to the target. More information will be added in future report updates.

Grades – In the future, we will assign a letter grade (A, B, C, D or F) to summarize our state's overall performance for each target. Once we have completed an independent review of our new grading methodology, we will re-issue this report with grade assignments. In the months and years ahead, we will continue to solicit input on this methodology and refine it as needed to ensure its fairness and objectivity.

Southeast Region – We defined the Southeast Region as encompassing the following ten states: Alabama, Florida, Georgia, Kentucky, Mississippi, North Carolina, South Carolina, Tennessee, Virginia and West Virginia.

Since there is no universally accepted scheme for determining which states should be in which regions, we defined the Southeast region using several criteria, including shared borders, proximity to North Carolina, geographic compactness and compatibility with existing federal regional structures (e.g., the Federal Reserve, Bureau of Economic Analysis, Department of Health and Human Services, Environmental Protection Agency, Transportation Department and FBI).

[1] We considered 14 states for the Southeast region: Alabama, Arkansas, Delaware, Florida, Georgia, Kentucky, Louisiana, Maryland, Mississippi, North Carolina, South Carolina, Tennessee, Virginia and West Virginia.

197

The Strategic Scorecard always will be a work in progress ... and, as we obtain new ... data, it will become a durable framework for assessing our state's competitiveness

Public Input – The most valuable strategic targets are those that best reflect the values and aspirations of all citizens. We did not develop the Strategic Scorecard on our own. Through the years, it has involved thousands of people: citizens across the state, civic leaders, policy makers, representatives of advocacy groups, and public policy specialists. They gave us their ideas, telling us what they thought was important and why. As we receive more input, we will continue to refine the Scorecard and shape it to the state's long-term needs.

Upcoming Enhancements – The Strategic Scorecard always will be a work in progress. We will need new goals to meet new challenges. We will refine targets and add new targets as we look further into the future and reassess what truly needs to be accomplished. We will modify those targets for which our public policies and investments produce desired outcomes. In the coming months, as resources permit, we will obtain, validate and analyze new, relevant data for our targets and update the Strategic Scorecard.

How We Are Doing

The Strategic Scorecard is designed to provide long-range milestones for assessing our competitiveness as a state, not to assess the term of any one Governor or General Assembly. In fact, by their very nature, the targets are long-range. They usually defy quick fixes, calling instead for bold, thoughtful and bi-partisan policy initiatives that span multiple administrations and legislative sessions, and need local government, business and non-profit collaboration.

Taking the long view...North Carolina has come a long way [but] the race is just beginning....

Taking the long view, it is beyond dispute that North Carolina has come a long way. In 1880, just as the US was overtaking Great Britain as the world's most efficient economy, North Carolina lagged way behind other states. A recent historical analysis of state economic productivity trends (Mitchener and McClean) concluded that, "Labor productivity in the least productive state (North Carolina)" was less than 25 percent of the most productive states (e.g., California and New York), similar to today's productivity gap between "developed and developing economies." In 1900, North Carolina had the highest illiteracy rate in the South and one of the highest in the nation. As C. Vann Woodward wrote in *Origins of the New South*, "Starting further behind than almost any other state, North Carolina began her [educational reforms] earlier" and emerged as the most prominent example of the South's "great educational awakening."

Since the Great Depression and World War II, our state has emerged from the economic and social backwater to become one of the fastest-growing states in the nation. And there are many reasons for our popularity as a place to live and work. Our economic potential, particularly in new, technology-fueled industry segments, is widely respected. Our public system of higher education remains the envy of the Southeast, and many other states throughout the country. Our public K-12 education system is making remarkable strides. Our state government has demonstrated an unshakeable commitment to improving our air and water quality. Our state and local governments enjoy a well-deserved reputation for sound fiscal stewardship.

Unforeseen events ... and an economic downturn ... made it difficult to achieve significant progress ...

Nevertheless, in this era of mounting global competition, breathtaking innovation and relentless economic upheaval, North Carolina cannot rest on its laurels. Too many other states are poised to overtake us, by making the requisite investments in health care, education, workforce development and infrastructure. And more and more countries want what we have, and are prepared to set ambitious goals and make enormous economic (and social) investments to achieve those goals. The race is not over, it is just beginning, and it will be won by those nations, states and communities that commit themselves to bold goals and strategies.

Where are we today? Since we issued the *North Carolina 20/20 Report*, North Carolina's progress toward its long-range targets has been mixed. Given the state's fiscal challenges the last four years, this is not surprising. After making some big investments and reducing many taxes during the 1990s, we were stunned by unforeseen events, including costly hurricanes and court rulings, and an economic downturn. Since 2001, state officials have scrambled to balance the annual budget, but fiscal constraints have significantly impaired their ability to make the kind of strategic investments that many leaders would like to make.

In the face of economic setbacks, we have maintained our competitive position for the race ahead...[but] we have a great deal of work to do to make our state a national—and global—leader...

Since 2000, profound changes in our economic landscape, including plant closures, worker dislocations and the virtual disintegration of some of our most cherished industries, have made it much tougher to maintain the progress we made during the 1990s. All of our strategic goals and targets are inter-related, but the importance of a prosperous economy cannot be understated. We all want good health care, safe neighborhoods, quality schools, pristine air and water, modern infrastructure and effective government, but our ability (and willingness) to pay for them is often a function of economic prosperity. That is, we are less inclined to pay for investments in our future without good jobs and plentiful tax resources.

How have we fared so far in the 21st century? The good news is that, in the face of jarring economic setbacks, we have hung in there and, more importantly, maintained our competitive position for the race ahead. The bad news is that our competitive standing is still not where it needs to be for most of our strategic indicators. As summarized by the text box below, we have many achievements of which we can be proud, but we also have a great deal of work to do to make our state the national—and global— leader we all want it to be.

Highlights of North Carolina's Recent Strategic Progress

1. **Healthy Children and Families** — Poverty continues to plague too many children. We are living longer in a state with strong medical resources, but a smaller portion of us have health insurance coverage and many health problems (e.g., smoking and obesity) persist.
2. **Safe and Vibrant Communities** — Our violent and property crime rates have plummeted over the last ten years, but our crime rates--especially property crime rates--remain high compared to other states in the nation and Southeast. Our homeownership rate remains stable and average housing costs in NC are lower than in many other states.
3. **Quality Education for All** — Our standardized reading, math and SAT scores continue to improve, but our public high school graduation and dropout rates remain unacceptable. Despite fiscal pressures, our higher education system still offers good access and quality.
4. **A High-Performance Workforce** — Our aggregate high school and college attainment rates are improving, yet remain relatively low for the nation and mediocre for the Southeast. Our workplace safety record continues to lead the nation and region.
5. **A Sustainable Environment** — Our air quality, as measured by the number of ozone exceedance days, is showing signs of improvement due in part to new air pollution controls and an expanded vehicle inspection program. Our drinking water quality, as measured by the public water system violation rate, merits serious attention.
6. **Prosperous Economy** — Our state appears to have regained its short-term economic momentum and our business climate continues to earn high marks, but concerns about global outsourcing and other factors that could increase unemployment linger.
7. **Modern Infrastructure** — Our transportation system continues to compare poorly to systems in other states in terms of such factors as average annual vehicle miles traveled per vehicle, average commute times and congestion. Our electricity and natural gas costs are surprisingly high compared to the rest of our region. However, we are making impressive strides in increasing private and public access to technology.
8. **Accountable Government** — Our state and local tax revenue ratio (taxes as a percent of personal income) is the 20th lowest in the nation and 6th lowest in the Southeast. Our per capita state and local government debt, while rising, remains relatively low.

North Carolina has made progress in some areas and lost ground in others.

As discussed in more detail in this report, North Carolina has made progress in some areas and lost ground in others. As of 2005, we have already attained 12 of our strategic targets for 2020, including those for violent crime, math proficiency, classroom resources, short-term economic growth, economic climate and government stewardship. We are making progress toward attaining several other targets, including child health care, reading proficiency, teacher recruitment, air quality, and technology access. For other strategic targets (e.g., health insurance coverage, high school graduation, higher education access, drinking water quality, manufacturing vitality and transportation efficiency), we have actually lost ground or failed to make real progress toward our targets.

As we are reporting on only 48 of our 84 approved targets, this is only an interim progress report. In many areas, we have no new data or are in the process of obtaining new data from federal agencies and other reliable data sources. For many goals, we are working with state agencies and other entities to develop more relevant measures and targets. For these strategic targets, we have indicated in the progress summary charts introducing each imperative that our update work is still in process.

No individual measure truly stands alone. The state's performance in one measure is often a function of its performance on another. All of our goals, measures and targets are part of a larger inter-related framework. Income is in part a function of educational attainment and workforce training. Many economic sectors, not just tourism, benefit from well-preserved natural resources. Healthy lifestyles affect employee productivity and government costs. We encourage all citizens to view the individual indicators in the context of the entire strategic scorecard.

During the last five years, we have experienced strategic gains and setbacks. We have withstood hurricanes, profound economic shocks and acute budget shortages. We are still standing, but we all know that we cannot stand still. We should note our resilience, set our sights higher and renew our commitment to a more prosperous future. Make no mistake, the future will have winners and it will have losers. The winners of global competition will be those who set a clear strategic course and make smart investments in the future, even during tough times.

The winners of global competition will ... set a clear strategic course and make smart investments in the future, even during tough times.

Overview of Progress

Our Vision

Families and individuals of all ages will thrive in North Carolina. From early childhood well past retirement, our citizens will be mentally and physically fit, with no significant differences in health across racial, ethnic, or geographic lines. Our most vulnerable citizens will be supported by strong families.

Our Goals

1. Foster financial self-reliance
2. Encourage healthy lifestyles
3. Ensure access to good health care services
4. Sustain stable & nurturing families

As summarized in the table below, North Carolina has realized mixed progress toward its long-range targets for this imperative. Poverty continues to plague too many of our children. We are living longer and we offer our citizens an impressive array of medical resources in many parts of the state. However, a smaller share of us have health insurance coverage than before and too many of us remain plagued by health problems, such as smoking and obesity.

Summary of Strategic Progress—Healthy Children & Families

Goals	Measures	Target	US Rank	SE Rank
1. Foster financial self-reliance	1. Child poverty		34th	2nd
	2. Family income		40th	6th
	3. Elder poverty	(Update in process)		
2. Encourage healthy lifestyles	1. Longevity		37th	3rd
	2. Weight		33rd	3rd
	3. Smoking		34th	4th
	4. Substance abuse	(Update in process)		
3. Ensure access to good health care services	1. Health insurance		34th	7th
	2. Primary care access		12th	2nd
	3. Child health care		4th	1st
	4. Mental health care	(Update in process)		
4. Sustain stable & nurturing families	1. Family stability	(Update in process)		
	2. Child neglect	(Update in process)		
	3. Domestic abuse	(Update in process)		

Note: Measures for which we have met or exceeded the target are marked with a "check" under the Target column. Measures for which we are awaiting new data are marked "update in process" and will be updated as new data becomes available.

Over the years, our elected officials have adopted several policies that advance the long-term goals for this imperative, including the following:

- Offer broader Medicaid coverage for children, pregnant women and the elderly than is required by federal law, and one of most comprehensive programs in the region;
- Created the *NC Health Choice for Children* plan to help working families obtain free or reduced price comprehensive health care for their children;
- Created the Community Care program to coordinate all services required by Medicaid clients (e.g., social services and hospital care);
- Provide vaccines for all children through 18 years of age (a universal vaccine state);
- Support child development with more developmental screening, referrals (as needed) and well child care visits;
- Established the NC Senior Care program to help older adults offset prescription drug costs for certain illnesses (e.g., diabetes, heart ailments and chronic lung disease);
- Encourage businesses to expand health care insurance by offering tax incentives to companies with health insurance plans for employees; and
- Enacted the Mental Health Reform to modernize our mental health system and create the Mental Health Trust Fund.

Federal efforts to shift Medicaid costs to the states have forced many states to cut benefits, a course largely resisted in NC. Many of our health care issues demand national solutions. For instance, improving health care insurance coverage will require concerted federal and private action. In the absence of meaningful federal reforms, North Carolina and other large states may have to lead efforts to spur collaborative health care initiatives with the private sector.

The state's progress on individual goals and measures for this imperative is discussed in more detail on the pages that follow.

The Transparent Accountability Paradigm

Goal — Foster financial self-reliance

Measure: Child Poverty

Target:
At least 90% of children live above poverty line

Actual: 82%

US Rank (2003): 34th

Southeast Rank (2003): 2nd

Definition: Percent of children aged 0–17 living in families below the federal poverty level which varies by family size (e.g., in 2003, it was $12,015 for a two-person family and $18,810 for a four-person family)

Source: US Census Bureau, American Community Survey, and Poverty Status by State

Notes: The federal poverty level does not account for geographic differences

Since 1994, the percent of children living above the poverty line in NC has not significantly changed. However, since 2000, NC's national ranking for this measure has improved to 34th and its regional rank, while fluctuating considerably, has improved from 7th to 2nd.

Percent of children living above the poverty line

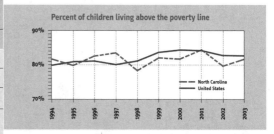

Poverty indicators for the general population provide added context for the child poverty trends shown above. In 2004, NC's three-year average poverty rate for all citizens rose from 13.1% to 14.2%. In 2004, NC had relatively fewer welfare recipients per 10,000 population than most states—only the 41st most in the US and 7th most in the SE region. In 2003, 8.6% of NC households received food stamps. Since the mid-1990s, immigration, especially the influx of poor, unskilled and unauthorized immigrants, has contributed significantly to NC's poverty levels. According to the Pew Hispanic Center, in 2004, NC had the 8th highest share (and one of the fastest-growing populations) of undocumented immigrants in the US.

Measure: Family Income

Target:
At least 100% of US average median household income

Actual: 88%

US Rank (2003): 40th

Southeast Rank (2003): 6th

Definition: Three-year average of median household income where household income includes the income of the householder and all other persons 15 years old and over in the household.

Source: US Census Bureau, American Community Survey

Notes: Average or median household income is usually less than average or median family income because many households consist of only one person.

After rising gradually through the 1990s, NC's median household income has leveled off since 2000 and fallen as a percent of the national average. From 2000 to 2003, NC's competitive ranking fell from 32nd to 40th in the US and 3rd to 6th in the SE region.

Median household income

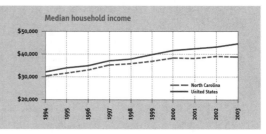

Nationally, in 2003, median family income rose at about the inflation rate, but income disparity between the rich and poor grew. Against this backdrop, NC fell in 2003 to 40th in the nation in median income. This decline was the result of several factors, including many beyond the state's direct control (and the reach of state public policies), such as immigration trends, global competition, federal trade policies and the collapse of our traditional manufacturing industries.

Goal — Encourage healthy lifestyles

Measure: Longevity

Target:
Less than 100% of US average age-adjusted death rate

Actual: 107%

US Rank (2003): 37th

Southeast Rank (2003): 3rd

Definition: Deaths per 100,000 population adjusted for age differences and averaged over the three most recent years

Source: US DHHS, National Center for Health Statistics, National Vital Statistics Reports

Notes: The Bureau of Vital Statistics changed the age-adjustment formula in 1999

NC is experiencing a steady increase in overall lifespans. Since 1999, when the formula for calculating this indicator was revised, NC's age-adjusted death rate has declined by nearly 4.0% and the national death rate has fallen by just over 4.1%. NC has improved slightly in relation to the national rankings, from 39th in 2000 to 37th in 2003, while remaining 3rd in the SE region.

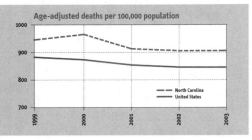
Age-adjusted deaths per 100,000 population

NC is only part of a larger regional problem. According to a 2004 United Health Foundation study, southern states accounted for the ten lowest states in overall health. Similarly, the US is beginning to suffer in comparison to other industrialized nations. In 2002, infant mortality rose in the US for the first time in 40 years, ranking the US 29th in the world in infant mortality rates. NC's infant mortality rates improved from 9.3 per 1,000 live births in 1998 to 8.2 in 2003, but the infant mortality rate for the non-white population is twice that of whites.

Measure: Weight

Target:
Less than 15% of adults are obese

Actual: 24%

US Rank (2003): 33rd (tie)

Southeast Rank (2003): 3rd

Definition: Percent of adults who are obese (a body mass index of over 30)

Source: US DHHS, Centers for Disease Control & Prevention, Behavioral Risk Factor Surveillance System

Notes: The CDC's BMI measure considers height and weight, but not frame size and muscle mass

NC, like the rest of the nation, is struggling with excess weight. Since 1994, the percent of adults who are classified as obese has been on the rise, both in NC and in the US. But, during that time, NC's adult obesity rate has fallen from 113% to 105% of the national average. Since 2000, NC's state obesity rankings have improved slightly from 40th to 37th in the nation and from 4th to 3rd in the region.

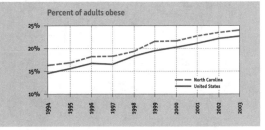
Percent of adults obese

From 1998 to 2003, the percent of low-income children aged 12-18 considered overweight increased from 23.5% to 26.5%. There is some good news. From 1998 to 2003, the percent of students in grades 9-12 who reported exercising regularly (i.e., at least 20 minutes per day, three days a week) increased from 55.3% to 61.2%. NC was one of only 11 states in the US and two states in the SE region awarded a B by the University of Baltimore for its overall efforts to combat obesity (no states earned an A).

203

Goal — Encourage healthy lifestyles

Measure: Adult Smoking

Target:
At least 90% of adults do not smoke

Actual: 75%

US Rank (2003): 34th (tie)

Southeast Rank (2003): 4th

Definition: Percent of persons 18 years and older who have not smoked at least 100 cigarettes and do not currently smoke

Source: US DHHS, Centers for Disease Control & Prevention, Behavioral Risk Factor Surveillance System

Since 1995, the percent of non-smoking adults has increased marginally from 74% to 75%. However, since 2000, as the rest of the nation has struggled with this issue, NC has improved its competitive position, rising from 44th to 34th in the US in the percent of non-smoking adults and from 8th to 4th in the SE region.

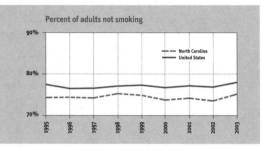

Percent of adults not smoking

From 1998 to 2003, the percent of students in grades 9-12 who reported smoking cigarettes in the last 30 days dropped from 35.8% to 25.0%. In 2004, NC had the 2nd lowest state cigarette tax in the US. However, in 2005, the General Assembly enacted a 25-cent increase.

Goal — Ensure access to good health care services

Measure: Health Insurance

Target:
At least 90% of citizens are covered by health insurance

Actual: 84%

US Rank (2003): 34th

Southeast Rank (2003): 7th

Definition: Percent of population who are covered by public or private health insurance at some time during the year

Source: US Census Bureau, Current Population Survey, and Historical Health Insurance Tables

The percent of population covered by health insurance in NC has declined since 1994, while the nation's coverage percentage has only marginally improved. NC's comparative ranking in health insurance coverage has fallen somewhat since 2000, both nationally and regionally; NC has the 7th lowest health insurance coverage ratio in the SE region.

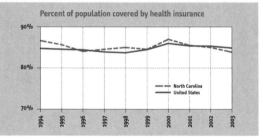

Percent of population covered by health insurance

Since 2000, NC's uninsured population has increased faster than in all but six states, but it could have been worse. According to the NC Child Advocacy Institute, the percent of NC's children lacking health insurance actually declined from 13.2% in 1998 to 11.9% in 2003. As state officials have resisted federal efforts to curtail public programs and their coverage, NC's Medicaid enrollment has increased by 30% and its Children's Health Insurance Program (CHIP) enrollment by over 100%. In lieu of NC's commitment to such public health insurance programs as Medicaid and Health Choice, the number of uninsured persons would have increased even more.

Goal — Ensure access to good health care services

Measure: Primary Care Access

Target:
At least 95% of citizens have access to primary health care

Actual: 92%

US Rank (2004): 12th

Southeast Rank (2004): 2nd

Definition: Percent of population with primary medical practitioners (e.g., family practice doctors, internists, OB/GYNs and pediatricians) within reasonable geographic bounds

Source: US DHHS, Division of Shortage Designation, Selected Statistics on Health Professional Shortage Areas

Notes: A plentiful supply of medical resources within reasonable geographic proximity does not ensure full access to needed health care services or resources

NC has been gradually climbing toward its primary health care access target since 2000, and, according to this indicator, has the 2nd best primary health care provider access in the region and the 12th best in the nation. In 2002, NC had the 6th highest per capita health and hospital spending rate in the US and the 3rd highest in the SE region.

Percent of population with access to primary health care

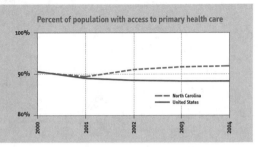

According to more specific indicators, some shortages persist. In 2003, NC was 38th in the US in the number of community hospital beds, 23rd in the US (4th in the SE) in the number of physicians and 27th in the US (6th in the SE) in the number of registered nurses per 100,000 population. While 13 counties have no acute care hospital beds, operating room, permanent-site MRI scanner or endoscopy room, the uneven distribution of care facilities across NC's 100 counties does not necessarily translate to access problems.

Measure: Child Health Care

Target:
At least 95% of infants are immunized

Actual: 89%

US Rank (2003): 4th

Southeast Rank (2003): 1st

Definition: Percent of children aged 19-35 months immunized using the 4:3:1:3 series (4 doses of DTP/DT/DTaP, 3 doses of OPV, 1 dose of MCV, and 3 doses of Hib)

Source: US DHHS, CDC, State Vaccination Coverage Levels, Morbidity and Mortality Weekly Report

NC's infant immunization rate continues to improve, as does the nation's. NC's infant immunization rate also remains well above that of most other states. Since 2002, NC's national rank slipped slightly from 1st to 4th, but its regional rank remained first.

Percent of infants immunized

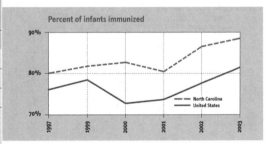

Due to the General Assembly's decision to make vaccines available at little or no cost, and the statewide involvement of public and private primary care providers, NC has one of the best child immunization rates in the nation. In 2003, NC's estimated MMR vaccination coverage for K-1 pupils was 100% and its immunization rate for children at school entry was 99.6%. In 2003, 80% of pregnant mothers in NC received adequate pre-natal care, the 17th best rating in the US and 4th best in the SE region.

Goal — Encourage healthy lifestyles

Measure: Adult Smoking

Since 1995, the percent of non-smoking adults has increased marginally from 74% to 75%. However, since 2000, as the rest of the nation has struggled with this issue, NC has improved its competitive position, rising from 44th to 34th in the US in the percent of non-smoking adults and from 8th to 4th in the SE region.

Target:
At least 90% of adults do not smoke

Actual: 75%

US Rank (2003): 34th (tie)

Southeast Rank (2003): 4th

Definition: Percent of persons 18 years and older who have not smoked at least 100 cigarettes and do not currently smoke

Source: US DHHS, Centers for Disease Control & Prevention, Behavioral Risk Factor Surveillance System

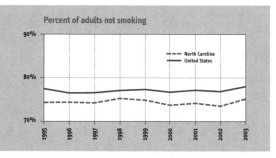

Percent of adults not smoking

From 1998 to 2003, the percent of students in grades 9-12 who reported smoking cigarettes in the last 30 days dropped from 35.8% to 25.0%. In 2004, NC had the 2nd lowest state cigarette tax in the US. However, in 2005, the General Assembly enacted a 25-cent increase.

Goal — Ensure access to good health care services

Measure: Health Insurance

The percent of population covered by health insurance in NC has declined since 1994, while the nation's coverage percentage has only marginally improved. NC's comparative ranking in health insurance coverage has fallen somewhat since 2000, both nationally and regionally; NC has the 7th lowest health insurance coverage ratio in the SE region.

Target:
At least 90% of citizens are covered by health insurance

Actual: 84%

US Rank (2003): 34th

Southeast Rank (2003): 7th

Definition: Percent of population who are covered by public or private health insurance at some time during the year

Source: US Census Bureau, Current Population Survey, and Historical Health Insurance Tables

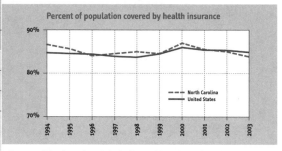

Percent of population covered by health insurance

Since 2000, NC's uninsured population has increased faster than in all but six states, but it could have been worse. According to the NC Child Advocacy Institute, the percent of NC's children lacking health insurance actually declined from 13.2% in 1998 to 11.9% in 2003. As state officials have resisted federal efforts to curtail public programs and their coverage, NC's Medicaid enrollment has increased by 30% and its Children's Health Insurance Program (CHIP) enrollment by over 100%. In lieu of NC's commitment to such public health insurance programs as Medicaid and Health Choice, the number of uninsured persons would have increased even more.

206

Goal — Maintain safe neighborhoods

Measure: Violent Crime

NC's violent crime rate has significantly declined over the last ten years, falling below the national average (and thereby attaining our target). Since 2000, NC's national ranking has improved from 33rd to 31st while its regional ranking has fallen from 6th to 7th.

Target:
Less than 100% of US average violent crime rate

Actual: 96%

US Rank (2003): 31st

Southeast Rank (2003): 7th

Definition: Reported number of violent crimes (e.g., murders, rapes, robberies and aggravated assaults) committed per 100,000 population

Source: US Federal Bureau of Investigation, Crime in US, Annual Uniform Crime Reports

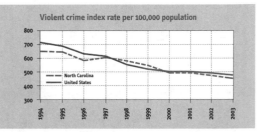

Violent crime index rate per 100,000 population

In 2004, the state's violent crime rate declined another 1.7%, with robberies falling 5.8%. However, the rate of intentional killings did not change and the reported number of rapes soared 7.5%. In 2003, the rate of violent crime fell 5.3% statewide. More specifically, NC's murder rate decreased by 10.3%, the rape rate declined 6%, the robbery rate decreased by 3.3% and the aggravated assault rate fell 6.1%.

Measure: Property Crime

NC's property crime rate has decreased considerably since 1994. Since 2000, our national rank for this indicator has improved from 43rd to 39th and our regional rank from 9th to 7th. Still, NC continues to exceed the national average property crime rate.

Target:
Less than 100% of US average property crime rate

Actual: 119%

US Rank (2003): 39th

Southeast Rank (2003): 7th

Definition: Reported number of property crimes committed per 100,000 population

Source: US Federal Bureau of Investigation, Crime in US, Annual Uniform Crime Reports

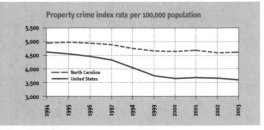

Property crime index rate per 100,000 population

In 2003, the rate of property crime decreased 2.1% across the state, with burglary decreasing 3.6%, larceny falling 2.2%, arson dropping 22.9% and motor vehicle theft increasing 4.8%. In 2004, the state's property crime rate declined another 3.1%, with the number of thefts dropping 4.3%. Despite these favorable trends, state officials have become increasingly concerned about some emerging crimes, such as illicit methamphetamine production, sales and distribution.

The Transparent Accountability Paradigm

Goal — Promote adequate & affordable housing

Measure: Home Ownership

Target:
At least 75% of homes are owned by occupants

Actual: 70%

US Rank (2004): 36th

Southeast Rank (2004): 10th

Definition: Percent of total occupied housing units that are owner-occupied

Source: US Census Bureau, Current Population Survey

Note: Home ownership does not necessarily reflect relative prosperity or asset accumulation, especially in states where relative housing values are low (e.g., Alabama or Mississippi); conversely, some states with low home ownership rates may enjoy high wealth ranks (e.g., California and New York)

NC's home ownership rate has remained relatively stable over the last ten years, but the national average has steadily increased. In 2004, NC remains slightly above the national average, but its state rank has slipped to 36th in the US and last in the SE region. Home ownership does not necessarily or fully reflect relative asset accumulation or economic prosperity.

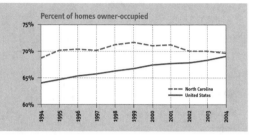

Percent of homes owner-occupied

Homeownership rates vary widely among specific population groups, in NC and throughout the nation. In 2004, the national homeownership rate varied widely depending on race—76.2% for white households, 49.1% for black households and 48.9% for Hispanic households. In 2002, NC's homeownership rate for persons aged 65 or more was 83.4%, the 9th highest in the US.

Measure: Housing Availability

Target:
Less than 2.0% of homes have over-crowded conditions

Actual: 2.4%

US Rank (2000): 28th

Southeast Rank (2000): 7th

Definition: Percent of occupied housing units with more than one person per room

Source: US Census Bureau

Notes: We are exploring alternative indicators for tracking housing availability

The incidence of over-crowded housing dramatically declined in NC from 1950 to 1990 and, after a slight reversal during the 1990s, appears to have continued to decline since 2000. While more recent state rankings are not yet available, in 2000, NC's national ranking for over-crowded housing conditions was 28th and its regional ranking was 7th. Since 2000, Census Bureau estimates indicate renewed progress, and NC remains well below the national averages.

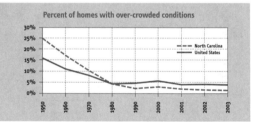

Percent of homes with over-crowded conditions

In 2004, NC's rental vacancy rate was the 9th highest in the nation and 4th highest in the SE region. Available housing must also meet basic living standards. In 2003, only 0.35% of NC's occupied housing units lacked complete plumbing facilities and only 0.32% lacked complete kitchen facilities, a slight improvement since 2000. In 2002, NC was ranked 23rd in the US and 2nd in the SE region in per capita state and local government housing and community development expenditures.

Goal — Promote adequate & affordable housing

Measure: Home Affordability

Target:
Less than 25% of homeowners pay excessive housing costs

Actual: 28%

US Rank (2003): 23rd

Southeast Rank (2003): 5th

Definition: Percent of owner-occupied households with mortgages spending more than 30% of their income on housing (e.g. mortgage, real estate taxes, property insurance, utilities & fuels)

Source: US Census Bureau, American Community Survey

Notes: We are exploring alternative measures for tracking home affordability, such as the National Low-Income Housing Coalition's housing affordability index and rental affordability

NC housing is gradually becoming less and less affordable, relative to income. Since 2000, the percentage of NC homeowners with mortgages spending more than 30% of their income for housing has increased from 25.5% to 27.8%. However, during the same period, NC's competitive rankings have improved, from 28th to 23rd nationally and from 6th to 5th in the Southeast region.

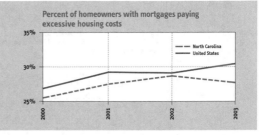

Percent of homeowners with mortgages paying excessive housing costs

In recent years, the housing affordability gap has grown in NC, but NC continues to have more affordable housing than many other states. From 2000 to 2003, for example, the ratio of renters in NC paying at least 30% of their income on housing rose from 39% to 45%. Moreover, from 1998 to 2003, NC's foreclosure rates increased dramatically. In 2003, the median monthly housing cost for renter-occupied housing in NC was the 28th highest in the US and 4th highest in the region. In 2004, NC was ranked 21st in the US in housing affordability by the National Low Income Housing Coalition.

Goal — Deliver responsive community-based care

Measure: Child Day Care

Target: At least 120% of US average regulated child day care rate

Actual: 132%

US Rank (2003): 4th

Southeast Rank (2003): 1st

Definition: Percent of children receiving day care in regulated settings through the federal Child Care and Development Fund (CCDF), the block grant program for low-income working families and families transitioning off welfare to work

Source: US DHHS, Administration for Children and Families, Child Care Bureau

NC has attained its long-range target. NC is one of the top states in the nation, and the leading state in the SE region, in the percent of children receiving day care in regulated settings, at least for services funded by the federal Child Care and Development Fund (CCDF). Since 1999, the percent of children receiving day care in regulated settings has improved from 95% to 98%.

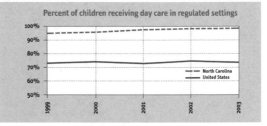

Percent of children receiving day care in regulated settings

In 2004, NC had 4,999 licensed family child care homes and 4,248 licensed child care centers. In 2003, 85% of the children enrolled in CCDF-funded programs in NC received day care by licensed centers and 13% by licensed family homes. In 2003, NC had the 12th most children in the US enrolled in Head Start programs, and the 4th most in the Southeast. In 2002, NC was ranked 37th in the nation and 9th in the region in the percent of three- and four-year olds enrolled in state pre-kindergarten. In 2001, NC instituted an academic pre-kindergarten program for at-risk four year olds.

Imperative 3: Quality Education for All

Overview of Progress

Our Vision

North Carolina will make sufficient investments in its public schools and institutions of higher education to give every student an an opportunity to succeed. Our education system will provide the tools to help citizens become solid contributors to the state's civic and cultural life, and prosper in the increasingly competitive workplace.

Our Goals

1. Offer a comprehensive public school (K–12) education
2. Make prudent investments in public education programs
3. Build a premier public higher education system

North Carolina is making substantial progress—with the notable exception of high school graduation rates—toward attaining the strategic targets for Quality Education for All. Our standardized reading and math scores continue to show dramatic improvement, our SAT scores and pupil-teacher ratios are approaching the national averages and our teacher pay is becoming more competitive. Despite recent fiscal pressures, our higher education system still offers relatively good access and our public investment in higher education is still competitive. In only one area have we failed to make progress—with our poor public high school graduation and dropout rates.

Summary of Strategic Progress – Quality Education for All

Goals	Measures	Target	US Rank	SE Rank
1. Offer a comprehensive public school (K–12) education	1. Reading proficiency		16th	2nd
	2. Math/science proficiency	✔	4th	1st
	3. College preparedness		14th (of 23)	2nd (of 5)
2. Make prudent investments in public education programs	1. Teacher recruitment		23rd	3rd
	2. Classroom resources	✔	30th	6th
	3. High school graduation		37th	4th
3. Build a premier public higher education system	1. Higher education access		18th	6th
	2. Community colleges	(Update in process)		
	3. University resources		20th	2nd
	4. University innovation	(Update in process)		

Note: Measures for which we have met or exceeded the target are marked with a "check" under the Target column. Measures for which we are awaiting new data are marked "update in process" and will be updated as new data becomes available.

Our Governor, General Assembly and other public leaders, have adopted several policies that advance the long-term goals for this imperative, including the following:

- Established a community-based, academic pre-kindergarten program to prepare disadvantaged four-year olds for success in school (the More at Four program);
- Reduced class sizes in the early elementary grades (kindergarten through third grade);
- Implemented a comprehensive program to improve educational practices and boost student performance (the ABCs Accountability Program);
- Established a National College Savings Program (the 529 college savings plan) to encourage families to save more for their children's higher education; and
- Won voter approval for the UNC Higher Education Bond Program in 2000 to expand facilities throughout the 16-campus UNC system.

The external pressures on state policy-makers to promote educational excellence will not likely dissipate. The courts have affirmed that the state has a constitutional duty to provide all school age children a sound basic education and, through the Leandro mandate, specified the educational resources that this duty entails. Mounting global competition will likely increase the need to make our public higher education system even better than it is today.

The state's progress on individual goals and measures for this imperative is discussed in more detail on the pages that follow.

Goal — Offer a first-class, comprehensive public K-12 education

**Measure:
Reading/Writing Proficiency**

The reading proficiency rate of NC's 4th graders improved from 27% in 1998 to 33% in 2003. Moreover, since 1998, NC's 4th grade reading proficiency rate has risen above the national rate, giving NC the 16th best score in the nation and the 2nd best score in the region.

**Target:
At least 120% of US average in reading proficiency**

Actual: 110%

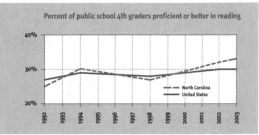

Percent of public school 4th graders proficient or better in reading

US Rank (2003): 16th (tie)

Southeast Rank (2003): 2nd

Definition: Percent of 4th graders rated proficient or better in reading per the National Assessment for Educational Progress (NAEP), where proficient represents a demonstrated academic mastery for specified grade level

Source: US Dept. of Education, National Center for Education Statistics (NCES), NAEP Reading Assessment

Notes: Since the differences among NAEP scores are small, future state rankings could change significantly (NCES cautions that NAEP reading score differences among many states are not statistically significant)

In 2003, according to NCES (the Nation's Report Card), NC had the 30th best average reading score for 8th graders in the US (where 11 state scores were not significantly different). In 2002, NC had the 6th best average writing score for 8th graders in the US (where 11 state scores were not significantly different). NC's English standards have won recognition from the Fordham Foundation for "being clear, specific and measurable, showing increasing difficulty over the grades and addressing almost all areas of the English language arts and reading satisfactorily."

**Measure:
Math/Science Proficiency**

Target: At least 120% of US average in math proficiency

The math proficiency rate of NC's 4th graders improved from 25% in 2000 to 41% in 2003. In addition, NC's 4th grade math proficiency rate is significantly higher than the national rate. In 2003, NC enjoyed the best math proficiency score for 4th graders in the region, and the 4th best in the nation.

Actual: 132%

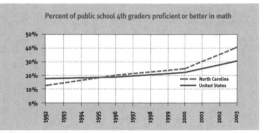

Percent of public school 4th graders proficient or better in math

US Rank (2003): 4th (tie)

Southeast Rank (2003): 1st

Definition: Percent of 4th graders rated proficient or better in math per the National Assessment for Educational Progress (NAEP), where proficient represents a demonstrated academic mastery for specified grade level

Source: US Dept. of Education, National Center for Education Statistics (NCES), NAEP Math Assessment

Notes: Since the differences among NAEP scores are small, future state rankings could change significantly (NCES cautions that NAEP math score differences among many states are not statistically significant)

In 2003, according to NCES (the Nation's Report Card), NC tied for the 18th highest average math score for 8th graders in the US (where 20 state scores were not significantly different). NC's math standards have been cited by the Fordham Foundation as better than those of most states.

Goal — Offer a first-class, comprehensive public K-12 education

Measure:
College Preparedness

Target:
At least 100% of US average SAT score

In 2005, NC continued to improve its SAT scores, narrowing its gap with the US average and climbing in the state rankings. Since 1998, NC has reduced the national SAT score differential by 20 points. From 2000 to 2005, NC improved its national ranking from 48th to 42nd and its regional ranking from 8th to 7th. However, among states with SAT participation rates of 50% or more (states with high SAT participation rates tend to have lower aggregate SAT scores than states with lower participation rates), NC is ranked 14th (of 23) in the US and 2nd (of 5) in the SE region.

Actual: 98%

US Rank (2004): 14th (of 23)

Southeast Rank (2004): 2nd (of 5)

Definition: Average combined math and verbal score on Scholastic Aptitude Test (SAT)

Source: The College Board

Notes: SAT scores provide one proxy indicator of public school quality, especially for high SAT participation states like NC, but should be reviewed in the context of other data; the above state ranks are only for states with more than 50% SAT participation

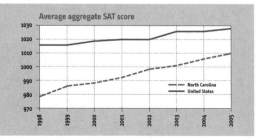

Average aggregate SAT score

NC's SAT rankings for math are higher than those for reading. In 2004, NC ranked 44th nationally and 8th regionally in verbal (508 score) and 41st nationally and 7th regionally in math (518 score). In 2003, NC ranked 46th nationally and 8th regionally in verbal (495 score) and 41st nationally and 7th regionally in math (506 score).

Goal — Make prudent investments in public education

Measure: Teacher Recruitment

Target:
At least 100% of US average teacher pay

Despite losing ground during the recent recession, NC has made great strides since 1997. Its average teacher pay has climbed from 81% of the US average in 1997 to 93% in 2004. During the same time period, NC's national rank has risen from 43rd to 23rd and its regional rank from 9th to 3rd.

Actual: 93%

US Rank (2004): 23rd

Southeast Rank (2004): 3rd

Definition: Average teacher pay, where pay is the average gross salary before any deductions for Social Security, retirement and health insurance

Source: National Education Association

Notes: ETS' nationally-recognized Praxis assessment series is used by many states for licensing purposes

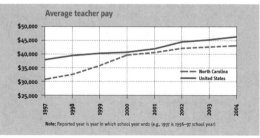

Average teacher pay

Note: Reported year is year in which school year ends (e.g., 1997 is 1996–97 school year)

In a recent national assessment of teacher quality, NC was awarded a "B" and a national ranking of 7th in improving teacher quality. In 2002, NC's average teacher pay was nearly 142% of the state's average wage, giving NC the 13th highest rating in the nation (and the 2nd highest rating in the region). NC is also near national averages in licensure and competency ratings. In 2003, NC's average Praxis teaching skills score was 98% of the US average and its average Praxis knowledge score was 100% of the US average. In 2003, 84% of NC's teachers satisfied applicable state licensure requirements, down slightly from 2002.

Goal — Make prudent investments in public education

Measure: Classroom Resources

Target: Less than 100% of US average pupil-teacher ratio

Actual:	99%

US Rank (2004):	30th

Southeast Rank (2004):	6th

Definition: Total reported public school students divided by the total classroom teachers (FTEs) assigned to instruct pupils in self-contained classes or classroom situations

Source: National Education Association, Rankings & Estimates, & US Dept. of Education, National Center for Education Statistics

Notes: The pupil-teacher ratio provides a rough indicator of a state's commitment to providing adequate instructional resources, but it may be smaller than actual class size; we are exploring other indicators (e.g., average classroom size)

NC's aggregate pupil-teacher ratio remains below the national average, but the margin is narrowing. As of 2004, NC's pupil-teacher ratio was 99% of the US average. Since 2000, even while experiencing one of the largest enrollment increases in the nation, NC's competitive rankings have not changed significantly.

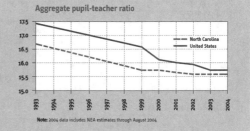

Aggregate pupil-teacher ratio

Note: 2004 data includes NEA estimates through August 2004

NC has developed its own comprehensive system for assessing the quality of its public schools (the ABC system). In 2003, the NC Department of Public Instruction found that 73% of public schools earned a "higher-than-expected improvement" grade on the ABC report card. In 2004, NC spent $6,727 in federal, state and local monies per pupil for public K–12 programs, 21% lower than the national average, ranking it 40th in the US and 5th in the SE region.

Measure: High School Graduation

Target: At least 100% of US average public high school graduation rate

Actual:	94%

US Rank (2002):	37th (tie)

Southeast Rank (2002):	4th

Definition: Estimated public high school graduates in current school year divided by 9th grade enrollment from four years earlier

Source: Manhattan Institute and US Dept. of Education, National Center for Education Statistics

Notes: There are numerous methods for calculating high school graduation rates, including four nationally-recognized methods: NCES, Manhattan Institute, Postsecondary Opportunity and Urban Institute; in 2005, a US Education Department task force recommended a standard formula for states (i.e., graduates with regular diplomas / 9th grade class adjusted for transfers)

Since 1993, NC (like most states) has made no real progress in improving high school graduation rates. NC's competitive rankings have changed little, leaving NC with the 37th lowest graduation rate in the US and 4th lowest rate in the SE region. According to the Manhattan Institute, the national graduation rate for public high school students fell from 72% in 1993 to 71% in 2002. During the same time period, the percent of students leaving high school with the requisite skills for college rose from 28% to 34%, an indication that higher state graduation standards can suppress graduation rates even as they produce more competent graduates.

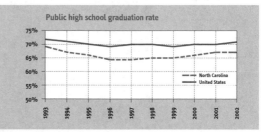

Public high school graduation rate

In 2004, after four years of decline, NC's high school dropout rate rose (and only 39% of 2004 graduates passed all five standard end-of-course exams). In 2003, NC's dropout rate for pupils aged 16 to 19 was the 16th highest in the US (tie). Graduation rates vary widely among racial groups, but NC's rate variances are considerably lower than the national variances. In 2002, according to Morgan Quitno Press, the national graduation rate differential was 24.6 percentage points between white and African-American students and 20.9 percentage points between white and Hispanic students. In contrast, the NC graduation rate differential was 16.5 percentage points between white and African-American students and 9.2 percentage points between white and Hispanic students.

Goal — Build a premier public higher education system

Measure:
Higher Education Access

Target:
Less than 80% of US average higher education costs

From 1994 to 2003, NC's rank for average public university tuition, room, board and fee costs fell from 2nd to 18th in the US and from 1st to 6th in the region. Still, NC continues to have some of the most affordable public universities (and best college bargains) in the nation. Its average student costs for public higher education are about 85% of the national average, and its average tuition and fees were only 21.5% of the median family income (for lowest quintile), compared to 29.9% for the US.

Actual: 85%

US Rank (2003): 18th

Southeast Rank (2003): 6th

Definition: Average in-state tuition, room and board and fees for full-time students in public four-year institutions of higher education for one academic year

Source: US Dept. of Education, National Center for Education Statistics, Digest of Education Statistics

Notes: Average costs per student roughly reflect college affordability (without adjustments for tuition assistance), but we are exploring alternative affordability indicators (e.g., the National Center on Higher Education Policy rating which considers multiple access factors)

Average student costs for public higher education

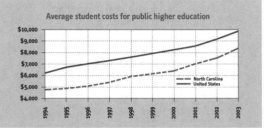

From 2000 to 2004, the average tuition for NC's public four-year institutions rose 71%, but this increase was partially offset by financial assistance (e.g., in 2002, the UNC System awarded $3,573 in grants and scholarships per undergraduate student). In 2004, per the National Center for Public Policy and Higher Education, NC's average tuition at public four-year institutions was $3,251—the 11th lowest in the US and 3rd lowest in the SE—and NC offered the 16th (tie) most affordable public universities in the US and 3rd most affordable in the SE (considering family income, college costs and tuition assistance). With 126 institutions of higher education, NC has the 8th most in the US and the 2nd most in the region, but this does not necessarily translate to high enrollments. In 2003, 30% of NC's adults aged 18 to 24 were enrolled in a two- or four-year institution, tying it for 43rd in the nation.

Measure:
University Resources

Target:
At least 120% of US average per capita higher education spending

NC's commitment to higher education, at least in terms of its per capita spending, remains relatively strong. In 2002, NC spent $619 per capita on public higher education, more than the national average—20th highest in the US and 2nd in the region.

Actual: 114%

US Rank (2002): 20th

Southeast Rank (2002): 2nd

Definition: Per capita state and local government expenditures (operating and capital outlays) for higher education

Source: US Census Bureau, Governments Division, State and Local Government Finances

Notes: Per capita higher education expenditures provide only one indicator of a state's relative commitment to higher education, and should be considered in the context of how student costs may affect higher education access

Per capita public higher education expenditures

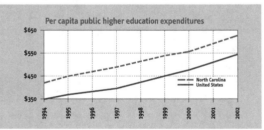

Despite some signs of erosion, NC's public financing for higher education remains strong. For FY04, NC state government spent the 5th most in the US per pupil (and the 2nd most in the SE) on Title IV institutions of higher education. In 2002, NC spent the 11th most in the US on higher education as a percent of personal income and the 2nd most in the SE region. In 2002, NC had the 8th highest per capita tax appropriations for higher education in the country and the highest in the SE region. However, NC's average faculty salary is only the 33rd highest in the US and 4th highest in the SE region.

Imperative 4: A High Performance Workforce

Overview of Progress

Our Vision

Our workers will possess the skills to adapt quickly to the changing demands of the global workplace, use technology, think analytically and participate in the emerging economy. Employers will provide the requisite compensation and work environments to ensure a competitive and productive workforce.

Our Goals

1. Produce workers with competitive skills
2. Offer innovative & accessible continuous learning
3. Support safe & rewarding work environment

North Carolina is making some progress toward attaining the targets for A High Performance Workforce for which we have recent data. Our aggregate high school and college attainment rates, while improving, remain relatively low for the nation and mediocre for the Southeast. Our wage levels are in the middle of the pack, both nationally and regionally. However, our workplace safety record continues to lead the nation and region.

Summary of Strategic Progress – A High Performance Workforce

Goals	Measures	Target	US Rank	SE Rank
1. Produce workers with competitive skills	1. Basic educational attainment		40th	5th
	2. Advanced educ. attainment		35th	4th
	3. Technical educ. attainment	(Update in process)		
2. Offer innovative & accessible continuous learning	1. Basic skills training	(Update in process)		
	2. Vocational training	(Update in process)		
	3. Technical training	(Update in process)		
3. Support safe & rewarding work environments	1. Competitive wages		28th	3rd
	2. Equitable pay	(Update in process)		
	3. Workplace safety	✔	3rd (of 41)	1st (of 9)

Note: Measures for which we have met or exceeded the target are marked with a "check" under the Target column. Measures for which we are awaiting new data are marked "update in process" and will be updated as new data becomes available.

In North Carolina, our leaders have adopted numerous strategies to further the long-term goals for this imperative, including the following:

- Established the NC Community College System's New and Expanding Industry Training (NEIT) program, to provide job training to individuals and companies;
- Created the Incumbent Workforce Development Program under the Commerce Department to encourage established businesses to train current workers in portable skills; and
- Funded a project to upgrade the Industrial Commission's computers to improve our ability to track workplace injuries and identify causal factors.

Much work remains to be done to enhance the competitiveness of our workforce. One such initiative under consideration by our elected officials is to examine the state's vast array of worker training programs and identify ways to improve overall effectiveness and reduce administrative costs.

The state's progress on individual goals and measures for this imperative is discussed in more detail on the pages that follow.

215

Goal — Produce workers with competitive skills

Measure: Basic Educational Attainment

NC's high school attainment rate has steadily increased from 74.8% in 1993 to 81.4% in 2003, but remains below the national average and slightly below target. Since 2000, NC has improved its national ranking from 46th to 40th and its regional rank from 7th to 5th.

Target:
At least 100% of US average high school attainment rate

Actual: 96%

US Rank (2003): 40th

Southeast Rank (2003): 5th

Definition: Percent of population aged 25 years or older who have graduated from high school or earned a General Equivalency Degree (GED)

Source: US Census Bureau, Educational Attainment in the US

Notes: We may limit this target to young adults (e.g., 25–35 years old) to better track our progress; it is very difficult to affect educational attainment levels among older adults

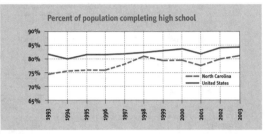

Percent of population completing high school

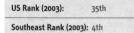

High school attainment, in and of itself, does not ensure competitive skills. For instance, in the most recent available survey of literacy rates, 52% of NC adults scored in the two lowest levels of literary proficiency. Fortunately, more North Carolinians are pursuing education beyond high school. From 2000 to 2003, the percent of NC adults attaining associate degrees increased from 6.9% to 7.7%.

Measure: Advanced Educational Attainment

From 1995 to 2003, NC's college attainment rate for all adults aged 25 years old or older improved from 20.6% to 23.8%, but never reached the national average. NC's national college attainment rank for adults 25 years old or older rose from 33rd in 1995 to as high as 23rd in 1998, before slipping to as low as 41st in 2002, and rebounding to 35th in 2003. During the same time period, NC's regional rank for adults aged 25 years or older fluctuated from as high as 2nd to as low as 6th. Among younger adults (aged 18-24), NC's college attainment rankings appear somewhat higher—in 2000, NC was ranked 30th in the US and 4th in the SE region. More notably, from 1990 to 2000, NC experienced the 14th best improvement in college attainment among young adults in the US and the 4th best improvement in the SE region.

Target:
At least 100% of US average college attainment rate

Actual: 88%

US Rank (2003): 35th

Southeast Rank (2003): 4th

Definition: Percent of population aged 25 years or older who hold college bachelor degrees

Source: US Census Bureau, Educational Attainment in the US

Notes: We may limit this target to young adults (e.g., 25–35 years old) to better track our progress; it is very difficult to affect educational attainment levels among older adults

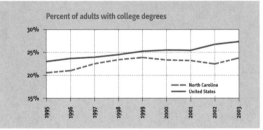

Percent of adults with college degrees

From 2000 to 2003, the graduate degree attainment ratio in NC increased from 6.7% to 7.8%. In 2002, 29.6% of NC's total workforce held college degrees, giving NC a national rank of 45th. The US Census Bureau has estimated that, on average, a college graduate will make at least $1 million more than a high school graduate over a lifetime.

216

Goal — Support safe & rewarding work environments

Measure: Competitive Wages

Target:
At least 100% of US average pay

Actual: 89%

US Rank (2004):   28th

Southeast Rank (2004): 3rd

Definition: Total annual wages, bonuses and other payments for employees covered by unemployment insurance divided by average monthly number of employees

Source: Bureau of Labor Statistics, Quarterly Census of Employment and Wages: Annual Data Tables

NC has made some progress over the last decade in its effort to pay competitive wages. Since 1994, NC's wages have risen from 87% to over 91% of the average national wage, its national rank has improved from 31st to 28th and its regional rank has jumped from 6th to 3rd. In 2004, NC ranked 28th in the nation and 3rd in the Southeast in this measure.

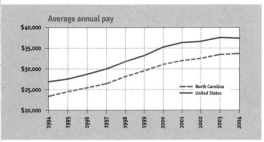

Average annual pay

The ability of the state economy to generate full-time jobs can significantly affect average wages. From 2000 to 2003, the percent of part-time workers wanting full-time jobs grew from 11.0% to 17.2%. In 2003, the percent of NC's labor force deemed under-employed was 11.1%-- higher than the rate for both the nation (10.1%) and South Atlantic states (9.0%). NC is one of 36 states with its minimum wage rate fixed at the national rate of $5.15; only one state in the SE region has a higher minimum wage (Florida with a rate of $6.15).

Measure: Workplace Safety

Target: Less than 90%
of US average
workplace incidence rate

Actual: 80%

US Rank (2003):   3rd (tie) (of 41)

Southeast Rank (2003): 1st (tie)

Definition: Number of nonfatal workplace injuries and illnesses reported by OSHA per 100 full-time workers

Source: Bureau of Labor Statistics, Survey of Occupational Injuries and Illnesses

NC achieved its worker safety target for the last two years. Its workplace injury and illness incidence rate fell from 6.2 per 100 workers in 1997 to 4.0 in 2002. Since 2002, NC has enjoyed the best worker safety rating in the SE region, and one of the best in the nation.

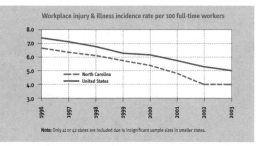

Workplace injury & illness incidence rate per 100 full-time workers

Note: Only 41 or 42 states are included due to insignificant sample sizes in smaller states.

In 2003, NC experienced a slight increase in workplace fatalities, the first such increase since 2000. Since 2000, NC's average worker compensation payments per covered worker have risen to about 2/3 of the national average, and its national and regional rankings for this indicator have slipped (such payments are made by law to a worker for job-related injury or illness).

Imperative 5: A Sustainable Environment

Overview of Progress

Our Vision

As stewards of the environment, North Carolinians will work together to preserve our state's vast natural resources, and make the requisite investments in environmental technology and monitoring capabilities to control pollutants. All of us will make it our calling to maintain and enhance the quality of the air, water and land we share.

Our Goals

1. Ensure clean air & water resources
2. Preserve precious & productive natural resources
3. Employ vigorous & cost-effective environmental strategies

North Carolina, despite many laudatory policy changes to address environmental quality issues in recent years, has yet to make significant progress toward attaining the strategic environmental targets for which we have current data. North Carolina's air quality, at least as it is measured by the ozone exceedance rate, is ranked among the worst in the nation and Southeast region. Similarly, our drinking water quality, as indicated by the public water system violation rate, merits serious attention.

Summary of Strategic Progress – A Sustainable Environment

Goals	Measures	Target	US Rank	SE Rank
1. Ensure clean air & water resources	1. Clean air		37th	8th
	2. Clean lakes and streams	(Update in process)		
	3. Safe drinking water		38th	9th
2. Preserve precious & productive natural resources	1. Coastal resource protection	(Update in process)		
	2. Natural lands preservation	(Update in process)		
	3. Efficient development	(Update in process)		
	4. Energy conservation	(Update in process)		
3. Employ vigorous & cost-effective environmental strategies	1. Pollution control	(Update in process)		
	2. Safe sewage disposal	(Update in process)		
	3. Solid waste management	(Update in process)		
	4. Hazardous waste control	(Update in process)		

Note: Measures for which we have met or exceeded the target are marked with a "check" under the Target column. Measures for which we are awaiting new data are marked "update in process" and will be updated as new data becomes available.

The Governor, Attorney General, General Assembly and other state officials have taken numerous measures to ensure a more sustainable environment, including the following:

- Enacted the Clean Air Bill of 1999 which required the expansion of our vehicle inspection and maintenance program from 9 to 48 counties;
- Enacted the Clean Smokestacks Act of 2002 to further reduce air pollution and help NC attain the federal 8-hour ozone and PM2.5 standards;
- Developed the 8th largest air quality monitoring program in the US and the 2nd largest in the SE region;
- Initiated legal action to invoke federal regulations to curb air pollution from out-of-state power plants;
- Established the Clean Water Management Trust Fund;
- Adopted rules requiring builders in 33 urban counties to install systems for controlling stormwater pollution; and
- Adopted the Coastal Habitat Protection Plan to guide the development of regulations for coastal waters, fisheries and wetlands.

Some of NC's metropolitan regions have promising collaborative initiatives with state and local government and business to improve air quality, including the Sustainable Environment for Quality of Life (SEQL) project in the Charlotte region, Triangle Tomorrow efforts in the Triangle Region and Air Quality Early Action Compact (EAC) programs in the Triad, Unifour, Fayetteville and Mountain areas. Such local initiatives, when coordinated with state and federal efforts, offer great potential for helping address NC's serious air quality issues.

We do not control all of the pollutants that adversely affect our natural resources. Without effective federal policy and inter-state cooperation, we cannot fully attain the targets for this imperative. Nevertheless, there is much that we can do make lasting progress.

The state's progress on individual goals and measures for this imperative is discussed in more detail on the next page.

Goal — Ensure clean air & water resources

Measure: Clean Air

Target:
Less than 100% of US average unhealthy smog day rate

Actual:	127%

US Rank (2003):	37th

Southeast Rank (2003):	8th

Definition: Number of days with state exceedances of USEPA ozone or unhealthy smog standard (0.085 smog parts per million over an eight-hour period)

Source: US Environmental Protection Agency

Notes: The EPA ozone standard exceedance day rate is an indicator of poor air quality, but state reporting systems vary widely and air quality rankings can be monitor-driven (i.e. states with the most rigorous monitoring systems may report the worst air quality)

Despite emissions from adjoining states, NC's air quality has steadily improved since 1998 (except for 2002 when a hot summer increased ozone levels). NC's ozone exceedance day rate is the 3rd highest in the SE and 15th highest in the US. States with large populations and monitoring programs often report the highest ozone rates. NC has the 3rd largest population in the SE and the 11th largest in the US.

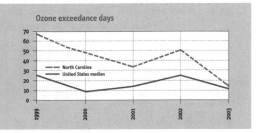

Ozone exceedance days

From 2001 to 2004, NC counties (with monitors) violating the 8-hour ozone standard fell from 21 to 12, and NC counties violating the fine particle (PM2.5) standard fell from 14 to 2. Still, our air quality remains a serious problem. In 2004, 26 NC counties, including our most urbanized counties (except New Hanover), had poor ozone grades and the Charlotte and Raleigh-Durham regions had the 14th and 23rd worst ozone scores in the US. That same year, the US EPA cited 3 NC counties (Davidson, Guilford and Catawba) for flunking air quality health standards for soot.

Measure: Safe Drinking Water

Target: Less than 100% of US average public water system violation rate

Actual:	146%

US Rank (2004):	38th

Southeast Rank (2004):	9th

Definition: Percent of community water systems reporting health-based violations of state or federal safe drinking water regulations to the EPA Safe Drinking Water Information System

Source: US Environmental Protection Agency

Notes: Some states may under-report community water system violations; state reporting systems vary widely and water quality rankings can be monitor-driven (i.e. states with the most rigorous monitoring systems may report the worst water quality)

From 1998 to 2004, the percent of NC's community water systems with health-based water safety violations rose from 2.6% to 12.1%, and NC's national drinking water quality ranking fell from 3rd to 38th and its regional ranking from 1st to 9th. This trend reflects several factors, including broader standards, more rigorous monitoring practices and fewer public systems.

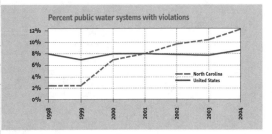

Percent public water systems with violations

In 2004, NC had 2,174 community water systems, the 5th highest number in the US (behind Texas, California, New York and Washington). From January, 2002 through June, 2003, NC had the 3rd highest percent of major facilities in the US (and highest in the SE region) exceeding their Clean Water Act permit limits at least once.

Imperative 6: A Prosperous Economy

Overview of Progress

Our Vision

North Carolina's growing, diversified economy will be competitive in the global marketplace. High-quality jobs will be plentiful across all economic, geographic and demographic sectors. Sound investments in people and infrastructure will accelerate our transition from traditional to knowledge-based economies. Through our willingness to think boldly, we will build a prosperous "New Economy" on the foundation of our traditional economic strengths.

Our Goals

1. Promote dynamic & sustainable economic growth
2. Attract & nurture emerging economy sectors
3. Revitalize traditional economic sectors

As shown in the table below, North Carolina is meeting four of its Prosperous Economy targets, but other targets remain elusive. Our five-year per capita gross state product growth rate is improving. Our state's short-term economic momentum appears to have improved, but concerns about unemployment persist. Our overall business climate continues to earn high marks for both the nation and region and, despite setbacks in traditional industries, we continue to lead certain indicators of manufacturing and agricultural vitality.

Summary of Strategic Progress – A Prosperous Economy

Goals	Measures	Target	US Rank	SE Rank
1. Promote dynamic & sustainable	1. Long-term growth		24th	2nd
economic growth	2. Short-term growth	✔	18th	4th
	3. Employment		32nd	6th
	4. Personal income		36th	5th
2. Attract & nurture emerging	1. Economic climate	✔	1st	1st
economy sectors	2. Innovation capacity	(Update in process)		
	3. New economy jobs	(Update in process)		
	4. Foreign capital	(Update in process)		
3. Revitalize traditional	1. Industrial transition	(Update in process)		
economic sectors	2. Manufacturing vitality	✔	8th	2nd
	3. Agricultural vitality	✔	7th	4th
	4. Global competitiveness	(Update in process)		

Note: Measures for which we have met or exceeded the target are marked with a "check" under the Target column. Measures for which we are awaiting new data are marked "update in process" and will be updated as new data becomes available.

The Governor and General Assembly have implemented numerous measures to revitalize our economy and achieve other goals of this imperative, including the following:

- Enacted the William S. Lee Quality Jobs and Expansion Act (the Lee Act) in 1996 to provide tax credits to companies that relocate, expand or upgrade facilities in North Carolina's economically distressed communities (over $66 million in tax credits were taken in 2004);
- Expanded the One North Carolina Fund in 2001 to empower the Governor to lure vital businesses on the verge of locating or expanding in North Carolina (nearly $11 million was awarded to businesses in 2004); and
- Enacted the Job Development Investment Grant (JDIG) Program in 2002 to provide financial assistance to new and expanding businesses up to 75 percent of the personal income taxes generated by the jobs they create (over $74 million in grants were awarded to businesses in 2004).

The Governor and General Assembly will likely continue to assess the costs and benefits of these economic incentive programs. The JDIG Program and Lee Act were slated to expire at the end of 2005 without legislative action, but both were extended. Some local governments offer supplemental incentives to businesses as well. The constitutionality of such state and local incentives may be tested in the courts. Such incentives apparently played a minor role in NC's most significant initiative of 2005, the announced plans to convert a textile mill in Kannapolis into the new North Carolina Research Center.

The private sector plays a critical role in promoting economic growth. For example, the Golden LEAF Foundation recently announced plans to invest over $70 million of national tobacco settlement funds in expanding the biotechnology industry.

The state's progress on individual goals and measures for this imperative is discussed in more detail on the pages that follow.

220

Goal — Promote dynamic & sustainable economic growth

Measure: Long-Term Economic Growth

Target: At least 110% of US average long-term growth rate

Actual:	98%

US Rank (2002):	24th

Southeast Rank (2002):	2nd

Definition: Average growth rate in per capita Gross State Product (GSP), the market value of all goods and services produced by labor and property located in state over last five years

Source: US Dept. of Commerce, Bureau of Economic Analysis, Gross State Product Data

Notes: As the state counterpart to the national Gross Domestic Product, the GSP is an important indicator of statewide economic strength

After two years of economic setbacks, NC showed signs of rebounding in 2002. Its economic growth rate bounced back to nearly the national average, and its competitive rankings climbed to 24th in the US and 2nd in the SE region. The impact of foreign trade policy continues to be particularly severe in NC.

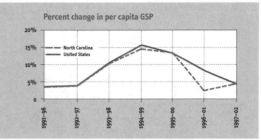

Percent change in per capita GSP

After leading the region in the early 1990s, and maintaining respectable growth in the late 1990s, NC experienced a dramatic economic setback in 2001. NC's per capita GSP fell from 99% of the US rate in 2000 to 94.6% in 2001. Nevertheless, despite some temporary reversals in our economic fortunes, our per capita GSP climbed to nearly 100% of the US rate in 2003 and our regional rank in per capita GSP has remained in the top three for over a decade. From 2000 to 2004, according to the Federal Reserve Bank of Cleveland, NC was 4th in the US (and 1st in the SE region) in average annual labor productivity growth, a measure of output per unit of work, and 17th in the US (and 4th in the SE region) in annual GSP growth.

Measure: Short-Term Economic Growth

Target: At least 120% of US average new employer firm rate

Actual:	125%

US Rank (2003):	18th

Southeast Rank (2003):	4th

Definition: Ratio of new employer firms started each year to existing firms at the beginning of each year, where multi-state firms are counted for more than one state

Source: US Small Business Administration, Small Business Indicators

Notes: We are exploring alternative indicators such as the State Economic Momentum Index

NC is well above the national average for new employer firms and is ranked 18th in the nation and 4th in the SE region in new employer firms. NC's new employer firm rate has declined slightly since 2000, but its national and regional rankings climbed one notch each in 2003.

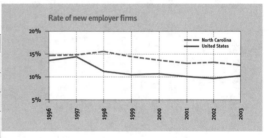

Rate of new employer firms

In 2005 (spring quarter), NC was ranked 23rd in the US and 3rd in the SE in the State Economic Momentum Index, rebounding from a national rank of 24th and regional rank of 5th in 2001. In 2004, NC had the 18th lowest personal bankruptcy rate in the nation and the 2nd lowest in the region.

Goal — Promote dynamic & sustainable economic growth

Measure: Employment

Target:
Less than 90% of US average unemployment rate

Actual:	96%
US Rank (2004):	32nd
Southeast Rank (2004):	6th

Definition: Aggregate state unemployment rate per the US Labor Department

Source: US Bureau of Labor Statistics, Regional and State Employment and Unemployment

Notes: The unemployment rate tracks adults looking for work, but not necessarily those who are out of work and no longer looking; we are exploring alternative indicators (e.g., the labor force participation rate)

After three years ranked among the 10 worst states in unemployment, NC improved in 2004 to the 32nd lowest rate and, for the first time since 2000, fell below the national average unemployment rate. In 2004, NC's monthly unemployment rate (seasonally adjusted) fell from 5.9% in January to 5.3% in December.

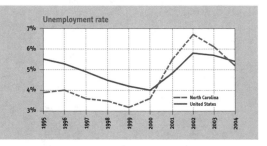

Unemployment rate

NC's aggregate adult employment rate has declined slightly in the last three years, even as the unemployment rate has improved; as of 2005, NC's employment rate remains below the national average, and our competitive rankings are 34th in the US and 3rd in the SE region. From 1993 to 2003, NC was 16th in the US and 4th in the SE region in non-agricultural employment growth.

Measure: Personal Income

Target:
At least 100% of US average per capita personal income

Actual:	90%
US Rank (2003):	36th
Southeast Rank (2003):	5th

Definition: Total income (i.e., wages, proprietor income, dividends, interest, rent and government payments) divided by total population

Source: US Bureau of Economic Analysis, Annual State Personal Income

Notes: Aggregate per capita income may obscure disparities among demographic, economic and geographic lines

After impressive per capita personal income increases during the 1990s, NC's national ranking for this indicator began to fall in 2000. Since 2000, NC's per capita personal income has continued to rise in actual dollars, but its competitive position has fallen from 31st to 36th nationally and from 4th to 5th regionally. NC's per capita personal income also fell slightly as a percent of the US average. Preliminary 2004 estimates indicate a continuation of this trend.

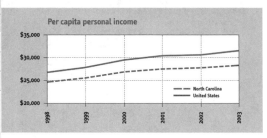

Per capita personal income

In 2003, NC was ranked 37th in the US and 5th in the region in per capita disposable personal income. In 2004, NC enjoyed a favorable competitive position in terms of personal bankruptcies—the 18th best rank in the US and the 2nd best rank in the SE.

222

Goal — Attract & nurture emerging economy sectors

Measure: Economic Climate

Target:
Rank among top 10 states
in overall business climate

In 2005, NC was ranked 1st in the US and Southeast in overall state business climate according to Site Selection Magazine. NC ranked among the national and regional leaders in state business climate for new and expanding business most of the last eight years, and earned the top national position in 2001, 2002, 2003 and 2005.

Actual:	1st

US Rank (2005):	1st

Southeast Rank (2005):	1st

Definition: Subjective ranking of desirability as place to do business based upon recent business plant expansion activity and a survey of corporate real estate executives regarding ease of doing business, overall business costs, state fiscal health and related factors

Source: Site Selection Magazine

Notes: The Site Selection ranking is more relevant for new and expanding businesses than traditional or declining industries

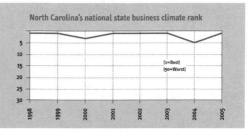

North Carolina's national state business climate rank

From 2001-03, NC had the 8th most corporate expansions and new facilities in the US and the most in the SE region. In 2002-03, Site Selection Magazine applauded several NC initiatives (e.g., the State Ports Credit, Qualified Business Venture Credit extension, and Economic Stimulus and Job Creation Act). In 2004, the Beacon Hill Institute (Suffolk University) ranked NC 26th in the nation and 3rd in the SE region in its ability to attract business and generate income. In 2004, the Tax Foundation ranked NC 30th in the US and 8th in the SE region in business tax climate, a business tax structure measure. In contrast, a Council on State Taxation/Ernst & Young study concluded that, as of 2004, NC (along with Delaware) had the lowest effective state and local business tax rate as a percent of private sector GSP.

Goal — Revitalize traditional economic sectors

Measure:
Manufacturing Vitality

Target: At least 120%
of US average
manufacturing job ratio

NC's preeminent position in manufacturing has been weakening over the last ten years, due in part to its long-standing concentration of textiles and other manufacturing industries vulnerable to global competition. From 1995 to 2004, the percent of manufacturing employees in NC fell from 24.6% to 14.8%. In 2004, NC was ranked 7th in the US in the percent of non-farm jobs in manufacturing, down from 6th in 2000 and 1st in 1995.

Actual:	136%

US Rank (2004):	8th

Southeast Rank (2004):	2nd

Definition: Manufacturing jobs as a percent of total non-farm jobs

Source: Bureau of Labor Statistics, Regional and State Employment and Unemployment

Notes: The manufacturing job ratio reflects the relative importance of a state's manufacturing jobs, but does not reflect net income or other indicators of industrial vitality; we are exploring other indicators

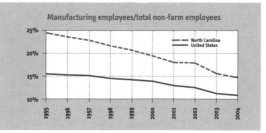

Manufacturing employees/total non-farm employees

Other indicators of industrial vitality help provide a more complete picture of NC's competitive position. For instance, in 2001, NC was ranked 14th in the US and 2nd in the SE region in manufacturing output per hour, a rough productivity measure for the manufacturing sector. More telling, NC ranked 37th in the US and 7th in the SE in average investment per manufacturing employee.

North Carolina 20/20 Update Report — January 31, 2005   29

Goal — Revitalize traditional economic sectors

Measure: Agricultural Vitality

NC's net farm income per acre has been steadily declining. Since 2000, the net farm income generated per acre in NC has fallen from $338 to $179, and NC's competitive rankings for this measure have fallen from 2nd to 7th in the US and from 1st to 4th in the SE region.

Target: At least 200% of US average net farm income per acre

Actual: 284%

US Rank (2003): 7th

Southeast Rank (2003): 4th

Definition: Net farm income (gross farm income less total production expenses) per acre, where a farm is any establishment from which at least $1,000 of agricultural products were sold during the year

Source: USDA, Economic Research Service, Net Farm Income for States

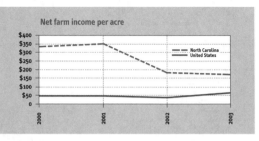

Net farm income per acre

NC continues to be one of the nation's leading agricultural states. In 2004, NC was 9th in the nation and 1st in the SE region in average farm value per acre, 19th in the nation and 2nd in the SE region (behind Kentucky) in total acres planted, and 2nd in the nation (behind Iowa) in hog and pig production. In 2003, NC ranked 10th in the nation and 3rd in the region in total net farm income (not adjusted for acreage).

Imperative 7: A Modern Infrastructure

Overview of Progress

Our Vision

North Carolina—long recognized as the good roads state—will win renewed acclaim for a globally competitive public infrastructure. Its hard infrastructure will effectively integrate efficient transportation modalities, reliable and affordable energy generation and distribution networks, and extensive water, sewer, storm water and solid waste management systems. Its soft infrastructure of low-cost, high-speed information and telecommunication networks will energize the state to compete in a dynamic, knowledge-based global environment.

Our Goals

1. Maintain a safe, efficient & balanced transportation system
2. Ensure abundant & affordable energy sources
3. Build ample & efficient public utility capacity
4. Stimulate thriving technology network

Despite many positive strides, North Carolina has yet to meet the strategic infrastructure targets for which we have current data. The competitiveness of our transportation system is being threatened by increases in mileage driven, commute times and congestion. Our electricity and natural gas costs are high compared to the rest of our region. Finally, our technology network, as measured by our access to internet technology, does not compare favorably to other states.

Summary of Strategic Progress – A Modern Infrastructure

Goals	Measures	Target	US Rank	SE Rank
1. Maintain a safe, efficient & balanced transportation system	1. Transportation efficiency		44th	9th
	2. Highway quality		30th	3rd
	3. Port & rail capacity	(Update in process)		
2. Ensure abundant & affordable energy sources	1. Energy efficiency	(Update in process)		
	2. Power access		30th	9th
	3. Natural gas access		39th	6th
3. Build ample & efficient public utility capacity	1. Infrastructure investment	(Update in process)		
	2. Water capacity	(Update in process)		
	3. Sewer capacity	(Update in process)		
4. Stimulate thriving technology network	1. Private technology access		37th	4th
	2. Public technology access		36th	7th

Note: Measures for which we have met or exceeded the target are marked with a "check" under the Target column. Measures for which we are awaiting new data are marked "update in process" and will be updated as new data becomes available.

The Governor and General Assembly have taken several important actions to improve our transportation system and achieve other goals establish for this imperative, including the following:

- Created the Highway Trust Fund to build and maintain highways within ten miles of most residents and reallocated $630 million in cash balances to accelerate road re-surfacing and repair projects (the NC Moving Ahead initiative);
- Open the state's first high-occupancy vehicle traffic lanes on Interstate 77 near Charlotte;
- Promoted several safety initiatives through the Governor's Highway Safety Program, such as the "Click It or Ticket" campaign for increasing safety belt and child seat use;
- Instituted regulations to encourage communities that rely on underground aquifers to control water usage and reduce over-pumping; and
- Supported the development of a liquefied natural gas terminal in Morehead City.

NC is reviewing the statutory formula for allocating highway funds. Transportation funds are distributed to 14 regions based on 3 major factors: 1) 1/2 based on each region's population, 2) 1/4 based on each region's uncompleted mileage and 3) 1/4 in 14 equal shares. Any changes in this formula could have profound effects on state and regional development plans. NCDOT's Long Range Transportation Plan anticipates a $29 billion funding shortfall over the next 25 years to upgrade system conditions and links, upgrade roadway safety and expand key routes.

The state government is but one actor in the infrastructure arena. NC's local governments (often with federal and state funding) are tackling traffic and other infrastructure issues. For instance, in Charlotte, voters approved a $3 billion transit system expansion (including a ten-mile light rail line to open in 2006), and officials are promoting car pooling, bus usage and telecommuting. In the Raleigh-Durham area, the Regional Transportation Alliance is promoting toll roads, car pool lanes and express buses and the Triangle Transit Authority is seeking federal funds to build a $700 million commuter rail line. Several communities are pursuing ways to manage water and sewer infrastructure more effectively, including water recycling programs and regional water and sewer authorities.

The state's progress on individual goals and measures for this imperative is discussed in more detail on the pages that follow.

225

Goal — Maintain a safe, efficient & balanced transportation system

Measure:
Transportation Efficiency

Target:
Less than 100% of US average vehicle miles traveled per vehicle

Actual: 123%

US Rank (2003): 44th

Southeast Rank (2003): 9th

Definition: Average annual vehicle miles traveled (VMT) per vehicle (i.e., autos, trucks, buses and motorcycles)

Source: US DOT, Federal Highway Administration, Highway Statistics

Notes: The vehicle miles traveled (VMT) per vehicle rate provides one potential indicator of the efficiency of a state's transportation system, but it is affected by many factors, including geographic diversity, historic developmental patterns and high population growth.

From 1994 to 2003, NC experienced a steady increase in average vehicle miles traveled (VMT) per vehicle, after similar increases during the 1980s and early 90s. Not surprisingly, NC has failed to make progress toward its target, and its competitive rankings for this indicator have fallen to 44th in the US and 9th in the SE region.

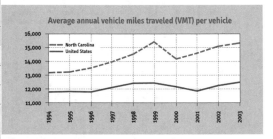

Average annual vehicle miles traveled (VMT) per vehicle

In 2003, NC had the 30th shortest average commute time in the US and the 5th shortest in the SE. In 2002, Charlotte had the 20th worst highway congestion among the country's 50 largest urban areas. In 2002, NC had the 25th highest urban transit (i.e., bus, rail and other) ridership in the US and the 4th highest in the SE region.

Measure: Highway Quality

Target:
Less than 90% of US average highway fatality rate

Actual: 110%

US Rank (2003): 30th

Southeast Rank (2003): 3rd

Definition: Number of fatalities per 100 million vehicle miles of travel on highways

Source: US DOT, Federal Highway Administration, Highway Statistics

Notes: We plan to replace the highway fatality rate with a nationally-recognized highway quality rating as soon as sufficient data for an acceptable indicator becomes available for a multi-year period

NC's highway fatality rate, an approximate reflection of highway quality and conditions, has gradually improved over the last ten years. Since 1994, NC's national highway safety rank has improved from 35th to 30th, but its regional rank has remained unchanged at 3rd. NC's highway fatality rate remains above the national average.

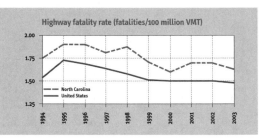

Highway fatality rate (fatalities/100 million VMT)

About 1/3 of NC's major roads need repair and 45% are congested during peak travel times. In 2003, according to the Federal Highway Administration, NC was 17th in the US and 7th in the SE region in highway condition ratings. In 2004, NC was ranked 35th in the US and 8th in the region in the percent of bridges meeting national standards. In 2002, NC spent 1.3% of personal income on highways, only the 32nd highest percent in the nation and 7th highest in the SE region. In 2003, NC had the 21st highest gas tax in the US and the 3rd highest in the SE (behind Florida and West Virginia). Over 78% of NC's roads are state-controlled, the 2nd highest state control ratio in the nation.

226

Goal — Ensure abundant & affordable energy sources

Measure: Power Access

Target:
Less than 90% of US average electricity costs

Actual: 93%

US Rank (2003): 30th

Southeast Rank (2003): 9th

Definition: Average aggregate electricity price for residential, commercial, industrial and other service in cents per 1,000 kilowatt hours

Source: US Dept. of Energy, Energy Information Administration, Annual Electric Utility Reports and Electric Power Monthly

Since 1995, NC's average electricity prices for all customers have increased slightly, yet remained below the national average. However, NC's electricity prices continue to be among the most expensive in the SE region, perhaps due to several factors, including the state's stranded costs attributable to prior nuclear energy investments.

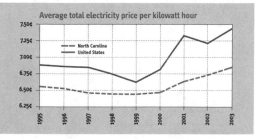

Average total electricity price per kilowatt hour

NC's electricity costs for residential customers remain high compared to other states. In 2003, NC had the 43rd lowest average monthly bill for residential customers in the US and the 6th lowest average monthly bill in the SE. NC's electricity costs for industrial customers are more competitive. In 2003, NC had the 33rd lowest electricity prices in the US and 3rd lowest prices in the SE for industrial customers.

Measure: Natural Gas Access

Target:
Less than 100% of US average residential natural gas costs

Actual: 118%

US Rank (2003): 39th

Southeast Rank (2003): 6th

Definition: Average price of natural gas delivered to residential customers per 1,000 cubic feet

Source: US Energy Department, Energy Information Administration, State Energy Data

NC has relatively expensive natural gas service for residential customers. In 2003, NC's average residential natural gas costs were nearly 20% higher than the national average, making it the 12th most costly state in the US and the 5th most costly state in the region. In recent years, however, NC's residential natural gas prices have risen at a slower pace than the US average.

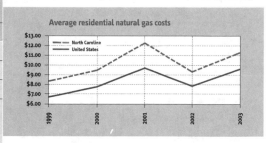

Average residential natural gas costs

NC is burdened by some of the highest natural gas prices in the nation and Southeast. In 2001, NC had the highest overall and industrial natural gas prices in the SE region, and the 8th highest aggregate prices and 14th highest industrial prices in the nation. NC uses less natural gas than most other states of comparable size. In 2001, NC was ranked 20th in total natural gas industry sales.

Goal — Stimulate thriving technology network

**Measure:
Private Technology Access**

**Target:
At least 100% of US average
household internet access rate**

Actual: 94%

US Rank (2003): 37th

Southeast Rank (2003): 4th

Definition: Percent of households with internet access

Source: US Commerce Dept., National Telecommunications &
Information Administration (NTIA) and US Census Bureau, Current
Population Survey, Internet and Computer Use Supplement

NC's household internet access rate is rapidly improving. In 2003, NC's private internet access rate rose to nearly 94% of the US average, ranking it 37th in the nation and 4th in the SE region. In 2004, NC continued to close the gap and, by some reports, may have surged ahead of the national average. A recent study by the e-NC Authority concluded that, by the end of 2004, NC's internet access rate had surpassed the US average.

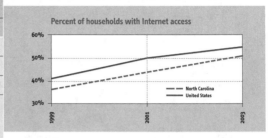

Percent of households with Internet access

In 2003, NC's high-speed access rate was the 17th highest in the US, and all of NC's counties had high-speed Internet service, but service availability varied widely by county. In 2003, 66.1% of the Raleigh/Durham population had internet access, ranking it 16th among metro areas and 18.1% had high-speed connections, ranking it 28th among metro areas. In 2003, 75% of NC's zip codes had at least one high-speed Internet subscriber, the 8th highest rate in the US and the 2nd highest in the SE region.

**Measure:
Public Technology Access**

**Target:
Less than 100% of US average public
school pupil-computer rate**

Actual: 107%

US Rank (2003): 36th

Southeast Rank (2003): 7th (tie)

Definition: Ratio of students per Internet-connected computer in
public schools

Source: Education Week, Education Counts

Notes: A decline in this ratio signifies greater Internet access

Since 2000, NC has dramatically increased the availability of internet-connected computers for students, from 11.0 students per internet-connected computer to 4.4, and steadily closed its gap with the national average. From 2000 to 2004, NC's competitive ranking in this indicator improved, from 46th in the US to 36th, and from 8th in the SE region to a tie for 7th.

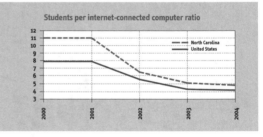

Students per internet-connected computer ratio

In 2004, the Center for Digital Government ranked NC 10th in the nation, and 3rd in the SE region (behind Virginia and Tennessee), in the use of digital technologies to streamline operations and serve citizens. In 2004, NC was ranked 36th in the nation in the ratio of instructional computers to students. In 2004, NC's state government website was rated the 31st best in the US (down from 11th in 2001) in terms of such factors as on-line services, credit card acceptance, privacy and security.

228

Imperative 8: Accountable Government

Overview of Progress

Our Vision

Knowledgeable citizens will actively participate in their communities and hold their state and local governments accountable for the revenues they receive and the services they provide. Our state and local governments will address the changing needs of their citizens in an efficient, effective, responsive and equitable manner.

Our Goals

1. Enhance citizen involvement in civic affairs
2. Promote effective & efficient government
3. Provide responsible & open government

North Carolina has attained 3 of the 7 strategic targets for Accountable Government. While we continue to lag other states in voter participation and civic engagement, our state and local governments incur lower per capita costs and debt than most governments in other parts of the country. Our state and local taxes (as a percent of personal income) are the 20th lowest in the nation and the 6th lowest in the Southeast. Our per capita state and local government debt, while rising, remains quite low compared to most other states.

Summary of Strategic Progress – Accountable Government

Goals	Measures	Target	US Rank	SE Rank
1. Enhance citizen involvement	1. Voter participation		35th	5th
in civic affairs	2. Community service		39th	8th
2. Promote effective & efficient	1. Government efficiency		20th	6th
government	2. State government performance	✔	16th	5th
	3. Local government performance		26th	9th
3. Provide responsible &	1. State government stewardship	✔	11th	4th
open government	2. Local government stewardship	✔	23rd	3rd

Note: Measures for which we have met or exceeded the target are marked with a "check" under the Target column. Measures for which we are awaiting new data are marked "update in process" and will be updated as new data becomes available.

North Carolina was the 2nd state in the US to enact legislation allowing eligible adults to register to vote upon renewing a driver's license (motor voter registration was required nationally by the National Voter Registration Act in 1995). This year, the General Assembly is considering several legislative reforms to enhance civic engagement, including bills to create an independent redistricting commission, tighten lobbying controls, improve voting systems and enhance procedures for correcting election errors.

The Governor has initiated several efforts designed to streamline state government, including a state government efficiency commission, a state government financing commission, a proposal to curb state borrowing and a proposal to revamp the state personnel system, but these efforts have not yet been fully implemented. Recent fiscal crises have forced state and local government officials throughout North Carolina to take short-term (and often painful) measures to cut costs, raise revenues and balance budgets. Nevertheless, North Carolina's state and local government structure has not been materially changed in many decades, and comprehensive strategies for revamping the way in which our governmental entities finance or manage their operations are not yet under serious consideration.

The state's progress on individual goals and measures for this imperative is discussed in more detail on the pages that follow.

Goal — Enhance citizen involvement in civic affairs

Measure: Voter Participation

Target:
At least 110% of US average voter turnout rate

Actual: 97%

US Rank (2004): 35th

Southeast Rank (2004): 5th

Definition: Percent of voting age population (but not necessarily eligible) voting in even-year elections

Source: Federal Election Commission, Voter Registration and Turnout

NC's voting participation continues to crest in 4-year cycles due to presidential elections, but remains below the US average. In 2004, NC's voter turnout increased dramatically and about 55% of NC's voting-aged citizens participated in the general election, the 35th highest turnout rate in the nation and the 5th highest rate in the SE region. The State Board of Elections reports that the turnout of NC's registered voters increased from 59% in 2000 to 64% in 2004.

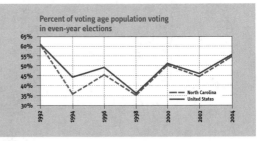

Percent of voting age population voting in even-year elections

After peaking at 88% in 2000, NC's voter registration rate fell in 2002, due in large part to the National Voter Registration Act which allowed states more latitude to update voter rolls. In 2004, NC experienced election problems, including lost votes in Carteret County and two disputed statewide races. The State Board of Elections promotes standard training and procedures, but NC counties use multiple voting practices and technologies, including direct record electronic equipment, optical scan machines, punch cards, lever machines and paper ballots.

Measure: Community Service

Target:
At least 100% of US average volunteerism rate

Actual: 90%

US Rank (2003): 39th

Southeast Rank (2003): 8th

Definition: Percent of adults aged 25 or older who volunteer at least 50 hours of free time per year to civic, community, charitable or other nonprofit activities

Source: US Census Bureau, American Community Survey

Notes: Estimated rate based on relatively small survey sample

The percent of NC adults who volunteer (i.e., the adult volunteerism rate), as tracked by the Census Bureau's American Community Survey, is well below the national average rate. In 2003, NC was tied for 39th in the US and 8th in the SE region in this indicator of civic engagement.

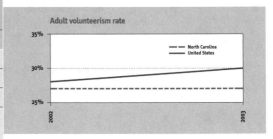

Adult volunteerism rate

In 2003, NC's volunteer rate for youth aged 16-19 years was about 23%, ranking it 45th in the US and 9th in the Southeast region. NC is highly ranked in charitable giving, another indicator of civic engagement. In 2002, NC was tied for 7th in the US, and ranked 4th in the Southeast, in charitable giving (as measured by itemized contributions as a percent of adjusted gross income).

Goal — Promote effective & efficient government

**Measure:
Government Efficiency**

**Target:
Less than 95% of US
average tax revenue ratio**

Over the past decade, NC's governmental tax revenues have declined marginally as a percent of personal income. Our state and local tax revenue ratio remains relatively low from a national perspective (we have the 20th lowest tax revenue ratio), but is relatively higher within the Southeast (we have the 6th lowest tax revenue ratio in the region).

Actual:	97%

US Rank (2004):	20th

Southeast Rank (2004): 6th

Definition: Total state and local tax revenues as a percent of total personal income

Source: US Census Bureau, Bureau of Economic Analysis, Annual State Personal Income, and US Census Bureau, State and Local Government Finances

Notes: The ratio of state and local tax revenues to total personal income reflects the relative size of government, but may only approximate government efficiency (i.e., a lower ratio may suggest greater efficiency); we are continuing to explore alternative indicators

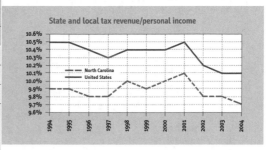

State and local tax revenue/personal income

In 2004, NC's total aggregate taxes (including federal taxes) were 26.4% of personal income, giving it the 19th lowest aggregate tax ratio in the US and the 7th lowest ratio in the Southeast region. In 2003, NC's per capita tax revenues and expenditures were the 7th lowest in the nation and the 4th lowest in the Southeast region.

**Measure: State
-Government Performance**

**Target: Less than 95%
of US average per capita
state government costs**

Since 1996, NC's per capita state government expenditures have steadily increased, but remain less than 90% of the national average. Since 2000, NC's per capita spending rate has improved from the 21st to the 16th lowest in the nation and improved from the 6th to the 5th lowest. In 2003, NC's state government tax revenue was 6.7% of personal income, the 34th lowest percent in the US and 7th lowest in the Southeast.

Actual:	87%

US Rank (2003):	16th

Southeast Rank (2003): 5th

Definition: Total state government expenditures, including all outlays except debt service, divided by total population

Source: US Census Bureau, Governments Division, State Government Finances

Notes: Per capita state government costs reflect the relative size of state government, but do not necessarily reflect government efficiency or effectiveness; this is merely a macro indicator of state government costs and should be viewed in the context of the state government's array of other performance indicators

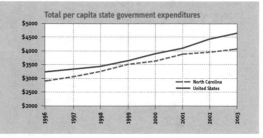

Total per capita state government expenditures

In 2005, *Governing Magazine's* Government Performance Project (GPP) assigned NC a grade of C+ for state government management (only 5 states nationally earned a lower grade, but 15 states received the same grade). NC received praise for its fiscal projection capabilities, e-procurement platform and asset management controls, but was chastised for information technology, employee recruitment, construction project reporting and strategic planning deficiencies. According to GPP, NC state government has a "very good long-term budgeting perspective," but its performance budgeting requirements have been eliminated and its use of performance data to make decisions varies.

Goal — Promote effective & efficient government

Measure: Local Government Performance

Target:
Less than 95% of US average local government employee ratio

Actual:	101%

US Rank (2003):	26th

Southeast Rank (2003): 9th

Definition: Total local government employees per 10,000 population

Source: US Bureau of Labor Statistics

Notes: The per capita number of local government employees roughly reflects the relative size of local government, but does not necessarily account for relative effectiveness and efficiency; large cities are defined as having a population of at least 25,000 and large counties are defined as those with at least 100,000 residents

In 2004, NC had 486 local government employees per 10,000 population, slightly more than the national average. Since 2001, the number of local government employees per 10,000 residents has declined in NC, giving NC the 26th fewest local government employees per capita in the US. However, NC still has the 9th fewest local government employees per capita in the Southeast.

Local government employees per 10,000 residents

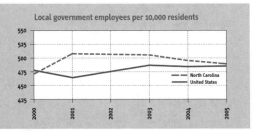

NC's local government expenditures are relatively low. From 1995 to 2002, NC's per capita local government expenditures ranged from 10% to 15% below the US average. In 2003, NC had the 26th highest average salary for local government employees in the US and the 3rd highest in the SE region. NC's local governments also have demonstrated a commitment to good management practices. For instance, in 2004, 37% of NC's large counties and 50% of NC's large cities earned the Government Finance Officers Association's Distinguished Budget Award.

Goal — Ensure fiscally prudent government

Measure: State Government Stewardship

Target: Less than 90% of US average per capita state government debt

Actual:	60%

US Rank (2003):	11th

Southeast Rank (2003): 4th

Definition: Total state government debt, including short-term, long-term, full faith and credit, non-guaranteed and public debt for private purposes, divided by total population

Source: US Census Bureau, State and Local Government Finances

Notes: Per capita state government debt, coupled with nationally-recognized credit ratings, provides an important gauge of state financial condition; the US Census Bureau debt definition is more inclusive than that of the NC Treasurer's Office and rating agencies, including all credit obligations incurred in the name of the government and its dependent agencies, even if non-guaranteed or issued for the direct benefit of the private sector

NC's per capita state government debt has increased significantly since 1996 due to numerous factors, including natural disasters, economic setbacks and major public investments (e.g., the higher education bonds). Still, NC's per capita state government debt is only 60% of the national average, giving NC the 11th lowest debt in the US and the 4th lowest in the region.

Per capita state government debt

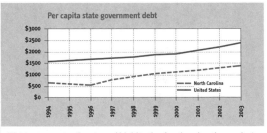

NC state government continues to earn high debt ratings from the major rating agencies. In 2004, NC earned an AAA bond rating from Standard and Poor's and Fitch, their highest rating, but dropped to an AA-1 rating (with a positive outlook) with Moody's, that agency's second highest rating. Since 2000, the state's debt service increased from $255 million to $483 million (from 1.9% to 3.0% of total spending) and has been projected to reach $656 million by 2006. In 2003, State Policy Research, Inc. concluded that NC state government had the 5th strongest fiscal condition (per its Solvency Index) in the US and the strongest in the SE region.

Goal — Ensure fiscally prudent government

Measure: Local Government Stewardship

Target: Less than 90% of US average per capita local government debt

Actual: 74%

US Rank (2002): 23rd

Southeast Rank (2002): 3rd

Definition: Total local government debt, including short-term, long-term, full faith and credit, non-guaranteed and public debt for private purposes, divided by total population

Source: US Census Bureau, State and Local Government Finances

Notes: Per capita local government debt, along with nationally-recognized credit ratings, provides a good overview of local government financial condition; large cities are defined as having a population of at least 25,000 and large counties are defined as those with at least 100,000 residents

NC's aggregate per capita local government debt has remained relatively stable over the past decade, but it has dropped relative to the national average. As of 2002, NC had the 23rd lowest per capita local government debt in the nation and the 3rd lowest in the Southeast.

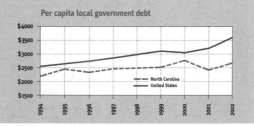

NC's largest local governments continue to earn favorable debt ratings from the major rating agencies. Many of the state's largest cities (i.e., Charlotte, Raleigh, Durham and Winston-Salem) and counties (i.e., Wake County) enjoy the highest bond ratings with all three rating agencies. The City of Greensboro, like the state government, earned an AAA rating from Standard & Poors and Fitch and an AA-1 with positive outlook from Moody's. NC's local governments also enjoy a good reputation for financial reporting . In 2004, for example, 87% of NC's large counties and 88% of NC's large cities earned the Government Finance Officers Association's Certificate of Achievement for Excellence in Financial Reporting.

Closing Comments

Why Scorecards Matter

The US GAO assessed 29 strategic indicator systems, including North Carolina's 20/20 project, ... and found that they offer great promise for improving accountability, decision-making and collaborative problem-solving

Since our nation's founding, the success of our democracy has depended in large part on our ability to obtain reliable and timely information about our governance processes. As the Comptroller General of the United States recently wrote, "there has been a long history—checkered by both success and failure—of attempts to create ever more advanced ways to inform our public dialogues and generate a context for civic choices..."

As the United States Government Accountability Office (GAO) found in its 2004 study, "Informing Our Nation: Improving How to Assess the USA's Position and Progress," strategic scorecards and other indicator systems are vital tools for informing citizens and their elected representatives. The GAO assessed 29 strategic indicator systems (i.e., systems that gauge the economic, social and environmental trends of states, regions and localities), including North Carolina's 20/20 project. In summary, the GAO concluded that strategic indicator systems offer great promise for improving public accountability, strategic decision-making and collaborative problem-solving.

That there is a growing interest in strategic indicator systems, especially those that offer comparative rankings and grades, there is little doubt. North Carolina and its communities are being measured, but not necessarily against benchmarks of our own choosing. We have listed below several national organizations that grade states on their strategic performance.

- The Morgan Quitno Press publishes annual rankings of the "most livable," "healthiest" and "smartest" states in the US using a broad array of factors for each index;
- The United Health Foundation publishes an annual report, "America's Health, State Health Rankings," rating the "healthiest" states in the US using such factors as mortality, obesity, smoking, health insurance, child poverty and violent crime rates;
- The Annie E. Casey Foundation's "Kids Count Data Book" ranks individual states in overall child well-being based on ten factors (e.g., infant mortality, low birthweight, high school dropout and parental employment rates);
- Education Week, in its annual 50-state report card on education, "Quality Counts", grades states in such areas as improving teacher quality, standards and accountability, school climate, resource adequacy and school equity;
- The National Center for Public Policy and Higher Education, in its biennial report card, "Measuring Up," grades all 50 states in six higher education performance categories;
- The Beacon Hill Institute at Suffolk University, in its annual "Metro Area and State Competitiveness Report," grades states on their ability to attract business and generate income;
- The Corporation for Enterprise Development (CFED)'s "Asset and Opportunities Scorecard" grades states on asset accumulation and distribution, based on a broad range of criteria, including financial security, business development, homeownership and education;
- Governing Magazine publishes an annual state management report card grading state governments on overall management, fiscal management, personnel management, infrastructure management and information management.

Governing Magazine's 2005 report card on state management concluded, "North Carolina has systematically dismantled much of its strategic planning apparatus. The Progress Board still looks at future needs, but the...entire [budget office's] planning unit... was eliminated."

Some strategic scorecards may be more agenda-driven than others. That is one more reason why we need our own scorecard system—one that best reflects our state's long-term priorities.

As more outsiders grade our state, and the pressures for strategic competitiveness mount, our ability to plan and track outcomes will be critical. Will we be up to this challenge?

Governing Magazine's 2005 report card on North Carolina's management practices concluded, "North Carolina has systematically dismantled much of its strategic planning apparatus in the past three years. The Progress Board still looks at future needs, but about 25 percent of the analytic capacity of the budget office was eliminated, including the entire planning unit. At the same time, the legislature also abolished existing requirements for performance budgeting." State officials contend that the planning unit's core functions (e.g., demographic analysis) have been retained, and that they are exploring better ways to link planning and budgeting. We contend that our ability to compete will depend in part on the effectiveness of our state's strategic planning and performance management processes.

What's Next?

Statement of Need – North Carolina faces daunting challenges, including escalating global economic competition, mounting investment needs and fiscally strained state and local governments. As we have learned from such bold, visionary decisions as university system consolidation, banking reform and the Research Triangle Park, thinking and acting strategically can give us a critical competitive edge.

We have enjoyed some of our greatest strategic successes—in child health care and education— where we have used strategic targets and actions...

Thinking strategically—taking the long view—requires us to face the future with a cohesive vision, measurable targets and sound strategies. In fact, it is where we have used strategic targets and actions that we have enjoyed some of our greatest successes. In health care, for instance, our state leaders raised our child immunization ranking from the bottom tier to the 4th best program in the nation and the best in the Southeast region. In education, we have increased our average teacher pay rank from 43rd to 23rd and earned some of the highest average reading/math proficiency scores in the Southeast region.

North Carolina has a proud history of rising to new challenges. Just as previous generations made tough choices that benefit us, we can now act on behalf of future generations. By asking hard questions about public policies, defining our expectations and ensuring accountability, we can give our children—and their children—a better state in which to live.

New Direction – In the hope of strengthening North Carolina's strategic capabilities and thereby promoting our competitiveness as a state, the North Carolina Progress Board has adopted the following four-point plan:

- Build a permanent, fact-based campaign for North Carolina's future around the new strategic scorecard and other useful value-added data products;
- Develop real-time data delivery and other enhanced communications capabilities for keeping leaders and citizens current on breaking developments and trends;
- Engage communities in enhancing their strategic capabilities and bridging the gap between Raleigh-centric policies and community interests; and
- Adopt a new entrepreneurial, sustainable business model to increase private sector involvement and make better use of fragmented or under-utilized public policy resources.

The North Carolina Progress Board will use the newly-designed strategic scorecard system as the foundation for a series of new dynamic, efficient and inter-related data products. The strategic scorecard system will serve as the primary tool for tracking our progress as well as the focal point for framing strategic issues. As a natural part of our ongoing work to update the strategic scorecard system, we will offer several new products in useful and visually compelling formats, such as the 2020 Update Report, public policy website profiles (Progress Links), research paper abstracts (Progress Digests), non-partisan issue summaries (Issue Scans) and practical menus of promising solutions (Progress Points). We will make the above products available to the public through our new website (the Progress Portal).

This year, we are undertaking several initiatives to [make] the Strategic Scorecard ... a durable framework for assessing our state's competitiveness ...

FY06 Plan – This year, we are undertaking several initiatives to improve the effectiveness of the Strategic Scorecard. We are designing a methodology for assigning grades. We are working to develop strategic targets for the key economic regions of our state. We are exploring ways to tap our state's vast academic resources in the public policy arena. We are migrating from a reliance on biennial printed reports to real-time website delivery. With our new electronic portal, we will be able to update our progress continuously, as new data are released. With such efforts, we hope that the Strategic Scorecard will become a durable framework for assessing our state's competitiveness on a continual basis.

To carry out our plan for this year, we will seek greater resources from the private sector and assistance from our state's academic institutions. If you would like to learn more about our strategic scorecard system, our new data products or ways in which you can help shape our state's future, visit our website at www.ncprogress.org or call us at 919-513-3900.

Acknowledgments

The North Carolina Progress Board, including our chairperson, Governor Mike Easley, and the other members listed on our website, would like to thank the staff and consultants who helped prepare this report (see our website for a full list of these contributors). The Board also would like to express its appreciation to the many federal and state agencies and other organizations that provided information and other invaluable assistance.

North Carolina Progress Board
Suite 3900, Partners I, Centennial Campus
1017 Main Campus Drive, Campus Box 7248
Raleigh, NC 27695-7248
Telephone: 919 513 3900
Website: www.ncprogress.org

236

Appendix B: Exercises in Exploring Transparency

The following questions and recommended assignments are designed to explore the concept of transparency in government and nonprofit organizations. Some of the examples are drawn from the corporate experience because they illustrate the underlying tension of revealing information that may prove to be damaging to the organization's reputation and future. The voluntary sharing of the information, however, may enable the organization to thwart threats to its very existence. A decision to disclose such significant information inevitably is expensive to the organization. It seldom destroys the entity. However, choosing to be secretive about important performance information may result in the destruction or serious weakening of the organization (the Catholic Church, Arthur Anderson Consulting Company, Enron, and Lehman Brothers brokerage firm).

Chapter 1: Introduction

1. Transparency is the disclosure of potentially damaging information to a person or organization that could subsequently use the information to negatively impact the individual being transparent. Provide three examples from your own life when individuals or organizations have demonstrated their honesty with you at some risk to their future relationship with you. What were the negative and positive consequences to the transparent person? Once you are able to conceptualize the idea of transparency at a personal level, it is easier to envision it at an agency, organization, or government level.

The key is to focus on "the dirty little secrets" which, if revealed, could cause major consequences. All organizations protect these secrets because they accurately fear the consequences. For example, in 2008, if the banks, brokerage firms, financial institutions, rating agencies, Federal Reserve, U.S. Treasury and business media would have warned investors of the true risk exposure of the stock market, millions of their customers would have shifted their investments to safer options. Such a response would have caused many of the financial institutions to become insolvent (as they ultimately did). They knew that their dirty little secret, if widely known, could seriously damage their customers and potentially destroy their organizations.

2. *The Harvard Business Review* uses case examples to simulate corporate decision making. Various executives provide unique

perspectives on a specific case example. The diverse responses create lively discussions regarding the differences in management approaches to the same presenting set of facts. This type of exercise trains new managers in clarifying their approach to management. This same approach is widely used in medicine, law, and other professional schools like social work.

The May 2008 edition of the *Harvard Business Review* included a case example on transparency and a corporate decision to either be more or less transparent and why. The case study was entitled *Will our customers bail us out?* (pgs. 37-48). The case focused on the question of a struggling college textbook publishing house and its strategy to share corporate information about its fragile financial condition with customers to solicit their support with product purchases during a transition period. This case study focused on how transparent the corporate president should be with customers and with what consequences for the company's future. Honest disclosure was presented as a way to secure trust from current customers who were expected to appreciate such disclosure and reward uncommon frankness with continued support. Read the case and prepare your response in approximately the same 600 words provided by the three respondents to the *Harvard Business Review* case.

3. Create your own case study from your own experience that illustrates how the disclosure of information can result in serious consequences for a government or nonprofit organization. The case study should focus on "dirty little secrets" that all organizations fear being widely known and because of their perceived highly negative consequences for future budgets or reputations. The information could become the basis for a scandal or highly visible press coverage as a misuse of public resources. The case study should be sufficiently detailed (3,000 words) so that the reader can appreciate different perspectives and proposed solutions within an organization. There usually are such differences within any agency among operational staff, accountants, lobbyists, public relations, and client advocate representatives.

Ultimately, the case study should focus on a specific issue or strategy with a specific decision point to limit readers to prepare their responses to the case example. Read an example of a *Harvard Business Review* case study to get some appreciation of the level of detail and the ability to bring a story to a focused question that requires a management decision. Once all case studies have been created, two or three should be distributed to class members for their analysis, response, and recommended management decision. A panel of best responses could provide a lively discussion surrounding the disclosure of information with high risk to the agency. It is remarkable how widely individuals will vary in their management decisions on this issue of transparency.

4. Johnson and Johnson, a large pharmaceutical company, produces and widely distributes Tylenol, the over-the-counter pain reliever. On September 29, 1982, Chicago drug stores sold Extra-Strength Tylenol to seven customers who subsequently died. This series of events was a national news item. Johnson and Johnson acted quickly and immediately removed all Tylenol from all stores across the country at high cost to the company. J&J admitted that it did not know the cause of the deadly consequence of taking Tylenol and assured the public that there would be a full investigation to determine the root cause. Ultimately, it was determined that someone had tampered with the product and had injected a deadly doze of cyanide into the containers before resetting them back on the store shelves for purchase by future consumers. This disclosure led to major repackaging to protect consumers against a repeat of this incident. This was an expensive alternative for both the company and future consumers. The case was never solved. The safer-packaged Tylenol was returned to all stores and has remained a product with a strong consumer loyalty and 35% of the pain reliever market. Go to Wikipedia and read coverage of this Tylenol incident. Try to imagine the discussions that must have ensued at Johnson and Johnson regarding the management decisions following this initial discovery of seven deaths. Create your version of the pros and cons of the four ultimate decision points:

1. taking Tylenol off the shelves,
2. pledging an investigation to get to the root cause,
3. repackaging, and
4. returning the product to the store shelves.

Your summary should be 600 words. Try to imagine a discussion between two or three individuals from the company who have different proposed strategies and solutions.

Chapter 2: Government Should Be More Like Baseball

1. Pick a sport and detail the performance level of your favorite player or team. You can obtain such outcome information

online or in most newspapers. Prioritize the most significant performance statistics for a given player or team, and indicate why a particular measure is more important than others to accurately reflect a high talent level. Try to remember when you first became aware of sports performance information. It will be difficult to isolate the time and circumstances because such information is a large part of the culture.

2. Go to Appendix A and review the various benchmarks used by North Carolina as indicators of progress. You can also use your specific state (Minnesota, Oregon, Florida, Maine, Connecticut, and Vermont) if they also have benchmarks. Select five of these benchmarks that you believe are the most important and that the United States should place among the top ten industrialized countries. Explore the Web to locate any international comparisons. One good source is the Organization for Economic Cooperation and Development (OECD) or the *Economist* magazine. How accurate were your predictions of the United States performance ranking?

Chapter 3: Transparent Accountability Paradigm

1. *The Transparent Accountability Paradigm* defines a significantly different future than exists in most communities. Do you have any examples to support this vision of government at the local, state, or national level? Describe your example in 600 words.

2. Critique one of the dimensions of *The Transparent Accountability Paradigm* in terms of your acceptance or rejection of this approach to government. For example, Walter Lippmann, a newspaper reporter and writer in the period before the Great Depression, would have rejected the willingness of the public to become knowledgeable about government. He believed that most Americans would not bother to be sufficiently well-informed about government. You may want to review the history of newspapers in Eric Alterman's "Out of Print" article in the *New Yorker* (March 31, 2008 pgs. 48-59). On the other hand, Barack Obama proposes an active citizen participation level by creating a Google-like database of every federal dollar spent. He would post online every non-emergency proposed legislation for five days before he signs it so that all Americans can comment. In addition, he envisions a White House blog for public input. You may want to review Marc Ambinder's "His Space" article in the *Atlantic* (June, 2008 pgs. 63-67).) The critique should be limited to 600 words.

3. The Government Performance and Results Act (1993), developed and shepherded through the Congress by Sen. William Roth (R-DE) and passed by Congress, created an accountable system for a set of federal programs. Have you ever heard of it? Why do you think this federal legislation was never widely publicized or followed by the media or general public? What are the biggest barriers to assuring that federal programs are working effectively?

4. The National Conference of State Legislatures has created a 13-question approach to guide the state level appropriations process for each program. What would be the three primary reasons for following this approach? What would be the three primary reasons not to follow this approach? If you were a legislator, what would be your approach? Call your state legislators' offices and ask what their involvement has been with the appropriations process. You will probably receive a very vague response.

In 2006, I provided the Carter seven accountability questions covered in Chapter Four to a member of the Appropriations Committee of the Michigan House of Representatives, and he forwarded them to the rest of the committee members. The members expressed that they were grateful to have something to guide them through an assessment of the various programs included in their committee's review and budget.

5. Select one of the following states: Oregon, Minnesota, North Carolina, Florida, Maine, Connecticut, and Vermont. They all have developed their own benchmarking systems. There may be additional states. Look up your state to see if it has initiated such an approach. The benchmarking program staff will generally be located within the Governor's office, or at one of the State's universities. Compare two of the states and select your preferred approach and the reasons for your choice. Then select the top ten benchmarks in terms of importance in reflecting progress. Choose one benchmark, and assess changes over a ten- to twenty-year period. This exercise will illustrate the benefits of focusing on defined expectations that can be measured over a significant timeframe. Why would a Governor choose to initiate a benchmarking system? Why would a Governor not initiate a benchmarking system?

6. Consider everyone you have met and select three individuals in whom you have the greatest trust. Review the seven charac-

teristics for trust presented in this chapter. Review your three selections and assess each in terms of these seven traits. Are there additional dimensions? If yes, describe the new criteria. These individuals may be your parents, spouses, or best friends. Do you have a set of different criteria for trust based on the kind of relationship you have with the individual? Prioritize the trust traits to see if the priorities change across the three individuals you trust the most. This exercise will alert you to why these special trust individuals have uncommon qualities. The second part of this exercise is to do the same type of assessment for an institution (church, school, city, fraternity/sorority, corporation, volunteer group, and club). This will be much harder than defining trust dimensions for special personal relationships.

7. Articulate the conditions under which you believe transparency would be the best strategy for government or a nonprofit organization. Be as specific as possible in presenting the context for transparency (budget setting process, millage request, and scandal), the content of the transparency (financial projections, revenue shortfalls, low program outcomes) and the benefits/risks involved in such a decision for a specific stakeholder's perspective (taxpayer, agency manager, program advocate). The rationale for and against transparency are listed at the end of this chapter. These lists should enable you to determine your own comfort level regarding transparency. You will be amazed how clearly others see themselves as managers along this dimension. It appears as if there are those who are much more comfortable with transparency than others. Both have strong arguments and reasons for their preferences and managerial styles.

Chapter 4: Intrinsic Goodness and Stewardship

1. Does your agency leadership accept the ethic of intrinsic goodness? How is it evident in the agency's public relations promotion material, agency policy, fundraising brochures, and rationale for continuing funding? Try to find explicit examples. In many ways, this ethic is so pervasive that it is difficult to describe as it penetrates the culture of the organization.

2. The first seven questions of the Carter-Richmond methodology are a more elaborate form of a logic model. Select a program you are familiar with and answer the seven questions for a set of ten clients or a larger sample so that you become more aware of the challenges of collecting and summarizing this informa-

tion. The employment program example used in the chapter will provide some helpful guidance in creating your own logic model. The employment program example is relatively straightforward in its design and ability to connect the dots between the different parts of the program. Many other programs are much more difficult to construct, especially in the area of outcomes.

3. The outcome question usually is the most difficult to answer because a program case has been closed long before a long-term outcome has been determined. There are many objections/barriers to collecting outcome information. Seven have been described in the chapter. Select your favorite and expand on why you believe it is a relevant barrier and how it needs to be resolved in order to collect the outcome data. You should also list any new objections or barriers.

4. Stewardship is often discussed in terms of an emotional commitment to a program. Rarely is it discussed in terms of actually measuring it by demonstrating the effectiveness of the program to improve the lives of clients or communities served. Are there additional components of stewardship other than the nine described in the Carter-Richmond methodology? How would you measure these additional factors and why are they important?

5. Logic models are very useful conceptual tools for describing program inputs, activities, outputs and outcomes (initial, intermediate and long term). Go to http://www.researchutilization. org/logicmodel/examples.html to see examples of logic models. Then select a program and create your own logic model for that program. It should look similar to these examples. It is much harder to do than it appears.

Chapter 5: Return on Investment

1. The Return on Investment concept assumes that you can attach a financial value to a specific outcome. This is relatively easy for such programs as employment or energy assistance. It is often more difficult for less tangible program outcomes such as improved quality of life, decrease in stress, improved quality of water, safety level, or improved family relationships. Select a program outcome and create an approach to determining a financial value. Select a dollar value or a reasonable range of financial value. It is helpful to think of the challenges facing trial lawyers and insurance companies as they establish a financial settlement for accidents involving a loss of function over a pro-

jected productive employment lifetime. It is also helpful to think in terms of financial obligations averted as a result of a prevention program. Family planning programs, for example, believe that averting an unwanted pregnancy and birth saves the medical community significant medical expenses.

2. Review the example of the ROI for employment programs. Do you consider the estimate's cost savings as an adequate reflection of the public expenses of a typical family of three living at 100% of poverty ($18,310 in 2010)? What additional expenses should be included in the calculation of the public safety net?

Chapter 6: Vergil and Clark

1. Have you ever met a manager like Vergil Pinckney or Clark Luster? If yes, what was your response to his or her approach to management by outcomes? If no, what would have been your own response to his or her approach to management by outcomes? Would you have perceived such a manager as naïve or courageous in his or her management style? Was there ever a time when you, as a manager, were requested to collect and use client outcome information to reflect the success of your program? If yes, describe the consequences for you personally and for the program's subsequent funding or changes as a result of the sharing of outcome performance data.

2. Clark Luster retired from Pressley Ridge. His successor believes the long term outcomes for the Pressley Ridge behavioral problem teenagers will not be determined until they have reached the age when they would graduated from high school. The current Pressley Ridge kid would be an average of 12-13 years of age. Is this an appropriate long term outcome for this program? What would you expect the graduation rate for these students? You can review the average graduation rates for white, African American, and Latino students in Chapter Nine's review of the most important benchmarks.

Chapter 7: Lessons in Transparency

1. This chapter focuses on several fears nursing home providers experienced as they became more transparent with the general public and future customers regarding their performance ratings. Which fear would have been the most important to you if you had been involved as a participating nursing home owner/operator? Are there additional fears or apprehensions you would

have had? Would you have been in favor or opposed to this initiative? For example, there is a group of hospital surgeons who have been willing to share the results of their operations with colleagues only with the condition that no specific hospital or surgeon be identified in the release of the performance information. All results would be reported anonymously. This allowed the participating hospitals and surgeons to learn collectively but not be at risk for the loss of their reputation if the results were shown to be less effective than their colleagues.

2. Which of the fears were most surprising to you? Which additional fears would you have expected?

3. Are you aware of other examples of transparency efforts and their results? For example, academic achievement scores for elementary and secondary schools have been widely available for 30 years. Such transparency has not led to any significant improvement level in the scores nationally. Why not? Another example is that many hospitals have been releasing performance scores for several years. What have been the consequences for the hospitals or other health care providers who have attempted this level of performance transparency? What are the implications of these new examples for future program managers interested in learning how to manage with increasing transparency?

Chapter 8: Connecting the Dots

1. The most interesting and unexpected lesson from the transparency experiment with the Consumer Guide to Michigan Nursing Homes was the realization that providers who were most successful were often totally unaware of their outlier status as high quality homes and had difficulty identifying what factors caused quality. This may be a relatively common consequence of operating a health facility in an isolated community and no standardized definition of success across peers. The annual inspection process was a standardized set of criteria conducted by a subjective set of inspectors. The family satisfaction survey scores were unique to each home's satisfaction questions. The new guide presented both performance measures in a standardized way so that consumers could compare different nursing homes along these two criteria.

Select a program you are most familiar with and choose the five factors you consider most important for causing long-term outcome success. Tell your story in 600 words and then document your conclusions with relevant information from various appropriate sources. What information would you have preferred to have to make your story more convincing?

The ten principles for telling your story are outlined in the chapter. The principles will help you organize your story. Have colleagues assess your story to see if they have alternative explanations.

2. Once you have developed your story by articulating the factors causing the best outcomes, you should develop a set of recommendations on how to improve your outcomes by making appropriate policy or practice changes. Some of these recommendations may simply be to stop using resources on factors that are irrelevant to improving outcomes. This alone could lead to focusing more resources on the most important causal factors for success.

Chapter 9: Enhancing the Public Good

1. Much of government is invisible. List the five government functions (fire, police, mail service, garbage pick-up, schools, universities, tax collection, vehicle registration, car license) that are most visible to you. How do you rate the effectiveness of these services for you? What functions of government would you like to be more visible to you and how would you like to observe these functions? For example, I would like to know the Security Exchange Commission's accurate assessment of the level of risk in investing in various retirement options (US Treasury bills, public bonds, corporate bonds, CDs, annuities, stocks, 401K investment firms). I would like to see this type of oversight risk assessment regularly published in the New York Times financial section Web site available 24/7. Another example would be to have my East Lansing high school routinely release its graduation rate relative to the Michigan average so that I can appreciate its use of my tax dollars. I would also like to know the percent of high school graduates who ultimately complete college so that I can assess if the short term graduation leads to college graduation. This type of exercise should provide a way to increase the awareness level of the reader to the existence of government and your expectation of results for government. It is very difficult for individuals to become aware of these functions since they are largely invisible.

2. Select any institution (government, military, business, church, school, university, medicine, other profession) that has lost your trust and tell your story in 600 words. Be specific in your story about what was done to secure your trust, lose your trust, and what would restore it to the original level. This exercise will help you become more aware of how fragile trust is and how difficult it is to restore once it is lost.

3. This chapter presents three predictors of trust in government:
   a. politicians who do the right thing most of the time,
   b. rating of government performance, and
   c. the public's connection to the political component of government.
Are any of these three important to your trust in government? Why? What other factors are important to you in establishing trust in government?

4. Benchmarks are measures of expected progress for government. Eight are used as examples in this chapter. Pick one that is most important to you. List three institutions that should be enhancing this benchmark measure. Which institution do you expect to take the lead responsibility for improving this measure? What would you recommend government and/or other institutions do to assure future progress on this measure? One recommendation may be to stop funding of programs that cannot define how they contribute to improvements in the benchmark measures. Reassigning these funds to more effective programs would be an improvement in the use of public resources. For example, the various benchmarks for educational achievement are largely centered on schools and universities as opposed to families and religious organizations.

5. This chapter prioritizes the most important benchmarks for three major areas of progress. However, there are two areas without current benchmarks:

   (i) infrastructure improvements, and
   (ii) independence from fossil fuel energy sources.

These two areas are comprised of many separate components. For example, infrastructure may include roads, bridges, railroad tracks, electricity grids, ports, levees, mass transit, and airports. There is no one indicator for infrastructure. But there are measures of individual components of the infrastructure. Identify three measures you would propose for specific components (i.e., percent of all highway miles of roads in good or better condition).

6. This chapter ends with specific recommendations about which everyone can choose to become involved with benchmarking as a measure of progress. Benchmarking assumes that this is a way to deliberately choose to use public resources most effectively to improve progress. It also assumes a high level of political consensus about the priority of benchmarks above competing agendas. It is not that other agendas are not important. They are just of lower importance since we can only advance progress in a limited set of areas at any given time. Once the collective priority is set, then our public resources should be focused on improving these benchmarks. Which of the recommended next steps are you most likely to be involved and why?

Chapter 10: Answers to Key Questions

1. Which of the questions and answers was most interesting to you and why?

2. What additional questions do you have that are not addressed in this chapter? Why is your question important to you? Where can you go to get a possible answer? Explore Internet resources and suggest a reasonable answer to your question.

Chapter 11: Next Steps

1. There are many advocate groups that support transparency in government. Several are mentioned in the book—Sunlight Foundation, OMB Watch, and the Center for Public Integrity. In each benchmark area, there are various advocate groups specializing in creating practical solutions to improve progress on these measures. For example, The Commonwealth Fund is focused on solutions to lower the cost of health care and increase the health outcomes in the United States. The Fund promotes transparency, makes the organization's research widely available, and is actively involved with political leadership to enact positive change. Pick a benchmark that interests you and prepare a list of advocate organizations and their Web sites. Summarize their proposed solutions and prioritize the initiatives in terms of most effective strategies to improve the benchmark measures. This will be a valuable exercise as it requires an ability to "connect

the dots" and to envision a set of steps, partnerships, and resources to actually introduce change.

2. Make a copy of the ten components of *The Transparent Accountability Paradigm* and send it to your mayor, state, or federal representative. Or send them a copy of the book. Ask them to support this type of government and to send you specific examples of how they do or will promote transparency and accountability. If enough citizens did this one act, the legislators and government agency managers would realize that there is a growing expectation that the taxpayers are interested in knowing what they are getting as a result of their investments. It does not take a lot of this type of direct "ask" to have a big impact.

3. Create your own editorial encouraging your audience to embrace the concepts of the new paradigm. Send the editorial to your newspaper, and

4. Submit it to your favorite blog, or put it on Facebook and start a dialogue with your friends.

Bibliography

AARP. (2002). *Trends in health security.* Washington, D.C: American Association of Retired Persons.

Ambinder, M. (2008). His space: How would Obama's success in online campaigning translate into governing? *The Atlantic.* Retrieved February 17 at: http://www.theatlantic.com/magazine/archive/2008/06/hisspace/6806/

APA. (2006). *Defining Medical Cost Offset: Policy Implications.* Practice Directorate, Washington, D.C.

Ballard, C., Courant, P., Drake, D., Fisher, R., & Gerber, E. (2003). *Michigan at the millennium: A benchmark and analysis of its fiscal and economic Structure.* East Lansing, Michigan: Michigan State University.

Beckwith, H. (1997). *Selling the invisible.* New York: Warner Business Books.

Benton, W. (1981). *The Ethic of intrinsic goodness.* Paper presented at the International Council on Social Welfare. Toronto, Ontario, Canada.

Berenson, A., & Henriques, D. (2008, December 17). S.E.C. issues mea culpa on Madoff. *New York Times,* B1, B5.

Brody, J. (2008, January 22). A basic hospital to-do list saves lives New York Times. Retrieved February 16, 2011 at: http://www.nytimes.com/2008/01/22/health/22brod.html

Bureau of Juvenile Justice. (2005). Recidivism study 2005. Lansing, Michigan: Department of Human Services.

Campbell, D., & Stanley, J. (1963). *Experimental and quasi-experimental designs for research.* Chicago: Rand McNally.

Carter, R. (1983). *The accountable agency.* Beverly Hills, California: Sage Publications.

Carter, R. (1984, Fall). Measuring up. *Public Welfare, 42* ,6-13.

Carter, R. (1994). Maximizing the use of evaluation results. In J. Wholey, H. Hatry, & K. Newcomer (Eds.), *Handbook of Practical Program Evaluation* (pp. 576-589). San Francisco: Jossey Bass.

Carter, R. (2004, April 21). *Quality: Connecting the dots.* Paper presented to Michigan chapter of Directors of Nursing Association. Mt. Pleasant, Michigan.

Colmers, J. (2007). *Public reporting and transparency.* New York: The Commonwealth Fund.

Committee on Government Affairs. (1993, June 16). Government Performance and Results Act of 1993. Washington, D.C.: U.S. Senate.

Common Cause. (1978). *Making government work: A Common Cause report on state sunset activities.* Washington, D.C.: Common Cause.

Consumer Reports. (2010, April 13). Don't buy: safety risk-2010 Lexus GX 460. Retrieved February 16, 2011 at: http://blogs.consumerreports.org/cars/2010/04/consumer-reports-2010-lexus-gx-dont-buy-safety-risk.html

Cooper, M. (2011, January 22). Mayors see no end to hard choices for cities, including bankruptcy. *New York Times,* pp. A10, A12.

Council for Excellence in Government. (2004). *A Matter of Trust. Americans and Their Government: 1958-2004.* Retrieved online at: http://www.excelgov.org/usermedia/images/uploads/PDFs/AMOT.pdf

Department of Housing and Urban Development. (2008, March 19). HUD's fiscal year 2008 notice of funding availability (NOVA). *Federal Register,* 73(54), p.14904.

Detroit Free Press. (1999, November 28). Nursing homes guide will be healthy for families and the industry. Detroit, Michigan: *The Detroit Free Press,* p. 14A.

Dingle, D. (1992, January). How to cut all of your taxes. *Money,* p. 69.

Donahue, J. (2002, September 22). Unchartered airspace [Letter to the editor]. *Economist.* pp. 51-52.

Dyer, J., & Chu, W. (1997). The economic value of trust in supplier-buyer relations. Draft paper. Philadelphia, PA: The Wharton School.

Economist. (January 6, 2011). Blame and shame. Retrieved February 17 at: http://www.economist.com/node/17857471

Fabry, B. (1994). Follow-up project 1993 report. Pittsburgh, PA: The Pressley Ridge Schools.

Fagan, P. (2007). *Outcome based evaluation: Faith-based social service organizations and stewardship.* Washington, D.C.: The Heritage Foundation.

Finch, J. (1995, June 27). Managing for results: Status of the Government Performance and Results Act. The House Subcommittee on Government Management, Information and Technology. Washington, D.C.: House of Representatives.

Fournies, F. (1999). *Why employees don't do what they are suppose to do and what to do about it.* New York: McGraw-Hill.

FoxNews.com. (2011, January 5). Poll: Fewer people say they're Democrats. Retrieved 1/14/2011 at: http://www.myfoxtwincities.com/dpps/news/poll-fewer-people-say-theyre-democrats-dpgonc-20110106-gc_11332030

Friedman, T. (2008, December 17). The great unraveling. *New York Times* p. A29.

Fung, A., Graham, M., & Weil, D. (2007). *Full disclosure: The perils of and promise of transparency.* Cambridge, England: Cambridge University Press.

Gannon, J. (2002, July 3). Luster leaves Pressley Ridge after 32-year tenure. Retrieved February 16, 2011 at: http://www.post-gazette.com/busine ssnews/20020703luster0703bnp2.asp

GASB. (2002). Report on the GASB citizen discussion groups on performance reporting. Norwalk, CT.: GASB.

GASB. (2005). *Service efforts and accomplishments performance reports: A guide to understanding.* Norwalk, CT.: GASB.

GASB. (2007). GASB adds project on performance reporting. Norwalk, CT.: GASB.

Gawande, A. (2007, December 10). The checklist. *The New Yorker,* pp. 85-95.

General Accountability Office. (2005). *Managing for results: Enhancing agency use of performance information for management decision making.* Washington, D.C.: General Accountability Office.

Gladwell, M. (2000). *The Tipping point: How little things can make a big difference.* NY: Hachette Book Group.

Gore, A. (1993). *From red tape to results: Creating a government that works better and costs less.* Washington, D.C.: National Partnership for Reinventing Government.

Great Lakes Marketing. (1996, 1998, 2000, 2002, 2004). HCAM family satisfaction survey. Toledo, Ohio.

Green, C. (2003, August, 4). A way to a better budget. *New York Times.* p. A17.

Greene, J. (2002). High school graduation rates in the United States. New York: The Manhattan Institute.

Greene, J. (2005). *Education myths.* Lanham, MA.: Rowman & Littlefield Publishers.

Greiner, J., Hatry, H., Koss, M., Millar, A., & Woodward, J. (1981). Productivity and motivation: A review of State and Local Government Initiatives. Washington, D.C.: The Urban Institute.

Health Care Association of Michigan. (1999). *Consumer guide to Michigan nursing homes.* Lansing, Michigan: HCAM.

Herbert, B. (2008, June 21). A dubious milestone. *New York Times,* p. A27.

Hosteller, M. (2007). Nursing home quality improvement: Issue of the month—Changing the culture of nursing homes. New York: The Commonwealth Fund.

Isaacs, J. (2008). *Economic mobility of families across generations.* Washington, D.C.: The Brookings Institute.

Kuhn, T. (1962). *The Structure of Scientific Revolutions.* The University of Chicago Press.

Leichter, H., & Tryens, J. (2002). *Achieving better health outcomes: The Oregon benchmark experience.* New York: The Millbank Memorial Fund.

Lendman, S. (2010). WikiLeaks Afghan war diaries. *Baltimore Chronicle and Sentinel.* Retrieved online 2/16/11 at: http://baltimorechronicle. com/2010/072810Lendman.shtml

Leonhardt, D. (2007, November 7). When trust in an expert is unwise. *New York Times*, p. C1.

Lippitt, L. (1998). *Preferred futuring.* San Francisco: Berrett-Koehler Publishers.

Millar, R., & Millar, A. (Eds.). (1981). *Developing client outcome monitoring systems: A guide for state and local social service agencies.* Washington, D.C.: The Urban Institute.

Misaras, L. (2007). Oregon state legislators' use of Oregon benchmark data in legislative decision-making. Eugene, Oregon: University of Oregon's Department of Planning, Public Policy and Management.

National Center for Education Statistics. (2007). Digest of education statistics: 2007. Table 389 (Average mathematics literacy, reading literacy, science literacy and problem solving scores of 15 year olds by sex and country: 2003). Retrieved February 16, 2011 at: http://nces.ed.gov/ pubs2008/2008022.pdf

National Poverty Center (no date). Poverty in the United States. Retrieved February 17, 2011 at: http://www.npc.umich.edu/poverty/

NCSL. (2003). *Legislating for results.* Denver, Colorado: NCSL.

New York Times. (2010, November 29). A note to readers: the decision to publish diplomatic documents. p. A8.

North Carolina Progress Board. (2006). North Carolina 20/20 Update report. Raleigh, North Carolina: Progress Board.

OMB Watch. (2004). Office of management and budget may be the only government programs' evaluator. Retrieved February 16, 2011 at: http://www. ombwatch.org/node/1898

Oregon Progress Board. (2007). Achieving the Oregon shine vision, Highlights, 2007 benchmark report to the people of Oregon. Retrieved February 16, 2011 at: http://www.oregon.gov/DAS/OPB/docs/2007Report/2007_Benchmark_Highlights.pdf?ga=t

Osborne, D. (1993, June 16). Government Performance and Results Act of 1993. Report of the Committee on Government Affairs. Washington, D.C.: US Senate. p. 58.

Osborne, D., & Gaebler, T. (1992). *Reinventing government: How the entrepreneurial spirit is transforming the public sector.* Reading, Massachusetts: Addison Wesley Publications.

Osborne, D., & Hutchinson, P. (2004). *The price of government: Getting results we need in an age of permanent fiscal crisis.* New York: Basic Books.

Payne, R. (2003). *A framework for understanding poverty.* Highlands, TX: Aha Process, Inc.

Pew Research Center. (2010). Distrust, anger and partisan rancor. Retrieved 2/16/11 at: http://people-press.org/report/606/trust-in-government

Pitt, H. (2002, November, 8). Speech by SEC chairman at Securities Industry Association annual meeting. Retrieved February 16, 2011 at http://www.sec.gov/news/speech/spch603.htm

Pollan, M. (2008, April 20). Why bother? Looking for a few good reasons to go green. *New York Times Magazine*, pp. 19-23, 88.

Pressley Ridge Schools. Retrieved November, 2007 at http://www.pressleyridge.org/research/research.html

Pronovost, P., Needham, D., Berenholtz, S., Sinopoli, D., Chu, H., Cosgrove, S., Sexton, B., Hyzy, R., Welsh, R., Roth, G., Bander, J., Kepros, J. & Goeschel, C. (2006, December 28). An intervention to decrease catheter-related bloodstream infections in the ICU. *New England Journal of Medicine*, 355(26), 2725-2732.

Reding, K. (1999). *Michigan families express satisfaction with nursing facility care.* Kalamazoo, Michigan: Western Michigan University.

Richmond, F. (2007). *Return on investment training for community action agencies.* Columbus, OH: Ohio Community Action Training Association.

Sack, K. (1994, November, 13). In post-loss interview, Cuomo has no excuses. *New York Times.* p. A17.

Sack, K. (2008, May 18). Doctors start to say "I'm sorry" before see you in court. *New York Times*, pp. A1, A17.

Schoen, C., Davis, K., How, S., and Schoenbaum, S. (2006). National score-card on U.S. health system performance: complete chartpack. N.Y.: Commonwealth Fund.

Sunlight Foundation. (2010). Retrieved July 8, 2010 at: http://sunlightfoundation.com

Sunstein, C. (2010). Disclosure and simplification as regulatory tools. Washington, D.C.: The White House memorandum for the heads of executive departments and agencies.

Torruellas, C. (2004). Oregon performance measure system assessment. Salem, Oregon: The Progress Board.

Trenholm, C., Devaney, B., Fortson, K., Quay, L., Wheeler, J., & Clark, M. (2007). Impacts of four Title V, Section 510 abstinence education programs: Executive summary. Princeton, NJ: Mathmatica Policy Research.

Trunzo, A. (undated). Outcome follow-up evaluation: Pressley Ridge a look back—5 years of follow-up data (2001-2005). Pittsburgh, PA: Pressley Ridge. Personal communication.

UPI.com. (2010, November 25). Poll: America headed in the wrong direction. Retrieved January 14, 2010 at: http://www.upi.com/Top_News/US/2010/11/25/Poll-America-headed-in-wrong-direction/UPI-28191290722648/

U.S. Census Bureau. (2008). Historical income tables-families. Retrieved February 16, 2011 at: http://www.census.gov/hhes/www/income/data/historical/families/index.html

U.S. Census Bureau. (2010). Poverty: 2008 and 2009. Retrieved February 16, 2010, 2008, at http://www.census.gov/prod/2010pubs/acsbr09-1.pdf

White House. (2009). Transparency and open government memorandum for the heads of executive departments and agencies. Retrieved 2/16/2011 at: http://www.whitehouse.gov/the_press_office/TransparencyandOpenGovernment/

Zelio, J. (2005). *Legislative use of performance information.* Denver, Colorado: National Conference of State Legislatures.

About the Author

Reginald Carter was born in Windsor, Ontario. He received his B.A. from the University of Windsor and M.A. from Bowling Green University in Ohio. He chose to become a naturalized American in 1981. This picture of Reg and his wife, Sandy, was taken during their recent trip to Israel and Egypt. They travel extensively. Reg plays golf and hockey; serves on the board of a continuing care retirement community; and consults with Public Policy Associates, a research and public policy firm in Lansing, Michigan.